Napoleon in Russia

BY THE SAME AUTHOR

METTERNICH, COUNCILLOR OF EUROPE
(Weidenfeld & Nicolson, 1972)

ALEXANDER I: TSAR OF WAR AND PEACE
(Weidenfeld & Nicolson, 1974)

THE KAISER
(Weidenfeld & Nicolson, 1978)

BERNADOTTE; NAPOLEON'S MARSHAL, SWEDEN'S KING
(John Murray, 1991)

THE DECLINE AND FALL OF THE OTTOMAN EMPIRE
(John Murray, 1992)

TWILIGHT OF THE HABSBURGS
(Weidenfeld & Nicolson, 1994)

DICTIONARY OF THE BRITISH EMPIRE AND COMMONWEALTH
(John Murray, 1996)

WHO'S WHO IN WORLD POLITICS FROM 1860
(Routledge, 1996)

Alan Palmer

NAPOLEON
IN
RUSSIA

*'Napoleon is a torrent which as yet
we are unable to stem. Moscow will
be the sponge that will suck him dry'*

KUTUZOV, SEPTEMBER 13, 1812

CONSTABLE · LONDON

First published in Great Britain by
Andre Deutsch Limited 1967
This edition published in Great Britain 1997
by Constable and Company Limited
3 The Lanchesters, 162 Fulham Palace Road
London W6 9ER
Copyright © Alan Palmer 1967
Reprinted 1998
ISBN 0 09 477560 5
Printed in Great Britain by
St Edmundsbury Press Ltd
Bury St Edmunds, Suffolk

A CIP catalogue record for this book
is available from the British Library

To Thomas Fox

Author's Note

It is my pleasure to record the help and encouragement given me in working upon this book. I am grateful to Mr Felix Markham, Fellow of Hertford College, Oxford, for advice on seeking illustrations; to Professor Tom Hammond of the University of Virginia for having generously made a gift to me of a book not easily obtainable in London; and to Mr Nicolas Bentley for his wise counsel. I also appreciate the assistance I have received from the staffs of the London Library, the British Museum and the Mansell Collection. United Press International have kindly given me permission to quote from Napoleon's letters to Marie-Louise, citing the edition of the correspondence mentioned in the bibliography. I would like, also, to acknowledge my indebtedness to the authors and editors of the memoirs and other eye-witness accounts which I have used as my main source material.

My wife, Veronica, assisted me at every stage and I have profited much from her comments and criticisms. Miss Patricia Kingaby typed the whole of the narrative and Mrs Janette Szemerenyi the bibliographical notes; I am grateful to both of them for their skill and patience. Finally I would like to express my gratitude to my friends in the Masters' Common Room at Highgate for their long-suffering tolerance of my obsession with the campaign of 1812; and I am glad to have the opportunity of dedicating this book to the most long-suffering and tolerant of them.

March 1967   A.W.P.

Contents

List of Illustrations

List of Illustrations

facing page 161

Rostopchin, Governor of Moscow
(Mansell Collection)

facing pages 192 & 193

The Burning of Moscow
(Photo Bulloz)

'Russians Teaching Boney to Dance', a contemporary English
cartoon
(Bodleian Library)

facing pages 224 & 225

Tsar Alexander I
(Mansell Collection)

A scene from the retreat
(Mansell Collection)

facing pages 256 & 257

Marshal Ney
(Mansell Collection)

Napoleon, by Meissonnier
Collection Viollet)

List of Maps

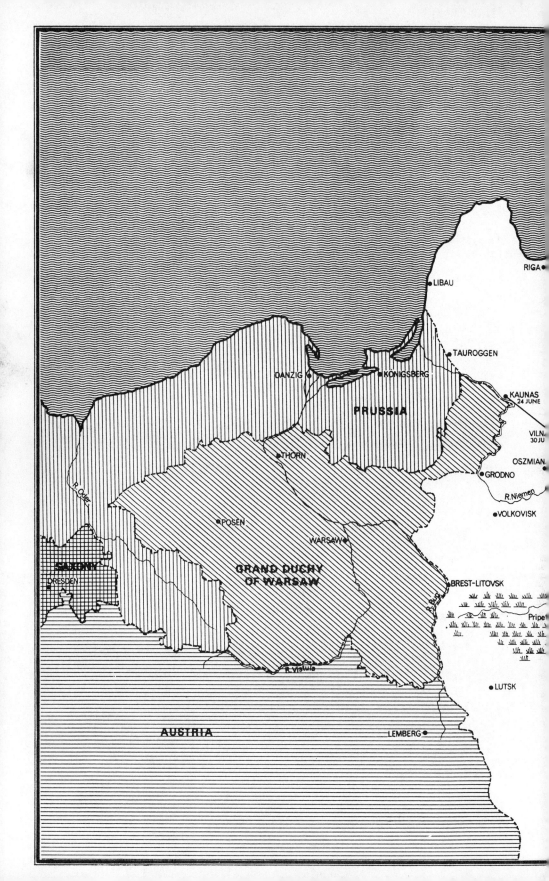

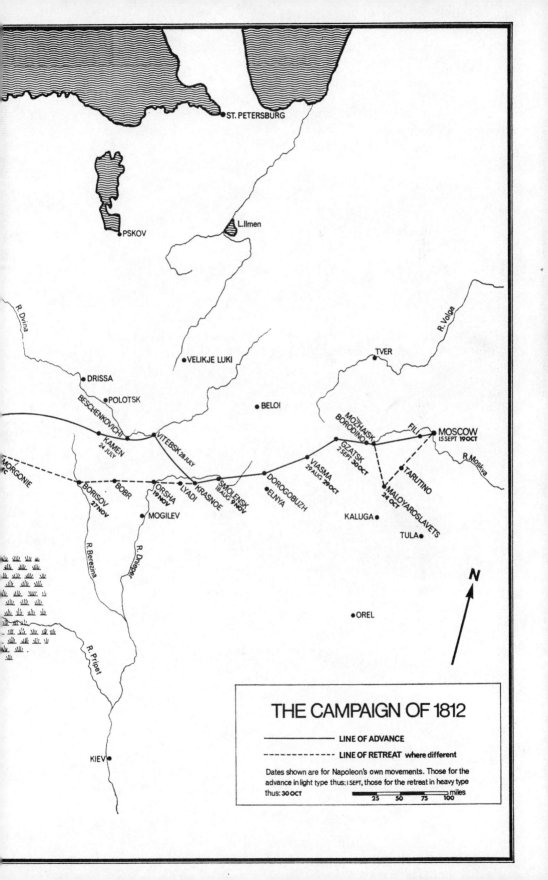

ST. PETERSBURG

PSKOV

L.Ilmen

R. Dvina

VELIKJE LUKI

R. Volga

DRISSA

TVER

BESCHENKOVICHI

POLOTSK

BELOI

MORGONIE

KAMEN
24 JULY

VITEBSK 28 JULY

MOZHAISK
BORODINO

FILI

MOSCOW
15 SEPT 19 OCT

R.Moskva

BORISOV
27 NOV

BOBR

ORSHA
19 NOV

LYADI

KRASNOE

SMOLENSK
18 AUG 9 NOV

DOROGOBUZH

ELNYA

VIASMA
29 AUG 29 OCT

GZATSK
2 SEPT 30 OCT

TARUTINO

MALOYAROSLAVETS
24 OCT

MOGILEV

R. Berezina

R. Dnieper

KALUGA

TULA

OREL

N

KIEV

R. Pripet

THE CAMPAIGN OF 1812

——————————— LINE OF ADVANCE

- - - - - - - - - - - LINE OF RETREAT where different

Dates shown are for Napoleon's own movements. Those for the
advance in light type thus: 1 SEPT, those for the retreat in heavy type
thus: 30 OCT

25   50   75   100

miles

List of the Main Participants in the Events of 1812

THE FRENCH AND THEIR ALLIES

NAPOLEON I, Emperor of the French and commander-in-chief of the Grand Army.

JÉRÔME Bonaparte, King of Westphalia (brother of Napoleon).

Joachim MURAT, King of Naples, Marshal of France, commander of the cavalry of the Grand Army (brother-in-law of Napoleon).

EUGÈNE de Beauharnais, Viceroy of Italy, commander of the 'Army of Italy' and of the 4th Corps (stepson of Napoleon)

Marshal Louis Alexandre BERTHIER, Prince of Neuchâtel, Prince of Wagram, chief-of-staff to Napoleon.

Marshal DAVOUT, Duke of Auerstadt, Prince of Eckmühl, commander of the 1st Corps.

Marshal NEY, Duke of Elchingen, commander of the 3rd Corps.

Marshal Claude VICTOR, Duke of Belluno, commander of the 9th Corps.

Marshal Alexandre MACDONALD, Duke of Tarento, commander of the 10th Corps.

General Armand de CAULAINCOURT, Duke of Vicenza, Grand Master of the Horse.

General Prince Joseph PONIATOWSKI, commander of the 5th Corps.

General Gouvion SAINT-CYR, commander of the 6th Corps (Marshal of France, August 1812).

General Andoche JUNOT, Duke of Abrantes, commander of the 8th Corps.

Hugues MARET, Duke of Bassano, French foreign minister.

General Jacques-Law LAURISTON, former ambassador to St Petersburg.

Field-Marshal Prince von SCHWARZENBERG, commander of the Austrian Auxiliary Corps.

Klemens METTERNICH, Count (later, Prince), Austrian foreign minister.

THE RUSSIANS AND THEIR FOREIGN ADVISERS

ALEXANDER I, Tsar of All the Russias.

Field-Marshal Prince Mikhail KUTUZOV, commander-in-chief of the Russian armies from August 20th, 1812.

General Mikhail BARCLAY DE TOLLY, Minister of War, commander of the Russian First Army, commander-in-chief until superseded by Kutuzov.

General Prince Peter BAGRATION, commander of the Russian Second Army (mortally wounded at the battle of Borodino).

General Count Levin BENNIGSEN, Russian chief-of-staff.

General Alexander TORMASSOV, commander of the Russian 3rd Army.

Admiral Pavel CHICHAGOV, commander of the Russian 'Army of Moldavia'.

General Ludwig von WITTGENSTEIN, commander of the Russian 1st Corps.

General RAEVSKI, commander of the Russian 7th Corps.

General DOCTUROV, commander of the Russian 5th Corps.

General MILORADOVICH, commander of the Russian rearguard and successor to Bagration.

General Andrey ERMOLOV, chief-of-staff to Barclay de Tolly.

Hetman PLATOV, commander of the Cossack units in the Russian 1st Army.

Colonel Karl von TOLL, Quartermaster-General to Barclay de Tolly and to Kutuzov.

Colonel (later, General) Ernst von PFUEL, special military adviser to the Tsar.

Theodore ROSTOPCHIN, Governor of Moscow.

General Sir Robert WILSON, British representative attached to Russian headquarters.

I

Dresden

It was a fine night in Dresden. The moon glinted on the baroque tower of the Hofkirche and threw the shadow of the Frauenkirche dome across a crowd in the Neumarkt. For six weeks the people of Saxony had prepared for the occasion, pressed into service by their restless king: potholes were filled in along the roads; carriages bearing tapestries and velvets clattered over the cobbles; cooks and maids of honour, equerries and court chamberlains were hustled through the twin courtyards of the royal palace in a flurry of confusion. Now all Dresden was watching for the Emperor of the French and his consort – all Dresden, that is, except King Frederick Augustus who, impatient to the end, had driven out to Freyberg to meet his guests a day too early. There were lights along the narrow streets and a line of torches flickered down the Annenstrasse to the solitary bridge across the Elbe. Shortly before eleven the bells began to peal and the windows rattled as cannon boomed a royal salute. From the suburb of Plauen came a sound of cheering and the strident braying of trumpets. A cavalcade of mounted men in helmets with horsehair tails escorted a carriage into the city. It passed under the arch of Augustus the Strong and halted in the courtyard; a stocky figure in grey cloak and cocked hat led a young Empress up the stairs of Frederick Augustus' palace; it was May 16, 1812, and after a week of dusty roads – for spring was dry that year – Napoleon and Marie-Louise had completed their journey from Saint Cloud.

The Emperor had spent five festive days in Dresden in the summer of 1807 after his men had driven Russia's finest troops into the river Alle at Friedland and he had charmed the Tsar into friendship at Tilsit. But alliance with France stifled Russia's trade and by the end of 1810 the two empires had drifted into hostility. Now it was said that Napoleon, with the Austrians and Prussians at his side, was marching once more against Russia. Soon, no doubt, the drums would go beating out across the Polish plains and the guns rumble relentlessly eastward. But this was still in the future. For the moment, central Europe was at peace and in the Emperor's baggage-train had travelled, not the apparatus of war, but half the court of France. 'Never had departure for the Army more resembled a voyage of pleasure,' wrote Baron Fain, Napoleon's secretary, when he looked back on the journey some years later. For a fortnight Dresden, a provincial though exquisitely attractive city, could bask in the reflected sun of Europe. There was every reason for the imperial couple to be welcomed that Saturday night.

Few as yet perceived that Napoleon's sun was already low in the sky. In May 1812 it seemed likely that Europe would lie for many years in the shadow of French pride. The French eagles were beside the Rhine at Cologne and above the Adriatic at Dubrovnik; Bremen and Genoa and Antwerp were ports hardly less French than Marseilles and Dunkirk; Lutheran Lübeck on the Baltic was a French city and Catholic Rome the capital of a French department. Only on the upper Tagus, where lurching ox-waggons carried British arms timelessly through the red Spanish dust, was the power of France faintly challenged. It is true that in Heidelberg and Göttingen and Leipzig young students were sullenly hostile to the existing order: but who could take seriously the nostalgic romanticism of university taverns? Certainly not the Emperor of the Revolution.

Yet did he still deserve such a title? By the spring of 1812 the months of Jacobin Terror seemed far distant; Napoleon was cushioned against recent realities by the sanctity of the legend he lived out from day to day. He had come to Dresden as Charlemagne incarnate. Here he would seek homage from his tributaries and impress his allies with the magnitude of his authority. A protracted pageant was mounted in which the kings and dukes of the German lands could rival each other in obsequious flattery. The Emperor of Austria, Francis I, and his Empress were invited to greet their omnipotent son-in-law and see their daughter 'with the world at her

18

feet' in the King of Saxony's palace; they arrived on May 18, placid and imperturbable, with the egregious Metternich in attendance. Permission was sought, and tardily given, for the King of Prussia to join the assembly. No doubt it was humiliating to reach Dresden ten days after the festivities had begun, but he came willingly enough; and Napoleon even found half an hour in which to give this great-nephew of Frederick II an audience and allowed the heir to the Prussian crown to be presented to him in a spare five minutes.

Some of the German rulers had already saluted Napoleon and Marie-Louise on their progress from the Rhine, but others hovered expectantly in the salons at Dresden, hoping for a nod of recognition from the cynosure of all Europe: the Dukes of Coburg and Mecklenburg were there; the Duke of Weimar; the Grand Duke of Würzburg, and the bearers of other resonant titles. Banquets and levées and receptions followed each other interminably, regulated by the stiff etiquette of German ceremonial.

At times, as he moved past the bowed heads of the princelings in the green and white uniform of his own Guard, the Emperor was graciously expansive – a shrewd aside to Metternich on the French craving for applause, even a kindly word for that 'blockhead, that drill sergeant' his royal 'cousin' from Berlin. One evening, with Paer's orchestra playing softly in the ante-chamber and the mirrors reflecting the flickering candelabra, memory slipped back twenty years and he remarked to his Imperial and Apostolic neighbour at dinner that things would have taken a different course if 'my poor uncle' had shown more strength of mind. Lieutenant Bonaparte had come far since that night he had watched a mob batter down the Tuileries gates to thrust a *bonnet rouge* into the hands of the king who had now posthumously gained this unlikely nephew by marriage.

Occasionally the assembly of sovereigns moved out of the palace and into the city. There was a grand hunt in the royal forest of Moritzburg, a performance at the Opera and a solemn apotheosis at the court theatre, with the central figure of the Sun bearing the inscription, 'Less great and less fair than He'. They heard Mass sung in the cathedral, and on the second Sunday of his visit Napoleon rode slowly through the streets and up to the heights above the river mounted on a white horse caparisoned in crimson and gold, followed, at a respectful distance, by an escort of Saxon cavalry in white uniforms and black breast-plates. Once more the cheers rang out and the good people of Saxony marvelled at the honour done to them by the Imperial Presence. At night, paper lanterns lit the sky, their reflected colours shimmering on the waters of the Elbe. All was brilliantly stage-managed, as each Napoleonic spectacle had been since the First Consul crowned himself in Notre Dame more than seven years before: no one sensed that they were witnessing the final gala performance of the Empire.

Napoleon was three months short of his forty-third birthday at the time of these festivities. Although still a commanding figure at the head of a procession, he was no longer the slim and almost handsome general whose lean looks and searching gaze are hallowed on the canvases of Ingres and David. We know his appearance from five sketches Girodet-Trioson had made in Paris that spring: the small mouth is petulantly tight; a lone forelock emphasizes thinning hair; flabby cheeks sunk on a high collar are as empty of expression as the sphinx. Yet behind those glazed eyes remained a riddle. The old vitality was still there and from time to time it flashed through in his conversation: a trenchant criticism of his brother Jérôme, the king of Westphalia, reduced his queen to tears; and, as he spoke of the war that was imminent, there was no hint of fading powers. He would advance this summer to Smolensk, he informed the Austrians, and wait for the economic burden of an army of occupation to bring the Tsar Alexander to his senses. Next year, perhaps, he might need to penetrate deeper into Russia, but, he added, 'We shall see which of us will tire first: I of feeding an army at the expense of Russia or Alexander of maintaining it at the expense of his own country . . . The affair is a question of time.' From Dresden east to the Vistula half a million men were on the move, but they were not yet ready for war. For the moment their commander was prepared to linger in Dresden – provided, of course, that the Russians did not strike first.

At that time the Russian armies were, in fact, concentrated some five hundred miles away. For Tsar Alexander, too, was holding court in a largely alien city. He had set out from St Petersburg in the third week of April to take up residence in the castle of Vilna, once a key citadel in the Polish-Lithuanian kingdom. With its dozen baroque churches and two cathedrals, Vilna had long been an outpost of Western Christendom, defended against predatory Muscovite incursions with ramparts thrown up by the Jagiellonian kings in the sixteenth century. Now, with the partition of Poland, diplomacy had succeeded where war had failed and Vilna was at last within the Russian Empire. But they were Polish peasants who laboured in the fields along the river Vileka and Polish magnates who hunted in the amphitheatre of wooded hills above the city. It would have been understandable had Alexander, the Russian autocrat, been received by the Poles with sullen passivity.

Yet, curiously enough, the Tsar was welcomed as Napoleon had been in Dresden: gay flags in the windows, spring garlands in the cobbled streets, garden parties and banquets organized by the Polish aristocracy; and in the midst of all this festivity the tall, fair figure of the Tsar, short-sighted and rather deaf for a man of thirty-five, but none the less radiating an almost boyish enthusiasm. Reconciliation was, for the present, fashionable, and Alexander took every opportunity of showing that he was well disposed towards the Polish and Lithuanian nobility. High Russian decorations were distributed to Polish princes and counts and they were made honorific dignitaries in the Russian administration. Even more was expected of Alexander: a rumour – which reached Napoleon in Dresden – said that he was about to be proclaimed king of Poland. Around him at Vilna there gathered exiles from the subject states of Europe – Prussians, Hanoverians, Neapolitans, disillusioned French liberals and even a delegate from insurgent Spain. It was almost as if History, with an ironic chuckle, had cast the Tsar as liberator of the continent while Bonaparte was fêted by the monarchs of the old order. As a reversal of roles it was hardly convincing.

On May 18 Napoleon's aide-de-camp, Count Louis de Narbonne, arrived unexpectedly at Vilna. Narbonne, who was alleged to be an illegitimate son of Louis xv and had served Louis xvi as Minister of War in 1792, was frequently employed by Napoleon on delicate diplomatic missions: he had received the first overtures from Metternich on the Austrian marriage and had gone to Vilna direct from Berlin where he had been seeking to thaw France's reluctant ally, Prussia. Now he had been entrusted with a fourfold task: to assure Alexander of Napoleon's wish to avoid war, while emphasizing the power of the massive army on the Vistula; to impress upon the Russians that, as a prerequisite of better relations with France, they must close their ports to trade with Britain; and to find out for himself the attitude of the Russian commanders towards the forthcoming campaign. Above all, he should seek to prevent the Tsar from anticipating events by ordering an advance into Prussia.

Alexander gave Narbonne an audience on the day of his arrival and accepted a letter from Napoleon which reiterated his desire for peace but added, significantly, that his personal regard for Alexander would remain unchanged even if fate forced the two empires into war. The Tsar received Narbonne amiably. Far from wanting war, he declared, he had been forced to mass his army in Poland because Napoleon 'was ranging all Europe against Russia.' 'I am under no illusions,' he said, 'I render too much justice to his military talents not to have calculated all the risks that an appeal to arms may involve for us, but having done all I could to preserve peace honourably and uphold a political system which might lead to universal peace, I will do nothing to besmirch the honour of the nation over which I rule . . . If the Emperor Napoleon is determined on war, and if fortune does not smile on our just cause, his hunt for peace will take him to the uttermost ends.'

On the following day Narbonne attended two military reviews and dined at the Tsar's table, again impressed by Alexander's rare resolution of purpose. The Frenchman was prepared to wait several days in Vilna but, on the morning of May 20, three members of the Tsar's entourage arrived to pay him a farewell visit, provisions and wines were sent for the return journey, and he was informed that his horses would be ready at six that evening. It was a polite, but effective, response to Napoleon's blandishments.

Five days later – it was the Tuesday on which the King of Prussia at last reached Dresden – Narbonne was back with Napoleon. Fain recalls that as Narbonne reported on his mission the Emperor paced briskly up and down, deep in thought. A long silence followed his account until, at last, Napoleon burst out, 'So all means of understanding are at an end! The spirit which dominates the Russian camp pushes us into war! . . . The princes who are here have told me as much: there is not one of them who has failed to receive information of this character . . . There is no more time to be lost in fruitless negotiations.'

Napoleon spent two more days in Dresden, while final preparations were made for the journey to the Vistula. His spare moments he gave to Marie-Louise, promising her that he would return in, at the most, two months' time. Then, at five in the morning of May 29, his carriage drove out of the palace courtyard and a waking city heard the clatter of cavalry as the Emperor's escort crossed the Elbe and disappeared up the long road to the east.

2

The Undeclared War

The chancelleries of Europe had long expected war to be renewed between Napoleon and Alexander, despite the formal friendship binding the two emperors together. Recent history had shown Russian policy capable of almost monumental vacillation. Fearing French dominance of the continent, Tsar Paul had entered the Second Coalition in 1798; his army won striking successes in Switzerland and Italy under the aged Suvorov until some quirk in Paul's feeble mind induced him to conclude a separate peace, laud Bonaparte as the champion of order over revolution and urge him to assume the crown of France. But in 1801 Paul was murdered in a palace conspiracy with the connivance of his son, Alexander, who believed that his assassination was essential for the salvation of Russia. The new Tsar responded to the enticements of Pitt – and a subsidy of £6¼ million – and brought half a million men into the Third Coalition against France. Russia survived the defeat of Austerlitz, but in the summer of 1807 with 20,000 dead at Friedland and his exchequer near bankruptcy, Alexander made peace with Napoleon at Tilsit and became, in name at all events, his ally against Britain. It is not surprising that a conservative journal in London should have described Alexander at this time as 'the acknowledged self-recorded tool of Europe's tyrant and oppressor, the promoter of his views, the instrument of his ambition, and the pander of his power.' Consistency was hardly one of his virtues.

Yet Tilsit was too dramatic a reversal of alliances to be true. The interests of Russia and France clashed at so many points that there was little prospect of a lasting peace. Neither side kept its pledges. Napoleon undertook to withdraw his garrisons from Prussia, where they were poised ominously along Russia's almost indefensible frontier: the garrisons remained there until ejected by force in 1813. Alexander agreed to support the continental blockade of Britain; but his authorities connived at smuggling on a grand scale and issued certificates to vessels flying the American flag and trading with English ports. In 1808 new protestations of mutual regard by the two emperors in conference at Erfurt deceived no one, least of all themselves. Erfurt had been intended by Napoleon as a preliminary gesture of solidarity before a joint invasion of Austria; but when war came, Alexander's assistance was so derisory that the Russian Army suffered precisely two casualties. Small wonder that, in the ensuing peace treaty, Napoleon showed scant regard for his ally's susceptibilities by enlarging the Grand Duchy of Warsaw and acquiring bases in southern Dalmatia. It was the Russians' turn to complain: they found it intolerable that the French, who had already made a satrapy of most of Poland, should now be encroaching on the Balkans as well. And, as if this were not enough, early in 1810 Napoleon preferred an Austrian princess to a Russian grand-duchess as his new empress. He might assure the Russian Ambassador that the Austrian marriage had no political significance, but Alexander knew better. Already he was beginning to think, as he said later, that two such men as Napoleon and himself 'could not reign together in this world.'

The rift became public at the close of 1810. On December 13 the French annexed all the German coast, except that in Prussia. Among the lands which thus changed sovereignty was the small duchy of Oldenburg, whose ruler had strong dynastic links with the Tsar, since he was himself Alexander's uncle and his heir-apparent had married Alexander's favourite sister, Ekaterina Pavlovna. So great was Romanov interest in Oldenburg that a clause had been inserted in the Treaty of Tilsit guaranteeing the rights of its reigning ducal house. When, however, the Russian Ambassador delivered a note of protest at this fresh breach of the Tilsit agreement, the French foreign minister refused to accept the message. This new double insult to his family stung Alexander. The French alliance had always been unpopular in St Petersburg – the landowners complained that they had no market for flax and hemp once they were cut off from England – and now the Tsar determined to make a bid for popularity and let his critics have their way. On December 31, 1810, an Imperial Ukase announced the opening of Russian ports and the imposition of a new tariff against French luxury goods. Russia would no longer play Napoleon's game against Britain: she had withdrawn from the Continental System.

'It seems that blood must flow again,' Alexander wrote that Christmas to his sister (who had fled from Oldenburg to Tver) and he added, a shade too complacently, 'But at least I have done everything that is humanly possible to avoid it.' This was, perhaps, the truth at that time; but it was a claim he could hardly have made a few weeks later. For, in the first months of 1811, the Tsar seriously considered a preventive war against France. Five divisions were hurriedly moved to the Polish frontier from Bessarabia, where they had been engaged in an interminable campaign against the Turks. At the same time, there was a flurry of diplomatic activity in St Petersburg as the Swedes and the Prussians and the Austrians were sounded out. The Polish aristocrat Czartoryski was received at the Winter Palace and discussed the possible effects a grant of autonomy to the Russian Poles would have on the subjects of the Grand-Duchy of Warsaw. The ordinances of the Church were waived so that the munition works at Alexandrovsk and Tula could continue to turn out guns on the great festivals of the Epiphany and the Annunciation – a small concession to the temper of the times, but in Holy Russia a significant one.

The alert was, however, premature. By Easter, Alexander had decided that it would be folly to precipitate war. The parade-ground punctilio of his regiments seemed barely adequate to carry them forward to the Oder; the mere prospect of operations had thrown the commissariat into decorous disorder. From a letter which he wrote that May it is clear that the Tsar had decided on a defensive strategy. 'I intend to follow the system which has made Wellington victorious in Spain and exhausted the French armies – avoid pitched battles and organize long lines of communication for retreat, leading to entrenched camps.' The topography was very different from the Iberian Peninsula and the entrenched camps still had to be created, but the basic principle was a sound one. Alexander had begun to sense that the strength of his Empire lay, not so much in the skill of its soldiery, as in its size.

Napoleon had not as yet finally decided on war with Russia. He had other troubles in 1811: an economic crisis in France herself; unemployment in Paris; and the persistent and intractable problem of Spain. That spring, however, he began to move more and more troops into Germany and he took every opportunity of emphasizing his military preparedness to the Russian diplomats in Paris. He also recalled Caulaincourt, his ambassador in St Petersburg, whom he regarded as too well disposed towards Alexander. On his return to France in June, Caulaincourt warned the Emperor of the new spirit animating the Russian court. Napoleon would have none of it; 'Puh! One good battle will see the end of all your friend Alexander's fine resolutions – and his castles of sand, as well!'

The Emperor had come to believe that Spencer Perceval's government in London was weaving a new coalition against him – a flattering tribute to an inept administration – and that, in Russia, the conservative landowners around the Tsar were no better than English agents. If it was necessary to fight Austerlitz and Friedland again, then he was prepared to give battle. And this time a second Tilsit would throw Russia out of Europe, turn her eyes towards Asia and send a Franco-Russian Army down the road to Samarkand to destroy England's hold on India. Such thoughts conjured up an old chimaera, a mirage from the sands of Egypt, where a dozen years before, a young general had dreamt of 'marching into Asia, riding an elephant, a turban on my head and in my hand the new Koran that I would have composed to suit my needs.'

But these fantasies were of the future, or the past; the present imposed a need for hard decisions of fact. If war came with Russia, what new conscripts were to be called to the colours and how many thousands of francs assigned to the War Ministry? It was on August 16, 1811, that Napoleon began the paper work on his Russian campaign. The previous afternoon there had been a reception of the diplomatic corps in the Tuileries to celebrate the Emperor's birthday and he had spent forty minutes castigating Kurakin, the Russian ambassador, for Alexander's alleged encouragement of Polish nationalism and his weakness in allowing England to drive a wedge between the allies of Tilsit. After this tirade the Emperor had driven out to Saint Cloud for the weekend. Maret, his foreign minister, was summoned that Saturday morning and together they went through all the correspondence with Russia since Tilsit. A Council of State met in the afternoon. The Emperor had decided on war. It was too late to begin operations that year; the winter must be used for planning and preparation. Austria and Prussia must put armies into the field and not be content with a gesture of co-belligerency, as Russia herself had been in 1809.

Napoleon spent the autumn of 1811 in the Netherlands and the Rhineland, but he returned to Paris in December and remained there for four months, as he had done in the two preceding years, immersing himself in the meticulous study which preceded each of his military undertakings. On December 19 his librarian was requested to send him 'good books with the best information about Russian topography, and especially Lithuania, dealing with marshes, rivers, woods, roads, etc' and also 'the most detailed account in French of the campaign of Charles XII [of Sweden] in Poland and Russia.' Slowly the huge machine of the Grand Army was constructed by the master-craftsman who was to operate it. Each morning, hour after hour, he would dictate instructions for couriers to carry to garrisons throughout his Empire: stores of grain are to be concentrated at Danzig; supplies of rice should be moved eastwards from Hamburg and Passau and Magdeburg; the route of the Army of Italy must be worked out kilometre by kilometre across the Alps and up to Pomerania; the Croat regiments must be retained at their depot for further training; 6,000 horses are to be transported from Holstein to the Vistula; waggons are assigned to units in Antwerp and Strasbourg and Delft. Few things were left to chance: they could not afford to be. As he became more and more absorbed in the problems of mobilization and supply, so Napoleon's awareness of the task ahead grew. 'I am embarking on the greatest and most difficult enterprise that I have so far attempted,' he remarked to a counsellor as he was setting out for Dresden and the Niemen. As a considered opinion, it was in striking contrast to his rejection of Caulaincourt's warnings less than a year before.

Alexander spent most of these months in St Petersburg, serene
behind the turquoise rococo of the Winter Palace. Occasionally he
would be displayed to his regiments at a review or to his God in
the cathedral – for autocracy imposed its quota of parades – but, for
the most part, he was content to look out at the artificial world of
St Petersburg from above the fluted pillars of a portico. It was
pleasant to present his grandmother's books to the massive new
library in the Nevsky Prospect and to study the statutes of the new
Imperial School at Tsarskoe Selo (where a youngster named Pushkin
had just been enrolled). At the end of January, braving the stinging
wind off the frozen gulf, he had travelled into the western provinces
and assumed a martial aspect before fortifications deep in snow; but
he knew that, however elegant he might appear in a tight uniform
in the Prussian style, he was at heart no soldier. It was a revelation
that had come to him, bitterly, at Austerlitz six years before, as he
led a broken army away from the field, tears coursing down his
cheeks.

At St Petersburg, Alexander had around him veterans who had
served under Potemkin and Suvorov. It was an impressive list,
headed by Bennigsen, who had almost defeated Napoleon at
Eylau, and Arakcheyev, the brilliant artilleryman now carrying into
civil administration the brutality of a gunner's mate. But Alexander,
with obstinacy bred of weakness, always preferred the advice of men
he had discovered himself. At Austerlitz he had trusted the intuition
of a young Austrian staff-officer named Weyrother rather than the
experience of his own commanders. Now he listened more and more
to a Prussian émigré, Colonel Pfuel, who had fled to Russia in 1806
and had an engaging habit of verbally re-fighting the battles of the
ancient world as if he had personally participated in them. It was
Pfuel who proposed the construction at Drissa, a small town on the
river Dvina between Riga and Smolensk, of an entrenched fortress
which would require investment by any invader, who could then be
attacked in the rear by a vastly superior relief force and made to
surrender. The plan hardly kindled enthusiasm among the Russian
generals but it appealed to Alexander, and thousands of serfs spent
that winter hacking away at the frozen soil along the Dvina. There
seemed no reason why a strategy which had failed Vercingetorix at

Alesia should succeed against the latterday Caesar: but Pfuel's reading of Roman history evidently stopped short of the Gallic Wars.

Throughout 1811 the Russian generals were, in fact, remarkably well-informed of Napoleon's military policy. For this good fortune they were indebted to Colonel Alexander Ivanovitch Tchernishev, a twenty-eight-year-old attaché at the Paris Embassy. Tchernishev possessed wit and initiative, as Napoleon who had accepted him as a personal friend appreciated. He also – and of this Napoleon was unaware – had ample supplies of money and was a man of utter ruthlessness (which he showed in later years when, as Minister of War, he became the scourge of all Russia's 'progressives').

The story runs true to form. In the Department of War Administration in Paris there was a clerk named Michel who had a fine palate for wine, although he lacked the cash to acquire it. Tchernishev and Michel became acquainted through the good offices of the Embassy concierge; and for thirteen months Tchernishev was able to purchase each fortnight from Michel a copy of the 'Summary of the Situation,' a report listing the movements of every unit of the Imperial Army. By February 1812 the French secret police had begun to suspect a leakage of information and Tchernishev having dutifully bidden the Emperor farewell at the Elysée Palace, discreetly hurried out of the country with, as he thought, all Michel's recent correspondence safely destroyed. But the police, searching Tchernishev's rooms after his departure, found a letter which had fallen under a rug and which bore the initial 'M' in place of a signature. The customary hunt for a poorly paid employee living beyond his means and the evidence of hand-writing experts led, inevitably, to the arrest of the unfortunate Michel.

With an interesting anticipation of later techniques, Napoleon decided on a show trial in public. Michel was duly condemned and guillotined on May 1 in the Place de Grève, outside the Hôtel-de-Ville. The French people were excited by this evidence of a nefarious Russian conspiracy; and Europe was solemnly informed that, since the abuse of trust by a spy is permissible only in wartime, the Russians were clearly planning hostilities against France. The logic of this argument may have been faulty but the tone of moral indignation was almost convincing: if we had not been assured by a

Soviet historian that Napoleon maintained spies in both St Petersburg and Moscow – and had his printers turning out counterfeit money with which, no doubt, to pay them – we might be tempted to accept it.

The Tchernishev incident, although satisfyingly melodramatic, made little difference to the course of events. Everything now rested with the diplomats. In February Napoleon had heard that Prussia would assign 20,000 men to the northern flank of the Grand Army and, a fortnight later, the Austrians promised a contingent of 30,000 in return for a guarantee of their existing territories. Elsewhere the French had less success. In Stockholm, Bernadotte, who had once been Napoleon's Marshal and now, as elected heir to the throne, directed Swedish policy, declined the bait of Finland and concluded a non-aggression pact with Russia. And in Bucharest the Turks, feeling that Napoleon's encouragement was distant and academic, began talks to end their seven-year conflict with Alexander's armies. Once Russia was assured of peace along her frontier with Sweden and at her outposts in Bessarabia, she could concentrate almost all her forces in the decisive theatre of operations, west of Smolensk.

There was little chance now of averting war; yet twice at the end of April Kurakin made proposals for a settlement between the two empires. Every possible solution broke, however, on one of two stumbling-blocks: the Russian insistence on freedom to trade with neutral states; and the French refusal to withdraw their troops from Prussian territory. Napoleon was not prepared to compromise on either of these questions. And on May 9, maintaining to his entourage that the Russian demand for the evacuation of Prussia was tantamount to an ultimatum, he set out for the hollow ceremonies of Dresden and, eventually, for Poland. The *Moniteur* might say that the Emperor had left Paris on a tour of inspection and Maret might continue to assure Kurakin that hostilities, although probable, were not yet certain; but, in reality, Napoleon had long since made up his mind. Ten months previously he had selected June, 1812, as his date to invade Russia: now war would follow at the moment of his choice.

Napoleon left Dresden, as we have seen, early on May 29. He travelled all that day, with breaks for luncheon and dinner, jolting along the dusty roads of eastern Saxony and, as night fell, on through the rich muddy clay of Silesia. The Emperor was accompanied by Berthier, his chief of staff, while orderly officers rode beside the carriage window. In a second coach came the Grand Marshal of the Empire, General Duroc, and the Master of the Horse, Caulaincourt who, as a former ambassador in St Petersburg, awaited the coming battles with unfashionable misgivings. Other dignitaries were in carriages ahead of the Emperor, heavy titles sitting lightly on their shoulders now that they were free from the pomp of Dresden.

The cavalcade maintained a steady seven miles an hour – 'I came very fast,' Napoleon wrote to Marie-Louise that night – and at two in the morning halted at Glogau on the Oder. Still the Emperor remained in his green-upholstered berlin, a four-wheeled upright carriage, with a covered seat behind for an aide-de-camp, drawn by six horses. He could sleep well enough there and, with dawn breaking early in that part of Europe, he would have time to study reports and dictate letters, for the Empire still had to be governed and he had arranged for couriers to travel at all speed with his orders and instructions. Generally, at such stops as these, he would enclose with his despatches a letter for Marie-Louise. Fain describes how 'in such cases he did not dictate, but wrote himself. Since he was not accustomed to this, it was a great labour for him to write legibly. "Give me a small sheet of fine paper," he would say to us, "and a good pen! For, after all, dear little Louise must be able to read what I write!" After writing, he would hand us the sheet folded in two and say, "For the Empress". And, when he was in a good mood, he would add, "To the Lady of my Dreams! To the Queen of my Heart!" At Glogau all was still well; and Marie-Louise received 120 words of husbandly consolation. Then, at eight-thirty, he was on his way again and the long line of carriages crossed into Poland.

His retinue received differing impressions of these Polish lands. Fain, who had been with the Grand Army in this region in the winter of 1806, was pleasantly surprised: 'Now spring covered it with greenness. It was no longer a desert losing itself in an emptiness of snow. Clusters of trees showed up on the horizon across the plain, and on all sides, we could see dwellings whose existence we had never suspected under the misty veil of December.' Castellane – a future Marshal of France but at that time a captain attached to the suite of one of Napoleon's aides – was less enthusiastic. On his last evening in Dresden he had met the pretty daughter of a grocer, but the romance had been cut short by the call of duty, Castellane having to slip out of her window as dawn was breaking. Now he looked with jaundiced eyes at the wastes of Poland: 'execrable roads, pine woods, mud huts, poor fields of corn and rye . . . A few one-storeyed houses of wood and mud, standing in gardens fenced in by boards, are what is called a town in Poland . . . It looks wretched.' He met veterans from the Peninsula sighing for the women and wine of Aragon: it was a little disheartening for a young romantic of twenty-four.

That night the Emperor reached Posen, 'a dismal town, one of the largest in Poland,' duly noted Castellane in his diary. But for Napoleon the reception was as enthusiastic as in Dresden. There were illuminated inscriptions, arches of flags and flowers, and cheering crowds 'celebrating his triumphs in anticipation' as a Polish officer wrote with the national gift for a felicitous phrase. Three days of such adulation raised the Emperor's spirits; he would destroy the Russians in one great battle as soon as he crossed the Niemen and Alexander would at once sue for peace. And to Marie-Louise (who was still in Dresden, amusing herself with gondola excursions on the Elbe) he wrote: 'You know I love you and how irritated I am not to be seeing you two or three times each day. But I think I shall be doing so in another three months time.'

On he went to the Vistula. At Thorn, which Napoleon reached on June 3, there were five regiments of the Old Guard to review, several squadrons of cavalry and a huge artillery park. 'With troops such as these, Sire,' said a major as he inspected the gunners, 'you could conquer the Indies.' It was at Thorn that his orderly officers, sleeping in the next room, were treated to a rare experience; they were awakened, one night, by the sound of their Emperor singing at the top of his voice the most inspiring verse of the *Chant du Départ*. When, on June 6, he came to leave Thorn he was so impatient that he set out an hour early, leaving the berlin to follow with his retinue as soon as they were able to collect themselves together. They caught

33

up with him before dusk but he insisted on the whole cavalcade pressing on through the night. Small wonder that the carriage broke a shaft next morning at Marienwerder. That evening he rode into Danzig having covered 130 miles in twenty-nine hours along roads thick with dust, for much of the time under a sweltering sun. The scent of battle was thrilling him once more and he expected those around him to quicken to its glamorous appeal.

At Danzig two of his veteran commanders, Davout and Murat, awaited the Emperor's arrival. Marshal Davout, Duke of Auerstadt and Prince of Eckmühl, came from a noble family whose members had served as officers of the kings of France for generations. Marshal Murat, King of Naples and Grand Duke of Berg, was the son of an innkeeper and had enlisted in the ranks of Louis xvi's cavalry twenty-five years before. The two marshals differed as much in personality as they did in provenance. Davout, short, stocky and prematurely bald, was the strictest and most just disciplinarian among the paladins of empire: he inspected his troops with cold eyes, peering short-sightedly through specially designed spectacles. His men never loved him, for he was far too austere and aloof, but they respected him because he was loyal to them and they knew – as Napoleon did – that what he set out to accomplish would be done methodically and efficiently. Already he had sent a detachment of bricklayers to the Niemen with his advance guard so that, when in a few days the main body of the First Corps moved forward, there would be kitchens for them and ovens in which their bread could be baked. In three months he had concentrated at the mouth of the Vistula an Army Corps of nearly 70,000 – Frenchmen, Germans, Poles, Dutch, Swiss and even a Spanish regiment. For this meticulous labour of improvisation he received scant praise from Napoleon; probably he never expected it.

With Murat it was different. Handsome, tall and dark, the King of Naples was a romantic hero personified. In a gold-trimmed blue coat and gold-braided red trousers, he was the most dashing cavalry leader in Europe. At the same time he was an ambitious intriguer, determined to preserve his impromptu throne in southern Italy. Napoleon, whose younger sister he had married, knew Murat's faults and virtues from nine campaigns: his courage in battle; his meek submission to a strong-willed wife; the expansive generosity which offset petty vanity; and the way he could fire the spirit of tired troops and yet court disaster by an impetuous disregard of common sense. 'He has a good heart,' Napoleon confided to Caulaincourt at Danzig. 'When he sees me he is mine, but away from me he sides, like all spineless men, with anyone who flatters or makes up to him. His wife . . . has stuffed his head with foolishness.' Relations between the brothers-in-law had been bad; Murat missed the Wagram Campaign in 1809 because of the political imbroglio in Naples; Napoleon reprimanded him for allowing evasion of the Continental System down the long coastline of his kingdom and refused him permission to come to Dresden. The affronts still rankled and they greeted each other frigidly in Danzig. Yet, if Napoleon needed Murat to lead his cavalry, the quarrel had to end and, with a swift change of mood, he used sentimental reminiscence to charm him into co-operation. There was an outward reconciliation and observers saw tears on Murat's cheeks; but the latent tensions remained.

Napoleon knew already the woods of birch and pine and the rush-fringed lakes in this borderland of Europe. Precisely five years before – it had been on June 14, the anniversary of Marengo – he had won the battle of Friedland in these forests and marshes. Five of the marshals who were with him now had fought in that campaign; the two opposites, Davout and Murat; the red-haired Ney; Oudinot, with his saintly face and diabolical temper; and Berthier, the incomparable chief-of-staff. But if the great names of the Empire were comfortably reassuring, the army itself had an unfamiliar aspect. At Friedland the presence of a foreign leavening among the mass of French troops had been a novelty which called for comment and, after the victory, for gratification. By 1812 the balance had changed. Over half the infantry and a third of the cavalry were not French. The Emperor spent nearly a fortnight inspecting the Grand Army in East Prussia. Some two dozen French regiments went past him in review, ten from Würtemberg, three from the north German states, Poles, Spaniards, Croats, impressed Portuguese, and Slovenes from the Illyrian Provinces. Had Napoleon gone further south he would have found an even higher proportion of foreign troops. The Second Army, which was nominally led by his stepson Eugène Beauharnais, was predominantly Italian and south German.

The Third Army, under his brother Jérôme, was two-thirds Polish and Saxon. And, in addition, there were the independent Prussian and Austrian divisions. With such a mixture of nationalities and languages it was easy to believe that continental Europe had turned against Asia.

On parade the Empire always bore itself with extravagant magnificence. That June, as the line swung past Napoleon behind eagle-topped sabres and bugle bands it still formed an impressive spectacle. There was an array of noble headgear – tall bearskins, row upon row of shakoes, the glittering helmets of the dragoons, the schapskas of the lancers. The uniforms themselves were no less colourful: the dragoons wore green cloaks, the grenadiers scarlet epaulettes and the Polish lancers crimson breastplates; and the sky blue braided jackets of the light hussars formed an appropriate contrast to the thick red chenille cord of the heavy cavalry. The troops, as Caulaincourt noted, 'received their Emperor with real enthusiasm' and seemed 'full of ardour and good health.' Napoleon would address them in a bluff and blunt manner. Then he would dismount and walk briefly down the ranks. Having familiarized himself with the record of the regiments he was inspecting, he would come to a stop before a veteran and make an allusion to Austerlitz or Jena or Wagram, emphasizing his words with a hearty slap on the shoulder. It was an effective way of identifying the man in the ranks with his commander. As Ségur, one of his aides, wrote in his refreshingly astringent memoirs, 'The veteran who thus assumed he had been recognized by the Emperor felt himself grow in stature and glory before his envious and less experienced comrades.'

Few of the men whom Napoleon inspected in Danzig or Insterburg or Gumbinnen seem to have known why they were marching against Russia; even fewer cared. To the old soldiers one campaign was much like another. Sergeant Bourgogne of the Imperial Guard had been seventeen hundred miles away in March, avoiding Wellington's bayonets at Almeida and the knives of the Spanish guerrillas in the mountain defiles. He had not expected to be hurried so far eastward, with only forty-eight hours' leave in Paris, but he was not surprised. So long as he had good quarters for the winter and the opportunity, as he put it, 'of making conquests of another nature,' he would be content. Moscow, no doubt, would prove as convenient as Madrid or Vienna or Berlin for his purposes. 'From war to love, and from love to war – such is the French soldier's character,' he wrote.

The rank and file of the other national contingents had a similar attitude, although the Poles were, to some extent, fired by a genuine patriotic enthusiasm (which would be satisfied in Vilna rather than Moscow). Some regiments, such as the Croats, had merely exchanged service with one foreign emperor for that of another; this one was a better soldier, had panache about him, and gave the impression of caring for the everyday details of their service life; what did it matter whom they were fighting, or why? But among the young French conscripts, for whom these reviews were a prelude to adventure, there was excitement and speculation about the ultimate objective of the expedition. None believed it was merely to defeat Tsar Alexander – 'We shall soon cook that little emperor's goose for him,' a fusilier wrote home to his parents. Some, with a sounder knowledge of history than geography, thought that Napoleon was off once more to Syria and Egypt. But the favourite destination corresponded with the fantasy that had beckoned Napoleon on for so many years. 'We are going to Greater India,' wrote the fusilier, and, being a knowledgeable lad he added, 'It is three thousand miles from Paris.'

On Sunday, June 21, at ten pm, Napoleon arrived coated with dust at a hunting lodge in a straggling village of thatched cottages on the borders of a pine forest. The Poles called the place Wilkowiszki, although Napoleon could only manage 'Wicowiski' in his letter to the Empress. There he was in the midst of the 60,000 men of Davout's First Corps who were to form the vanguard of the invading army. At Wilkowiszki Napoleon was slightly more than four hundred miles from St Petersburg and five hundred from Moscow. He had already travelled a thousand miles since leaving Saint Cloud six weeks before.

That Monday, in a summer pavilion shaded by lofty poplars, he dictated a proclamation which was to be read to all the units of the

Grand Army, except for the Prussian and Austrian contingents, at dawn on June 24. It rang with all the old fire, evoking the victories of the recent past as a promise of triumph in the new crusade and solemnly placing the responsibility for war on the perfidious Russians:

> Soldiers! the second Polish War has begun. The first was brought to an end at Friedland and at Tilsit. It was at Tilsit that Russia swore eternal alliance with France and war with England. Today she is breaking her plighted word . . . Does she think that we are degenerate? Are we no longer the soldiers of Austerlitz? She confronts us with war or dishonour: there can be no doubt about our choice. Let us then go forward! We will cross the Niemen and carry war into her territory. The second Polish War will be as glorious for French arms as the first. But the peace which we shall make will carry a guarantee and will put an end to the baleful influence which Russia has exercised for fifty years on the affairs of Europe.

It was, apparently, to be a war for the liberation of Poland, the sanctity of treaties and the self-esteem of the French Empire. Like most such documents, the proclamation treated the facts a little freely but, at all events, it did so with impeccable style.

After working all day in intolerable heat – 'We are in the dog days,' he wrote to Marie-Louise – the Emperor, who was in a testy mood, rode out that evening into the woods with Berthier, Caulaincourt, Castellane and three other officers. They took supper in a clearing beside the home of the local priest. Napoleon, having a Polish interpreter with him, decided to examine the priest. 'For whom do you pray?' he asked. 'For me or the Russians?' 'For your Majesty,' came the dutiful reply. 'And so you ought,' responded Napoleon blandly, 'as a Pole and a Catholic.' He gave him 40,000 francs to indemnify him for the damage caused by the passage of the troops and returned to his headquarters. He had done something for Poland, after all.

Later that night, in the small hours of Tuesday, Napoleon rode down to the river. The woods were full of troops. Beneath the pines long columns of infantry and more than a thousand guns were waiting and the auxiliary battalions which had been sent to throw pontoon bridges across the Niemen stood ready. More than 160,000 men were massed along thirty miles of river, in a bend facing the city of Kaunas. But, as yet, this concentration was unsuspected by the Russians. They knew, of course, that Napoleon had been inspecting the Army of the Vistula and they had received reports of Jérôme Bonaparte's Army moving up from the Bug towards Grodno, but they had no idea of the scale of preparation on the borders of Lithuania. The only troops on the actual river bank were Polish lancers; for Napoleon had expressly ordered that the first French troops to show themselves to the enemy must be the engineers of General Eblé who were to assemble the bridges; thus would there be complete surprise.

Napoleon personally played a part in this deception. When he and Berthier reached the Niemen they disguised themselves in the long coats and black hats of Polish lancers for fear that in the clear moonlight they might be seen by Cossack patrols on the other side. For some hours they looked out on Kaunas through the window of a cottage and watched dawn come up behind the towers and white walls of an abbey church. There was no sign of Russian activity to left or right of them, only the still waters of the winding river, no breeze and little current. They came out of the cottage, joined other staff officers and together rode for four miles along the left bank. It was then that Napoleon selected the points at which he wished the bridges to be sited. As he was cantering back through a field, a hare rushed out from beneath his horse, which was startled and threw Napoleon on the soft, sandy soil. He swiftly remounted and said little about the incident, but his staff, who were as superstitious as campaigners of the ancient world, were despondent. Berthier turned to Caulaincourt and remarked grimly, 'It would be as well if we did not cross the Niemen. This fall is a bad omen.' The news spread quickly around headquarters; and rumour added that the horse from which the Emperor had tumbled was the charger named Friedland.

After his reconnaissance, Napoleon decided to send the main body of his troops across the river on the following day, Wednesday, June 24. Caulaincourt says that throughout the Tuesday he was silent and pre-occupied, as though disturbed by his misadventure, and

Ségur describes how he tried in vain to take a siesta in the humid atmosphere. However, he found time to dictate a five-thousand-word directive with minute instructions for crossing the Niemen and entering Kaunas; and in the evening, as the hour for action drew nearer, his spirits rose. He sent for Caulaincourt and tried to convince him that it would be a short campaign. 'Russia will sue for peace in less than two months,' he said. 'The big landowners will be terrified and some of them ruined. Tsar Alexander will be in a very awkward position.' And, mounting Friedland, he rode out to watch the sappers bring the pontoons up to the river bank.

The crossing of the Niemen was a brilliant operation. It was not a wide river, no broader in fact than the Seine at Paris, but it was essential to move the troops across before the Russians could bring up cannon to the other bank. Some of Davout's corps had reported seeing Russian guns facing them, but Davout himself discounted the idea and, after his ride along the river-bank, Napoleon had every reason for agreeing with him. He was himself inclined to believe, as he told Caulaincourt, that the Russians had already retreated, but prudence dictated a speedy crossing.

All went according to plan. At ten that night there was no bridge across the Niemen: by midnight the sappers had erected three. There was no opposition, but a commotion could be heard downstream at Kaunas: 'The entire city heard it and beyond a doubt everyone guessed that such a din could be produced only by the march of a great army,' a Russian observer wrote. A patrol cautiously went forward and, shortly after the advance party had reached the right bank, a lone Cossack officer came down to them from the woods, 'What do you want?' he asked, 'Why do you come to Russia?' And he received the blunt reply, 'To make war on you! To take Vilna and set Poland free!' Then, like a bear who has scented enemies, he disappeared among the trees. The men were excited; three random shots rang out, but from the Russian patrol there was no response. In this curious and almost casual way, hostilities began between two great empires. It was the nearest the French came to a declaration of war.

Three hills overlooked the French position. On the highest of them was the blue and white rectangular tent which accompanied the Emperor when he went into the field. Outside it, dominating the main route down to the river, some of his guards had erected an improvised throne of branches and turf on a dais of foliage. It was, no doubt, an appropriate saluting base for a midsummer's night, but Napoleon was in no mood to play Oberon. He soon left it and at five in the morning rode Friedland across to the Russian side of the river and cantered off for some three miles towards Kaunas. He returned to the tent for breakfast in fine spirits and stood watching the steady procession of men and guns and horses pass down to the river, impatiently snapping his riding whip and humming to himself the simple tympanic rhythm of *Malbrouck s'enva-t-en guerre*.

All that morning the troops went by, the sun glinting on their weapons. Things occasionally went wrong – guns stuck in the sandy soil, infantrymen lost their footing on the slopes and arrived at the bridge with precipitate inelegance – but, for the most part, it might well have been yet one more of the Emperor's endless reviews with Napoleon himself solemnly acknowledging the salute of regiment after regiment. By noon he had had enough of this and he rode across the bridge again and waited on the Russian bank while the Old Guard was mustered; and, in the evening, mounted, significantly, on Moscow, he accompanied them into Kaunas.

That night Napoleon slept in a Russian monastery three-quarters of a mile outside the town. A letter duly went off to the Empress, who was with her family in Prague: 'I crossed the Niemen on the twenty-fourth. I have seized Kaunas. No serious engagement took place. My health is good but the heat is extreme.' And, turning to other problems, he added, 'By all means, present the University with a collection of books and engravings. This will please it enormously and cost you nothing. I have plenty of them.' With an undefended Russian city in his hands, the master of Europe felt well able to permit his wife such regal munificence.

3

Vilna and Drissa

While Napoleon was progressing from Dresden to Danzig and on to the banks of the Niemen, Tsar Alexander remained at Vilna, barely seventy-five miles from the point where the Grand Army eventually crossed the river. His arrival in the old Lithuanian capital two months before had been marked by fêtes and ornate receptions; and the visit had continued as it began. There was a succession of balls and entertainments. An attitude of feverish irrelevance, of almost hysterical contempt for the menace which had fetched the Tsar to this outlandish city, seemed to grip all who were there. Throughout the sultry summer days carriages clattered in from the north with the young ladies of St Petersburg society, intent on outshining the pretentious Polish nobility and oblivious to all danger of invasion. Amid guttering candles and accompanied by the ceaseless sound of polonaises, rank and fashion gossiped, gambled and flirted night after night.

Yet despite this background of frivolous unreality, something was done to prepare for the campaign. The Tsar had plenty of counsellors. Arakcheyev and Bennigsen were there and so were his Minister of Police, General Balashov, and his Secretary of State, Admiral Shishkov. And when he wished, Alexander could seek the opinion of the Minister of War, Barclay de Tolly, or of some of the émigrés who had taken service with the Russians, men like the Swedish general, Armfeldt, or the Würtemberger, Wintzingerode.

The experts pored over the maps and sought to analyse the intelligence reports of French movements which reached them. Consistently they underestimated the size of the Grand Army and were woefully ignorant of its concentration in the woods beyond

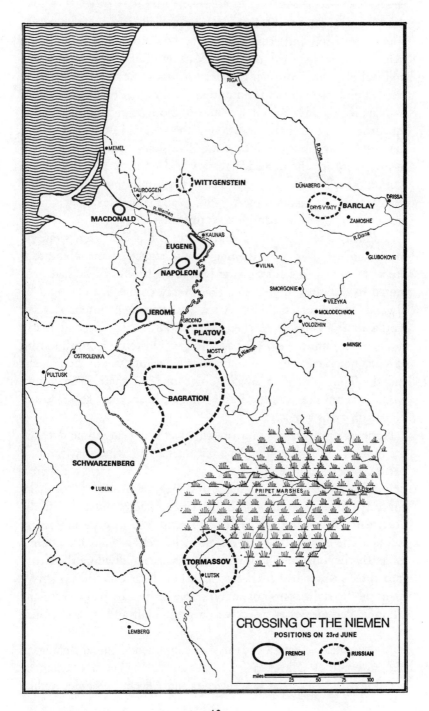

RIGA

MEMEL

TAUROGGEN

WITTGENSTEIN

DÜNABERG

DRISSA

DRYS VYATY

BARCLAY

ZAMOSHE

R.Niemen

MACDONALD

KAUNAS

R.Diana

EUGENE

GLUBOKOYE

NAPOLEON

VILNA

SMORGONIE

VILEYKA

JEROME

MOLODECHNOK

GRODNO

VOLOZHIN

PLATOV

MINSK

MOSTY

R.Niemen

OSTROLENKA

PULTUSK

BAGRATION

SCHWARZENBERG

LUBLIN

PRIPET MARSHES

R.Pripet

TORMASSOV

LUTSK

LEMBERG

CROSSING OF THE NIEMEN

POSITIONS ON 23rd JUNE

FRENCH   RUSSIAN

miles

25   50   75   100

43

the Niemen. Some of the Tsar's advisers even believed that he should take the initiative and order Barclay, as the senior commander in the field, to press forward towards Warsaw. But there were grave political objections to such a course: it would have resurrected the whole Polish problem and committed Austria and Prussia irrevocably to Napoleon's side. Alexander himself thought of sending a naval squadron to the Adriatic and raising the standard of revolt among the South Slavs: but this interesting diversion – which owed much in inspiration to the precedent Orlov had set in Greece during his grandmother's reign –would need not only time, but vessels which could reach the Mediterranean; and, in the end, Alexander got no farther than finding an admiral to command them.

Gradually the Tsar decided to settle for a defensive strategy. More and more he was listening to the advice of the ubiquitous Pfuel, whom, to the fury of the Russian staff officers, he had promoted to the rank of General. The 'Army of the West' would be divided into three: the First Army (118,000 men) under Barclay would retire to the entrenched camp at Drissa; the Second Army (35,000 men) under General Bagration would retire from the south of Vilna north-eastwards so as to attack the right flank of the French; and the Third Army, a smaller force under General Tormassov, would concentrate south of the Pripet Marshes, so as to watch Napoleon's Austrian allies.

None of the Russian commanders liked this plan: some detested the notion of abandoning the Lithuanian provinces without a battle; others discounted the likelihood of the Drissa defences defying Napoleon long enough for Bagration's army to make contact; and all were convinced that, since it had originated with the doctrinaire Pfuel, the whole concept must *ipso facto* be inherently wrong. The debate dragged on inconclusively around the council table. By the fourth week of June the principle of dividing the Army into three groups had been accepted, but there was still no agreement on the right course of action once the invader had crossed the frontier. Perhaps, after all, it was a great bluff and he would not come.

Meanwhile, the round of festivities continued. General Bennigsen had an estate at Zakret, a few miles outside Vilna, and when he heard that the officers at headquarters and Alexander's aides wished to give a grand ball, he put his house at their disposal. Zakret was a rare gem in that part of Europe; its elegance belonged to the west. There were fine grounds, with fountains and lakes and waterfalls, and the grass was as green as the turf of an English landscape garden. The mansion itself was, however, small and the officers decided to give the ball on the lawns under a huge awning. They selected the night of Wednesday, June 24, when a full moon would show everything to advantage. While preparations were being made on the Monday – that same Monday on which, a hundred miles away, Napoleon was dictating his proclamation to the Grand Army – the roof of the improvised ballroom suddenly collapsed.

This minor catastrophe seemed an omen to the Jeremiahs, of course; but, two days later, the festivities went ahead as planned, with the dances beginning under the evening sky on the lawns. When night fell the guests moved indoors, filling the candle-lit ballroom. It was there that General Balashov was seen to go up to the Tsar and speak softly to him: a messenger had come from Kaunas to tell them that a massive French army had crossed the river that morning. There was no change in the Tsar's expression. He told Balashov to keep the news to himself and gave his attention once more to the intricacies of a mazurka. Then, stepping into the gardens, he admired the decorative lanterns in the trees and the set-piece fireworks; and someone saw him look up at the moon in the clear sky and heard him say, 'That is the finest illumination of them all.' Soon after he took his carriage back to Vilna. Balashov broke his silence. And suddenly the ball was over.

Alexander spent the rest of that night at work in his study, sending staff officers to resolve, if possible, the doubts of his generals about Pfuel's strategy. All were agreed that they must retire from the Vilna region; and, since withdrawal to the camp at Drissa at least placed Barclay in a position to guard either the road to St Petersburg or the road to Moscow, it was decided to carry out the first stages of the plan. But Alexander still thought that there might be a faint possibility of negotiating a settlement. On the Thursday night he sent for Balashov and gave him a letter for Napoleon. He was to inform the Emperor that, as soon as his armies withdrew across the frontier, negotiations could at once begin; but otherwise, 'the Tsar gives his word of honour that he will neither utter nor

45

listen to a single word about peace so long as an armed French soldier remains on Russian soil.' It was a proud sentiment for a man who, after Austerlitz, had been contemptuously dismissed by his generals as no better than a coward.

Balashov set out along the Kaunas road within an hour of receiving his orders from Alexander. He reached the Russian outposts at the village of Rykonty as the sun came up on Friday morning. Escorted by a junior officer, a Cossack and a trumpeter, he continued for an hour through the silent countryside until he was halted by two surprised hussars from the French advanced headquarters. They eventually took him to Murat, who, wearing a 'highly theatrical costume' of red and gold, of which Balashov strongly disapproved, received him amiably although he showed little desire to conduct him to Napoleon. At last, he was allowed to proceed farther up the road to the next village, only to be detained again by guards who brought him before Davout. This time his reception was openly hostile. Davout had little to say to him, but demanded that the letter from the Tsar to Napoleon should be handed over. Under protest, Balashov gave Davout the message and it was forwarded to the Emperor at Kaunas; but Balashov remained at Davout's head-quarters virtually under open arrest. In all, he was kept with Davout's staff for four days.

This treatment of the Tsar's emissary is curious. There is little doubt that Davout thought his mission a ruse; he believed that he had been sent to find out all he could about the composition and organization of the Grand Army. But the responsibility for the protracted delay was not Davout's alone. On the Saturday Napoleon himself rode out from Kaunas and, although Balashov did not know it, conferred with both Davout and Murat. Had he wished, Napoleon could easily have sent for Balashov that afternoon. He preferred to keep Alexander's representative waiting until he had more to show than the mere occupation of Kaunas and a few border villages. Moreover, there were sound reasons why Balashov should not see what was happening to the Grand Army just then.

'My health is good. My affairs are going well,' Napoleon had written to Marie-Louise on the previous day. But were they? There was still no sign of the big, decisive battle that he had confidently predicted would be fought and won as soon as he set foot on Russian soil. Indeed, there was very little sign of the enemy at all. He had ordered Oudinot with the Second Corps and Ney with the Third to cross the Niemen at the same point as Davout's First Corps for fear that, if they sought to bridge it elsewhere, they might be defeated in isolated actions. But this caution was needless; the Russian army appeared to have dissolved into the sun-baked infinity of an endless plain. Around him was nothing but empty fields, deserted forests and an uncanny silence.

Disengagement was bad enough; it was even worse that the troops should be moving forward in a heat that none of them had ever known before, except the veterans of Egypt. Moreover, since crossing the Niemen, the supply system had come under a severe strain; rations were not getting through to the weary men and horses, and there was little enough for them to gather from the fields as they went. Some of the cavalry tried feeding their horses on green corn and many, in consequence, died. Count Anatole de Montesquiou, one of the junior officers on Napoleon's staff, counted the bodies of 1,240 horses as he rode twelve miles down the road towards Vilna. It was a sorry start to the campaign.

Even after the privations of the following winter, men still remembered the shock of those first days when they came to write their memoirs. Despite all the detailed planning which had preceded the campaign, convoys of food were delayed on the roads – hardly more than cart-tracks – from the towns of east Prussia to Kaunas, and the approaches to the bridges became choked. Moreover, once they had crossed the river, there was confusion about their destination, for the various regiments had been hustled forward at a far more rapid rate than anyone had contemplated when it was assumed that the Russians would offer early battle. Some units had fared well, but others were in desperate straits. Every man had been issued with subsistence rations for at least five days, but too much was expected from some of the least experienced troops and they began to fall out along the roads. Many went off into the forests and pillaged isolated cottages – a development which particularly infuriated Napoleon, who was anxious to placate the Polish and Lithuanian inhabitants of this disputed frontier region. The weather was treacherous: the stifling heat of the days was followed by raw nights, and sudden storms of heavy rain began to blow up on the Saturday afternoon, turning the dusty roads into squelching tracks of mud. Worst hit were the recruits of the Young Guard, the pick of French conscripts for the preceding two years. Caulaincourt wrote later, 'Their commanders wished these young men to rival the veterans who had come through so much peril and borne so many privations and burdens; and the youth of the army thus became the victims of misplaced zeal. Many of the Young Guard perished along the road from cold and hunger and fatigue.' By the small hours of Sunday morning, when the hussars approached the outskirts of Vilna, the Grand Army had already lost much of the panache that had carried it across the Niemen only four days before. It is hardly surprising that Davout sought to hide all this from the eyes of Alexander's emissary. He was expressly ordered by Napoleon to convey Balashov back to Vilna by 'a different route from that followed by the army.'

Napoleon arrived at Vilna on Sunday afternoon (June 30). It was a dismal scene. Heavy rain was beating down with almost tropical force. Smoke was still curling upwards from stores fired by Barclay's men before they evacuated the city on the previous day. The bridge had been destroyed by the Russians and Napoleon's own troops had pillaged the town for food and drink as soon as they arrived. The shutters were up in the houses and not a face peered down at the Emperor. His own feelings were mixed: here was the last of the great Polish cities handed over to him without a fight; and yet, instead of being welcomed as a liberator as he had anticipated, he was shunned as a foreign conqueror. 'These Poles,' he remarked, ruefully, 'are not like those in the Duchy of Warsaw.' As for the Russians, they must be cowards to have surrendered such a prize. Balashov deserved to be kept waiting for a few days: perhaps by then there would be some Russian prisoners brought in, and the townspeople might have begun to appreciate the advantages of being despoiled by the French.

In the hope of establishing contact with the main Russian army, Napoleon sent out reconnaissance forces in strength but they made slow progress through the heavy rain and achieved little, apart from

Napoleon and the Empress of Austria at Dresden

Marshal Murat, the King of Naples

Marshal Davout

The Grand Army crossing the Niemen

bringing him information about conditions to the north-east of the city. He also set about turning Vilna into an advanced base and spent a couple of days touring the neighbourhood. Still there were no signs of enthusiasm from the people of Vilna; they remained totally apathetic, although the entry of Polish lancers had, at first, aroused a few cheers from their compatriots. The town officials had to be summoned to the Emperor's residence before they would commit themselves to any act of co-operation. To the people of Vilna, with looting marauders quartered among them, the festive weeks of Tsar Alexander's visit seemed in retrospect to have held promise of a golden age; their loyalty remained with him.

Napoleon's failure to win the support of the Poles and Lithuanians in Vilna explains, in part, his behaviour towards Balashov. On July 1 he at last granted the Russian an audience. It took place in the very room from which Alexander had despatched him on his mission five days previously. No attempt was made to hide the irony of the situation. It was a strange meeting. Napoleon began the conversation with patronizing self-confidence: he regretted that the Tsar's bad advisers should have made war inevitable between the two empires, even though 'neither he nor I know what we are fighting for.' But Napoleon could not maintain this gracious, imperial manner for long. As Balashov began to answer his charges, he became more and more agitated. Why had Alexander demanded a French withdrawal from Prussia? Why had he made him concentrate so many men in Poland at a time when he had intended to go to Spain and dispose of Wellington's army? The Emperor paced up and down the room, glowering at the Russian. Once a window blew open. Napoleon shut it angrily and resumed his denunciations. Why had Alexander allowed himself to be surrounded by 'banished scoundrels' who were the sworn enemies of France? The window blew open again. Napoleon wrenched it from its hinges and the sound of shattering glass echoed through the courtyard as it hit the cobbles. And, in the room above, the rhetorical questions still continued, each of them making clear Napoleon's basic uncertainty and irritation. Why had the Russians assembled stores at Vilna if they only intended to burn them? Were not the Russians ashamed at having abandoned Vilna without a battle? Was this how they sought to inspire their people? There were answers to many of these points, but Napoleon was not interested in them. Each time Balashov attempted to reply, the Emperor cut him short. All Europe, he said, was behind him; had not Balashov seen the enthusiasm with which the Poles, for example, welcomed the opportunity of serving him? He knew the size of Russia's army: her cause was hopeless. 'Tell the Emperor Alexander I can assure him, on my word of honour, that I have 550,000 men this side of the Vistula.' If Alexander wished to avoid a protracted and costly campaign, he would understand his sentiments, for he was himself neither against negotiations nor against peace. And then, reverting to his earlier mood, he courteously dismissed Balashov; 'In the course of the day, I shall prepare a letter for the Emperor Alexander,' he added.

That night Balashov dined with Napoleon and his entourage. The Emperor was in good spirits. He had reviewed three regiments on the outskirts of the city in the early evening and, as he returned through Vilna, there had been cheers from some Polish volunteers. At dinner he was arrogant and intransigent, basking in the glamour of making history; he was also – and this was characteristic – childishly mischievous. 'Is it true,' he inquired with facetious innocence, 'that the Emperor Alexander spent his days at Vilna taking tea with a local beauty?' And turning to his chamberlain he asked, 'What was her name, Turenne?' 'Soulistrowska, Sire,' Turenne dutifully replied. 'Ah, yes, Soulistrowska,' echoed Napoleon, cocking his eye at Balashov to see if he resented the innuendo on his sovereign's private life. Other questions followed. Did Alexander really allow the foreign exiles to eat at this table with him? How could the autocrat of Russia tolerate the close companionship of Armfeldt and that incorrigible trouble-maker from Prussia, Heinrich vom Stein? The conversation – if such it can be called – then took a curious turn. The French intelligence services had kept Napoleon well informed of Russian conditions; he had already boasted of his knowledge of the Russian army to Balashov. But now he began to ask elementary questions about Moscow – how many inhabitants? How many houses? How many churches? And finally, glaring fixedly at his guest, 'What is the road to Moscow?'

The Russian had had enough. He was left in little doubt of the purpose of this interrogation: he was to inform the Tsar that Napoleon had every intention of marching on Russia's greatest city.

At last Balashov was able to make an adequate rejoinder: 'Sire, that question embarrasses me a little. Just as the French say "All roads lead to Rome", so in Russia all roads lead to Moscow. One chooses the road one wishes: Charles the Twelfth chose the road through Poltava.' The point cannot have been lost on Napoleon. He had read his Voltaire; he knew that, at Poltava, the Swedish king had been put to flight by Peter the Great. They adjourned for coffee to Napoleon's study, and the conversation moved to less dangerous ground. Eventually, Balashov was given horses for his journey back to the Russian camp and handed a letter he was to bear to Alexander. The parley was at an end.

Napoleon's letter to the Tsar shows the same nervous uncertainty as his conversation with Balashov. For nearly a thousand words Napoleon seeks to put all the blame for the war on the Russians. This was to be expected. But the Emperor was still convinced that Alexander would reverse his policy suddenly, as he had done after Friedland. Napoleon hoped that he might be able to keep in touch with Alexander even while invading his empire. The last section has a special significance:

Should Your Majesty wish to end hostilities, you will find me ready to do so. If Your Majesty is determined to continue the war, and would like to draw up an agreement on liberal lines, such as that men in hospital shall not be considered prisoners, or such as a fortnightly exchange of prisoners, rank for rank . . . or any other stipulations commonly allowed by the rules of war between civilized nations; then Your Majesty will find me ready for anything. And, even if, despite hostilities, Your Majesty wishes to maintain direct communication with me, that also could be provided for and regulated by the agreement. It only remains for me to end by begging Your Majesty to believe that . . . my private feelings towards you remain unaffected by these events, and that, should fortune again favour my arms, you will find me, as at Tilsit and Erfurt, full of friendship and esteem for your good and great qualities, and anxious only to prove it.

To such a message Alexander thought it unworthy to reply. He had already pledged himself to continue the war until the French had been thrown out of his realm. There was to be no further communication between the two emperors until Moscow had gone up in flames.

Napoleon remained in Vilna for two and a half weeks. There were many reasons for this delay. Some, perhaps, were unavoidable; heavy rain had made the roads almost impassable and transport was disorganized. Others were political; he had to set up a provisional government for these Lithuanian provinces of Poland, linking it with the puppet administration in the Grand-Duchy of Warsaw. He had also to transform Vilna into an advanced staging-post for his empire. From Vilna it was possible for couriers to reach Paris in ten days' hard riding. But this was not good enough. Some of the services of the capital had to cross Europe and establish offices here in Lithuania. Maret, the Foreign Minister, came for a time and he was accompanied by the diplomatic representatives of five of France's European allies and, rather unexpectedly, by the American Minister in Paris. And, of course, supplies and stores had to be moved into Vilna from the depots already established at Warsaw, Thorn, Marienburg and Danzig. The city grew out of all recognition.

Yet the prime reason for Napoleon's protracted stay was military. Confused and contradictory reports reached him from the surrounding countryside. Disappointed at being denied a second Wagram on the outskirts of Vilna, Napoleon decided that his main task must still be to bring Barclay's army to battle as soon as possible, and preferably west of the river Dvina. As he had informed Metternich at Dresden, he had every intention of advancing that summer as far as Smolensk, a city almost equidistant from Vilna and Moscow. But it was essential to have gained a striking victory over the Russians before entering Smolensk. Provided that he had destroyed Barclay's army, he could well afford to halt there and await overtures for peace from Alexander. Barclay de Tolly was therefore his principal adversary and he assigned the two army corps of Ney and Oudinot, supported by Murat's cavalry, for the advance to the Dvina. Anxiously, he waited in Vilna for news that they had made contact with the main force of the enemy. He waited in vain.

Meanwhile, he became more and more concerned with the activities of the Russian Second Army, commanded by Prince Bagration. Originally he had given little attention to Bagration's force since his spies told him that it was less than 40,000 strong. He had hoped that his brother Jérôme, who had concentrated an army twice as large around Warsaw, would dispose of Bagration in the early days of the campaign. Jérôme seemed to have begun well enough. He met a Russian corps around the town of Grodno, which fell to him without much difficulty, at the same time as Murat entered Vilna. But it soon became clear that Jérôme's opponents were not part of the Second Army at all; he had met the cavalry corps of Platov, who was attached to Barclay's force in much the same way as Murat was to Napoleon's.

Where, then, was Bagration? On June 29 a brigade of Polish lancers and French chasseurs stumbled across a Russian rearguard holding the small town of Oszmiana, thirty-five miles south-east of Vilna. At once there was a general alert at Napoleon's headquarters. Couriers were sent out to Jérôme ordering him to hasten to Oszmiana; and Davout was sent off there with the whole of the First Army Corps. They hastened as fast as they could through the torrential rain into a heavily wooded countryside. There were no Russians to be found. Once again the information had been wrong. The troops defending Oszmiana were a detachment of the Russian Fifth Corps under Docturov, which in the appalling weather had lost touch with the main body of Barclay's army. Docturov withdrew hastily at the approach of Davout and, while his men were scouring the forests, the Fifth Corps was already some forty miles away and moving northwards.

At Oszmiana on July 1 Davout received an urgent message from Napoleon. By now the Emperor was certain that Bagration was retiring on Minsk and he ordered Davout to head to the south. This time the French had made an accurate prediction although, curiously enough, they had done so in error. For the troops whose detailed movements Napoleon sent to Davout were not Bagration's rearguard, but Platov's Cossacks, who had abandoned all attempt to reunite with the Russian First Army and were screening Bagration from the north. It made little difference. Davout moved remorselessly forward with three columns towards Minsk while, to his west, a Westphalian army corps from Jérôme's force was pressing forward under General Vandamme. All through the first week of July two of Napoleon's armies converged on the elusive Bagration, moving across a grey and green landscape with the freedom of naval squadrons on the open sea. Everything was poised for a great battle; it seemed impossible for Bagration to escape destruction.

Day after day the Emperor himself, still at Vilna, rode relentlessly around the surrounding hills or sat with Berthier impatiently sifting fact from rumour in the messages that reached him. His greatest concern was his brother, Jérôme, the King of Westphalia. At heart he knew that Jérôme, the youngest of the Bonaparte family, was an amateur soldier, totally unsuited for the responsibilities involved in leading an army into Russia. On June 30 Napoleon had heard that Jérôme was safely in Grodno, barely eighty miles away, but for the next three days he had no news of him. How far had Vandamme progressed? Was Poniatowski in pursuit with the Polish cavalry? Napoleon did not know. Then, on the Friday afternoon (July 3), a messenger at last rode in from Grodno. But the only information that he had brought was that Jérôme had dismissed General Vandamme from his command for suspected embezzlement. Napoleon was beside himself with rage. On the Saturday a stinging rebuke went off to Grodno:

> I can only show my displeasure at the little information you have sent me . . . My operations are held up for lack of news from Grodno . . . It is impossible to wage war like this. You think and talk of nothing but trifles. I am sorry to see how petty all your interests are . . . You are compromising the success of the whole campaign on the right flank. It is impossible to wage war like this.

It is small wonder that Napoleon was angry. Jérôme's dispute with Vandamme had halted the Westphalian corps at a crucial moment. Bagration was slipping away south of Minsk and Jérôme, who did not even leave Grodno until after receiving his brother's letter on the Sunday, was far too distant to put pressure on him. Again there was an angry scene at Vilna and Berthier was ordered to send another imperial blast to the unfortunate King of Westphalia: 'Tell him,' said Napoleon, 'that the fruits of my manœuvres and the most magnificent chance in the war have been lost through his strange ignorance of the elementary principles of strategy.' And, at the same time Davout was secretly authorized to assume command of Jérôme's army if Bagration could be brought to battle.

Yet, even allowing for the unpardonable inactivity of Jérôme, the odds were still against Bagration. Davout's corps was forcing him inexorably towards the northern edge of the Pripet Marshes, a region where men could move only slowly along a narrow causeway, knowing that any accident to horse or vehicle would leave them floundering in a bottomless expanse of reeds and stagnant water. But Bagration had no intention of leading his men into such a disaster. He was better informed of his opponent's movements than they were of his own. Davout hoped to catch him in Minsk. He entered the city on Wednesday, July 8, and captured a considerable quantity of Russian stores; but there was no sign of Bagration. Two days previously, learning from his scouts of Davout's advance, he had changed his line of march and, while the French were hungrily pillaging his depots, Bagration was sixty miles away to the southwest in the small town of Nesvizh. Once again he had slipped away.

A fortnight had now passed since Napoleon had watched Davout's corps cross the Niemen. They had moved swiftly, averaging a dozen miles a day in sultry weather with frequent storms of almost tropical intensity. But, apart from skirmishes between patrols, there had been little activity. And the same was true of every other unit in the Grand Army. It was a strange war of movement – and no action.

The Emperor lingered in Vilna: that evening (July 8), with the sun still high in the sky at eight o'clock in the northern latitude, he took the salute as three divisions of the Guard filed past him a mile outside the city. It was, as ever, a fine spectacle; but with each day that he spent in Vilna the chances of a rapid, victorious campaign became more and more remote. His messages to Marie-Louise no longer contained the optimistic promise that he would be with her in a couple of months. The same formula crept in, in letter after letter – 'My affairs are going well. My health is good.' It was an elaborate euphemism for indicating that nothing had happened. He continued to hope for news that Murat had made contact with Barclay's army as it moved towards the Dvina. But Barclay, like

Bagration, had eluded his pursuers. Somewhere, a hundred thousand men were following their Tsar eastwards: where exactly they were, Napoleon had no idea. The boundless undulating plain, with towns fifty miles apart and villages mere collections of wooden huts, seemed to have swallowed them up in its sullen emptiness.

If Napoleon was perplexed, so too was Tsar Alexander. On that same Wednesday he at last reached Pfuel's vaunted entrenched camp at Drissa, two days ahead of Barclay de Tolly and the main body of the First Army. He had long intended to give battle to Napoleon there: that, after all, was the reason why for so many months the peasants had worked at throwing up three lines of fortifications behind the swamps facing the river.

When Barclay and his staff arrived, they soon saw the folly of Pfuel's plan. On one side of the camp there were no fortifications whatsoever. Moreover, the original strategic concept had assumed that, once Drissa was invested, the Second Army, under Bagration, would catch its attackers on the flank. But at that moment Bagration was 180 miles away, and cut off from the First Army by Davout's corps in Minsk. To remain in Drissa was to invite annihilation. Barclay was sure of it and so were the émigré officers attached to the Tsar's entourage. Clausewitz, greatest of all the theorists of war, inspected the camp in that first week of July. He had few illusions about his fellow Prussian's brain-child: 'If the Russians had not abandoned this position of their own accord,' he wrote later, 'they would have been attacked from the rear . . . driven into the semi-circle of trenches, and forced to surrender.'

There were hurried military conferences. Much time was spent in recrimination. To blame Pfuel would have been tactless, for it implied criticism of the Tsar, who had given him his confidence. Almost inevitably the absent Bagration was made the scapegoat. For years there had been a feud between Bagration and Barclay: now Barclay had his chance. He was, of course, not only commander of the First Army, but Minister of War; and he complained that Bagration had wasted time in questioning his instructions and had abandoned Minsk to Davout, thereby losing all the supplies accumulated there. To some extent, Bagration had expected this criticism and he had already despatched an angry apologia to Arakcheyev, which he must have known would reach the Tsar: 'I am not to blame for anything,' he had written. 'First they stretch me like a bow-string while the enemy breaks into our lines without firing a shot. Then we begin to retreat – nobody knows why . . . I alone cannot defend all of Russia. The First Army should, without fail, advance on Vilna at once. What is there to fear? . . . I implore you to advance . . . It ill suits Russians to run . . . One feels ashamed.'

The Tsar wished, if possible, to avoid a choice between Barclay and Bagration. There was little doubt which was the abler commander. Bagration had made his reputation under Suvorov in Switzerland and northern Italy when Barclay was no more than a hard-working and conscientious colonel. Similarly, there was no question that Bagration, although at times a fire-eating braggart, was a leader whom his men would follow, whereas they despised Barclay de Tolly – 'Bark-and-no-bite,' as they had punningly labelled him. Even his chief-of-staff, Andrey Ermolov, loathed him and maintained a treacherous correspondence with his rival Bagration. But Alexander knew that Barclay de Tolly, for all his faults, was a good organizer with great strength of character. He had no deep knowledge of strategy, but he did possess an almost uncanny instinct for avoiding a blunder. And now that Alexander's faith in Pfuel had been destroyed, it was to Barclay that he listened in Drissa.

Barclay assumed that Napoleon would advance along the 'Big One', the road that Catherine had ordered to be constructed from Poland to Moscow through Minsk and Smolensk. He was convinced that ultimately Moscow, rather than St Petersburg, was Napoleon's objective; and he therefore proposed to move the bulk of his army down the Dvina to Vitebsk (where it would be on the left flank of the highway) while Bagration was to break out of the net which was closing upon him, and retreat north-eastwards towards the highway. Fearing, however, that the French forces along the lower Niemen might make a dangerous diversion towards St Petersburg, he detached an army corps of 25,000 men, under General Ludwig Wittgenstein, to guard the road to Pskov and the capital. He was thus left with a mere 75,000 men to oppose the Grand Army at Vitebsk. The prospect looked bleak.

Throughout July 15 every cart and pack-horse in Drissa was loaded with stores and supplies; and next morning they started to move slowly down the Dvina towards Vitebsk, a hundred miles away. It was a strange procession, in its colourful variety suggesting an eastern caravan crawling across the expanse of White Russia. The carriages of the Tsar and the staff officers, four-wheeled open droskys and hooded britzskas, rarely travelled any faster than walking pace; behind and in front of them, stretched mile upon mile of infantrymen, some in the smart white trousers of a fashionable regiment, but a few in a simple grey uniform and carrying only a pike. There were powder-waggons, teams of horses dragging twelve-pounders and smaller cannon (for Barclay had nearly 500 guns), carts loaded with bread, and all the other paraphernalia of an army on the march. Normally the Russian soldiers would plod along for six hours and rest for the following four hours; but in the stifling heat along a crowded road, they could not maintain the pace. Late that afternoon the Tsar with the Semenovski Guard rode into Polotsk, forty miles from Drissa; but less favoured regiments were bivouacked far to the rear, down the river. It would take ten days, in all, for the First Army to reach Vitebsk.

Meanwhile, the Tsar's ministers had for weeks been wrestling with a difficult problem. They had always known that Alexander's understanding of war was limited; the folly of the Drissa camp had confirmed their belief and filled them with apprehension for the future. For, when the Tsar was in the field, his personal retinue was a source of mischief and intrigue, a burden which no commander-in-chief could bear. Yet, provided that he held fast to his present mood of resolution, he might in Moscow or Petersburg rally the timid to defiance of Napoleon. It was essential for the Tsar to leave the army.

Unfortunately Alexander had no intention of retiring from the field; he had convinced himself that, with Napoleon personally in command of the invading army, the prestige of the Russian monarchy demanded his presence with the troops. Even before his arrival at Drissa, his sister Ekaterina had written a long letter to him begging him to return to his palace 'as sole arbiter of the destiny of the Empire'; but he coldly rejected her plea. He had, in fact, drafted a manifesto promising his men, 'I shall be with you always; I shall never desert you' – an unsolicited assurance which, fortunately, his Secretary of State succeeded in amending.

At Polotsk, however, three of the Tsar's most trusted advisers waited on him with a four-page petition: Arakcheyev, Balashov and Admiral Shishkov urged him, with exquisite tact and a wealth of flattery, that since he had assumed the imperial crown by right and not (as Napoleon had done) by chance, his place was in the capital. Silently the Tsar listened to them and studied the document. And a few hours later, the Lord Chamberlain came up to Shishkov and confidentially told him that a carriage had been ordered for Moscow that evening. 'My joy was indescribable,' wrote Shishkov later, 'and the warmest prayer poured from my lips to the Bestower of all blessings, the Heavenly Creator.' Five months were to elapse before the Tsar returned to his army; and by then it stood once more on the wooded slopes looking out across the Niemen. Much was to happen in the interval.

While Alexander was at Drissa, Napoleon in Vilna was developing his plan to bring the Russians into battle. He, too, had decided to make for Vitebsk. Murat and Ney were to harry the First Army down the Dvina, Davout (supported by Jérôme's army) was to keep Bagration on the Dnieper, and Napoleon himself with the Guard Regiments and the two army corps of Eugène Beauharnais and Saint-Cyr would strike directly eastwards towards Smolensk. An increasing feeling of urgency was apparent at Headquarters. But the weather delayed his departure. On Monday, July 13, he was soaked to the skin while riding back – at full gallop, says Castellane – from an inspection of Saint-Cyr's Bavarians. There was no sense in setting out along the cart-tracks if the horses laden with heavy packs could only slip and slither in the mud. He would wait till the skies cleared and the hot sun blazed down again on the sandy uplands.

At this point, however, Napoleon was faced by a crisis in command. Davout believed that he had at last caught Bagration; if he could swing the hammer of Jérôme's men at the Russians he would then break them on his own anvil at Mogilev. Hence, on that same Monday, he notified Jérôme that he was assuming full command of the troops serving under him in order to complete this complicated manœuvre. Davout had received authority from the Emperor to take over Jérôme's corps seven days previously, but he did not realize that, by a singular inadvertence, Napoleon had neglected to inform the King of Westphalia of the proposed re-alignment.

Jérôme was angry. For weeks he had received little but abuse from the Emperor: now he was being robbed of his own subjects. It was intolerable; and he did not hesitate to vent his feelings on the unfortunate courier who had brought him Davout's orders. At once he halted all movement of his troops; a spirited letter was despatched to Vilna informing Napoleon that the King had 'resolved not to serve under anyone but him.' And on the Thursday, gathering his bodyguard around him in one last gesture of affronted dignity, Jérôme began the long journey back to Westphalia. Davout, in consequence, was unable to destroy Bagration, who escaped southwards to Bobruisk. It was an episode for which Napoleon never forgave his brother.

Jérôme's outcries had hardly reached Vilna before the Emperor set out for Vitebsk. He made good progress. Three nights at a Carmelite convent in Glubokoye – he heard Mass that Sunday and requisitioned a daughter-house as a hospital – and then on to a pleasant country house at Uscaez. 'A frightful route: endless swamps, execrable bridges,' noted Castellane with eloquent brevity in his diary. Now they were getting nearer to Murat, whose cavalry were in frequent skirmishes with Russian patrols; but the marshland hampered lateral communications and for two days Napoleon was completely out of touch with Murat.

Napoleon was finding the pace exhausting. At Kamen on July 24, he reached the last low hills before the Dvina, and, at noon, sent a hasty message to the Empress; 'We are having much rain, the weather is stifling, always we keep marching. I have not received any couriers since yesterday; I have marched too far.' His retinue had noticed a change in the villages through which they passed. All was quiet. Even the greater houses along the route were empty. The inhabitants had fled, in the wake of Barclay's army. Caulaincourt and the Emperor's staff were certain that this mass evacuation was part of a systematic plan. It was ominous, for they were at last approaching the genuine Russian lands, the old realm of Muscovy. Would all the cities be abandoned, too?

Athough the Emperor commented on this development, his

spirits were high. Barclay and the First Russian Army could not be far ahead now. And on July 25, when he was at Beschenkovichi, less than thirty miles from Vitebsk, he learned what he most wanted to hear. That day Murat's patrols stumbled across the Russian Fourth Corps, under General Ostermann-Tolstoy, at Ostrovno. There, only sixteen miles ahead of the Emperor's camp, a confused mêlée of French cavalry and Russian hussars fought all day on the edge of a wood of pine and birch. Eventually Ostermann pulled away towards Vitebsk; but he left eight cannon and several hundred prisoners on the field. From the prisoners, Murat discovered that the whole of the First Russian Army was in Vitebsk. He hastened to inform Napoleon: to both it seemed a decision could not long be delayed.

The Ostrovno skirmish – for it was hardly a battle – sent a thrill of anticipation through the Guard Regiments. Young Lieutenant Lyautey (whose grandson was to bring a Marshal's baton to Morocco) had journeyed from the Rhine to the Dvina without seeing the enemy. At Ostrovno, for him as for others, the campaign had suddenly assumed a new reality. 'Each of us,' he wrote later, 'weary of running point-to-point with the enemy, hoped for a battle on the morrow.' The Emperor, too, sensed the excitement. That night he dictated a letter, to be sent at once to his Foreign Minister, who had remained in Vilna: 'All the Russian Army is in Vitebsk . . . We are on the eve of great events. It is preferable that they should not be announced; but that news of them should follow results.'

Ten miles away in Vitebsk Barclay and the Russian staff saw the glow of camp fires in the western sky; and began to assess their chances.

4

Phantom of Victory

Vitebsk was an administrative centre on the banks of the Dvina with a population, in normal times, of twenty thousand. Like many other towns in this part of Russia, it was in origin a clearing in the forest; and the obstacles of geography, which had for centuries protected its inhabitants from wolves and bears, now made it an ideal site for a defensive camp. In the west the trees came down almost to the banks of the river Luchosa, which, although not a broad stream, had cut a deep channel. Behind this convenient moat an open plateau, broken by several ravines and isolated thickets, sloped gently towards the outskirts of the town. With the river Dvina running along its northern extremity and a range of low hills to its south, the plateau seemed a natural arena for a battle.

When Barclay de Tolly reached Vitebsk with the Russian First Army on July 23 he had every intention of awaiting the arrival of Bagration with the Second Army and then of offering battle there to the French. With Ermolov, his chief of staff, Barclay inspected the defence in front of Vitebsk on the Sunday morning (July 26). There was no doubt that the position was a good one, far better than at Drissa; but the Russians were uneasy. The Ostrovno skirmish of the previous day and the evidence of their own intelligence service convinced them that they were outnumbered. Their limited resources were dangerously taxed; and there was still no news of Bagration. Ermolov, for his part, was convinced that to fight a major battle at Vitebsk without Bagration's men would be to court disaster. Barclay, however, was prepared to wait on the events of that Sunday. If his rearguard could delay the French until the two Russian armies were united, then he would as soon fight Napoleon at Vitebsk as at Smolensk or anywhere nearer to Moscow.

Meanwhile, ten miles to the west, General Konovnitsin had rushed a division of infantry to the assistance of Ostermann-Tolstoy's hussars, falling back from Ostrovno. For seven hours Konovnitsin's men desperately held off cavalry thrusts by both Murat and Eugène Beauharnais. But gradually they were forced back towards the Luchosa, their reeling columns raked by cannon once they left the cover of the woods, a trail of dead and dying men and horses strewing the ground down to the river. By evening Barclay learned that there was nothing but the Luchosa between him and the main body of invaders. And a few hours later one of Bagration's aides, Count Menschikov, galloped into Vitebsk from the south with the news that Davout held Mogilev and that Bagration would not be able to join the First Army anywhere west of Smolensk. Inexorably, retreat was being forced on Barclay, yet again.

Napoleon, however, remained convinced that the fierce skirmishes on the Saturday and the Sunday were the preliminaries to a great battle. Most of that Sunday night he spent in the saddle, his tent pitched on the edge of the Vitebsk woods. So far there was no indication of a Russian withdrawal. Two more sharp clashes took place on Monday morning: Murat was checked by Russian cavalry; and a company of French light infantry, some two hundred strong, held out against wave upon wave of Russian lancers, seeking to thrust them back from the plateau into the Luchosa in what was, in many ways, a reversal of the previous day's encounter. At last the infantry formed up behind a rampart of dead and wounded and, faced by such stubborn defiance, the Russian horsemen withdrew back across the dusty plain. There followed the famous incident which was, in due course, broadcast in the Tenth Bulletin of the Grand Army and so embalmed in legend. From a knoll on their right the Emperor himself watched the savage fighting. As the Russian lancers fell back, he asked his staff to discover which of his regiments had so distinguished itself. 'The Ninth,' he was told, 'and three-quarters of them are from Paris.' 'Tell them,' he replied, 'that they are fine lads: each one of them deserves the cross.' He still knew how to kindle the flame of victory in those who were willing for it to consume them.

Yet, before noon, Napoleon had halted all operations. French losses in these three days of isolated action had been heavy: a whole battalion of Croats, attached to Eugène's army, had been wiped out in one Russian charge; and there had been a dismal moment on the Sunday evening when Murat found it difficult to keep his men from fleeing back through the woods. Not all had the valour of the Ninth. Moreover, many foreign troops had been unable to keep up with the main body of the army. General Junot, who had just taken over the Eighth Corps – mostly Würtembergers and Poles – was some eighty miles in the rear, and other units were hardly better placed. Napoleon wanted to wait so that all his forces might come up from Beschenkovichi and Krupki.

That afternoon he studied the Russian positions carefully from the crest of his hillock and rode down to inspect the troops waiting to go forward, as they had been on that other Monday, five weeks before, beyond the Niemen. At 10 pm he parted from Murat with the heart-warming injunction, 'Till tomorrow at five – the sun of Austerlitz!' And confident that on the Tuesday the Grand Army would add a new name to its battle-honours, the Emperor retired to his tent. It was pitched above the Luchosa and beside the shell of a burned-out mill, so that the sweet smell of charred wood mingled with the scent of the pines and almost drove the stench of dead horses from the nostrils.

Three hours later he was in the saddle again. There was a glare in the night sky somewhere north of the town, where the road to Petersburg bridged the Dvina, and a dull rumble from across the plain suggested that the Russians were still in Vitebsk, waiting no doubt, as he was, for the dawn. But with the first light an orderly rode up to the Emperor's tent with a message from Murat. His patrols had gone forward across the plateau towards Vitebsk. All was still. Murat was convinced that during the night the Russian First Army, which the Emperor himself had observed with such care twelve hours previously, had slipped away and left only glowing embers as proof that it had been something more than a phantom of the mind. The sun of Austerlitz would not shine that day.

Napoleon did not believe the news: it was a trap, a gigantic ambush; the Russians must have hidden their cannon in the trees and placed the lancers in the hills to the south; once the Grand Army advanced across the plain they would sweep in on it from either flank. He held the main body back, allowing only the advance-guard to creep cautiously towards the town. But shortly before noon Napoleon himself rode into Vitebsk and saw that the incredible had indeed happened. There were no enemy units there, not even a deserter to give any indication which way Barclay's men had gone. Staff officers dismounted to examine the ruts along the roads, like trackers in the bush. It seemed almost certain that the Russians had taken the route towards Smolensk and Murat was sent in pursuit, the Emperor following him for some miles east of the town. Contact was made that afternoon with the Russian rearguard under Pahlen, but Murat's cavalry was so mauled in the encounter that the French broke off the chase and contented themselves with the occupation of Vitebsk. 'A Russian soldier, who was surprised asleep under a bush, was the solitary result of that day, which was expected to be so decisive,' recalls Ségur dryly in his memoirs.

For the Emperor it was all bitterly discouraging. His personal staff, hopefully seeking for consolation, began to congratulate themselves on the ease with which the administrative capital of White Russia had fallen into French hands. Napoleon peremptorily cut them short: 'Do you think I have come so far to conquer these huts?' he demanded angrily. That Tuesday evening Count Anatole de Montesquiou found him slumped in an armchair at a dacha in a village east of the town; his hat was still on his head and he looked pale and pensive, with an expression of intense concentration on his face. For a moment faith in himself – the only enduring article in his *Credo* – seemed to have deserted him. Wearily he conferred with Murat, with Berthier and with Eugène.

It looked, after this evening council, as if the French might go no farther into Russia that summer. Napoleon argued that many units in his army were exhausted by long marches through clouds of dust under a parching sun. The supply train had broken down: waggons, constructed for use on metalled roads, were heavily laden because of the distances involved and, as soon as they encountered the soft soil of western Russia, both horses and vehicles began to sink into the sand. Supplies were not getting through: even Murat, who was as much a fire-eater as ever, had to admit that he was short of ammunition. Moreover, discipline was bad: there had been instances of looting in Vitebsk that very day and some hardened veterans among the officers were alarmed at the callous behaviour of the soldiery in the occupied villages. Many divisions were seriously depleted by stragglers. When Ney's cosmopolitan corps of Würtembergers, Portuguese and Slovenes reached Beschenkovichi, no less than 17,000 men were missing from its musters. Wastage on this scale could not continue.

On July 29 Napoleon ordered Berthier to inform the corps commanders that his main intention was 'to give the army seven or eight days rest in which to organize supplies.' But did the situation call for a more drastic solution? Common sense argued that the time had come to call a halt to this strangest of all wars in modern times. White Russia and Lithuania must be organized as conquered territory with the Dvina and upper Dnieper forming a natural frontier. Reserves should be brought across Europe and Vitebsk made into a fortified outpost, as Vilna had been. Ségur records that as Napoleon entered the Governor's palace at Vitebsk that Wednesday morning, he unbuckled his sword, laid it on the maps spread out before him and declared, 'Here I stop! . . . The campaign of 1812 is finished; the campaign of 1813 will do the rest!'

Napoleon kept to this decision for several days. It seemed folly to Murat, who wished to push on and destroy Barclay in front of Smolensk. He travelled back to Vitebsk to beg Napoleon to resume the advance. But the Emperor was adamant. With a weary smile, he said to him, 'Murat! The first campaign in Russia is over; let us here plant our eagles where two great rivers mark out our position . . . 1813 will see us at Moscow: 1814 in Petersburg. The Russian war is a war of three years!' And while Murat rode disconsolately back to his cavalry outposts along the Smolensk road, the Old Guard and the Young Guard resumed with relief the familiar routine of garrison duty. After all, a morning parade in the town square at 7 am was preferable to endless marching across a featureless plain with the temperature in the eighties.

For a fortnight life was tolerable again. Captain Castellane, while duly noting the Emperor's disapproval of pillaging in his diary, was glad that generous friends of his had become possessors of a large quantity of soap; and Sergeant Bourgogne's company even found a vat, some hops and a hand-mill, from which they brewed five barrels of beer.

With the Emperor in residence, Vitebsk became the capital of Europe, as Vilna had been earlier in the month. Through the tiny palace of the Governors of White Russia momentarily passed the affairs of a whole continent, earning a few curt words of dictated instructions from the restless figure in green and white. His three secretaries were with him morning after morning, starting work at any time he might choose to summon them and sometimes disposing of a hundred letters before their master took his evening ride, down to the supply depot, across the pontoon bridge and up one of the hillocks. And each monotonous day the couriers carried the despatches back to Maret in Vilna or Warsaw and through fourteen hundred miles of subject lands to the city on the Seine. A speedy courier could do the journey from Vitebsk to Paris in a fortnight. It was a cumbersome way to run an empire, but an effective one.

Meanwhile, the Russian war seemed almost as if it might become as interminable and indecisive as the long duel down in the Peninsula. There was, however, still some movement on the edge of the territories which the French had occupied. Ninety miles north of Vitebsk, Oudinot with the Second Corps found himself in contact with the detached section of the Russian First Army under Wittgenstein; the opposing sides wheeled in a long circle between Drissa and Klyastitsy and for a whole week the war blazed up in a series of sharp actions until Oudinot, tired and over-cautious, broke off the encounter at Jakabovo on July 30 and retired on Polotsk, thus permitting the Russians to claim their first victory. And sixty miles to Napoleon's south, Davout pressed slowly north-eastwards in a parallel column to Bagration as he fell back on Smolensk, thick forests keeping the two armies apart. There was little fighting in that direction, nor indeed along the main Moscow road where, on August 2, Sébastiani's cavalry corps had incurred the Emperor's official displeasure by a raid that carried them to within fifteen miles of Smolensk itself. For a few days the whole expedition seemed jeopardized by an alarm in the Grand-Duchy of Warsaw, several hundred miles in its rear: General Tormassov, rather clumsily, advanced with the Russian Third Army along the western edge of the Pripet Marshes so as to threaten the town of Brest and ultimately perhaps even Warsaw itself. If he had shown a little more initiative and if Wittgenstein had started a simultaneous offensive in the north – as rumour said that he intended to do – this could have been serious. But Wittgenstein remained inactive and, with Schwarzenberg and his Austrians moving round the marshes, Tormassov's challenge to the southern flank faded as swiftly as it had come; and the Emperor was left wrestling with his problems in the little town above the Dvina.

As a sultry July passed into a sweltering August, Napoleon became disgruntled and bored. His staff found him querulous and unapproachable. He would take up despatches and set them aside; pace aimlessly through the drab rooms; resume his work; dictate a letter; look at the weather; question the accuracy of the muster returns; ask the time; hum a tune with an absent air; and, hands clasped behind his back, walk yet again from the desk to the door and the door to the window and the window to the desk. The monotony was, of course, occasionally broken: once, a report that Tsar Alexander had been assassinated at Velikje Luki provided a few hours of eager speculation before it was found to be groundless; and on another day there was excitement of a different kind when a serious experiment on two guardsmen to check dysentery, by seeing whether rye was more acceptable to the stomach if newly roasted, proved an embarrassing failure, even though the Emperor himself plied the guardsmen with the best wine in the hope of soothing the digestive juices.

But such diversions brought no relaxation to the mind. His secretaries, Méneval and Fain, were acutely aware of the Emperor's peevish restlessness; and on August 7 the courier for Paris bore an unusual letter from Méneval for the Imperial Librarian:

> The Emperor wishes to have some light books. If you have some good new novels, or older ones that he does not know, or memoirs that make pleasant reading, you should send them to us, for here we have moments of leisure that it is not easy to fill.

The tedium of inactivity was testing Napoleon's patience. If the Russian Question demanded a three-year war, as he had blithely told Murat, could he possibly endure winter caged up in Vitebsk, a town already deserted by most of its inhabitants? Perhaps, he wondered, some women might come over from Warsaw or Vilna, and a troupe of actors make the journey from Paris? But then he began to reflect what would happen to Europe – and even to his very throne – while the Grand Army stood guard over the frozen borderlands of the continent. Disturbing thoughts troubled his hours of leisure. No one around him mentioned the long route to India, now.

One evening in that first week of August, he summoned an informal council of the generals who were in Vitebsk. The Emperor was excited. With face flushed and eyes bright with ambition, his fingers stubbed at the maps spread out before him. The affairs of Europe, he explained, demanded that he should end the Russian war in 1812, but he must first win a victory in the field; accordingly he was determined to push on to Smolensk and, if necessary, to 'the great Moscow, the holy city,' where he would dictate peace to Alexander.

The generals were ill at ease. Murat, who would have approved of every sentiment, was not present; and nobody in that room agreed at heart with their Emperor. Cautiously they began to reason with him. Berthier stressed the difficulty of getting fodder from the wasteland through which they would have to pass, and of the possible consequences in the German states of even the slightest reverse. Napoleon turned angrily upon him and the Prince of Wagram was silenced, tears in his eyes. General Duroc (who had been at the Emperor's side for more than seven years) and Caulaincourt (who knew Russia better than anyone else in his entourage) continued to stress the folly of penetrating farther into the great and empty plains. They were rebuked as harshly as Berthier. Finally, General Mouton – Count Lobau as he preferred to be called nowadays – bluntly warned the Emperor of disaster. Once, on a happier occasion, Napoleon had punned, 'My mouton is a lion:' now the Emperor treated him as if he were a sheep after all. Scathingly, he dismissed them from his presence: 'I have made my generals too rich,' he shouted. 'They think only of their pleasures, of hunting, of rolling through Paris in brilliant carriages! They have become sick of war!' It was a singular explosion, with just sufficient verisimilitude to disturb their consciences.

Next day Berthier again waited on Napoleon and this time he brought with him Count Bruno Daru who, as Minister Secretary of

State for the past fifteen months, knew every administrative detail of the Grand Army. Napoleon was in a calmer mood and for eight hours the three men discussed his plans. Daru marshalled his evidence coldly and methodically: 8,000 horses dead between Vilna and Vitebsk; no fodder within thirty miles of Vitebsk itself; no forges for shoeing the cavalry; no surgical lint for the medical service; no certainty that the supply waggons or the baggage train would get through, even in good weather. 'If provisions fail in Vitebsk, what will happen later on . . . with a people almost savage?' he asked. And he went on to make other points: the motives for war were not understood in France or the Empire; and, even without a battle, the Grand Army had lost a third of its effectives through desertion, disease and hunger. 'Everything indicates that we should call a halt now.'

Napoleon listened to Daru with surprising patience and when he made his reply, it is clear that he was, in a sense, soliloquizing. Clearly these fears had been in his own mind and he had wrestled with the problems they posed as he hesitated in Vitebsk. He was convinced that Lithuania and White Russia were regions too wild to be fortified and too sparse to feed his Grand Army through a bitter winter. He must either retire to the Vistula, which would be tantamount to acknowledging defeat, or press forward. At Smolensk he would at least gain a fortress and a position on the Dnieper; and, at the gates of Moscow, peace awaited him. He knew that Moscow hated Petersburg and, if Alexander should prove slow to negotiate, he would set the merchants of Moscow against the gentry of Petersburg: 'The results of such jealousy are incalculable,' he said. Yet there was one bogey which haunted him – the fate of Charles XII of Sweden, whose army had been scattered by Peter the Great around the marshes of Poltava. But, argued Napoleon, the Swedes had failed because they lacked a leader capable of success: fortune had never smiled on Charles XII. 'Blood has not yet been spilled and Russia is too mighty to surrender without fighting. Alexander can only seek peace after a great battle.' The Grand Army must resume its advance.

But the Emperor still hesitated. He continued to hope that the Russians would resolve his problems by launching an attack. Alexander, after all, had begun the battle of Austerlitz. On August 8

Napoleon heard that Barclay had sent out a strong force of cavalry and Cossacks against Sébastiani's outposts. The French withdrew, with over four hundred casualties. But Napoleon was delighted by the news of the Russian action. Once again he believed he was to have his great battle. That weekend he finally took his decision; and at two in the morning of August 13, his carriage pulled out of Vitebsk along the road to Smolensk, eighty miles to the south-east. Storm clouds brought a little rain that day: and over to his left, there was thunder.

Napoleon never saw Vitebsk again. But, four months later to the day, as the sledge on which they were travelling back to Paris sped across the snows of Silesia, he turned to his companion, Caulaincourt, sought to tweak his ear and remarked, 'This war with Russia is an unfortunate affair . . . I should have remained at Vitebsk. By now Alexander would have been on his knees to me.' And Caulaincourt, loyal as ever, forbore to recall a stormy council table and an Emperor who had believed his generals were sick of war.

After their retreat from Vitebsk, the Russian commanders were no less hesitant than Napoleon. Instinctively, Barclay de Tolly shrank from a major battle. The massive mediaeval walls of Smolensk looked comfortingly secure. The harvest had been gathered in and it was a good one. Given time, perhaps Smolensk might withstand a siege as the city had done two centuries before, when it had taken the Poles twenty-one months to break through those grim ramparts. There was much to be said for a defensive strategy.

But Barclay de Tolly was a lonely figure. He had been unpopular before the campaign began and nothing that had happened in the five weeks since Napoleon crossed the Niemen had endeared him to his men. His character and reputation became the victim of the xenophobia which lies so near the surface in every Russian. He bore a foreign name, he came from some outlandish spot in Estonia, he spoke the Russian language with a heavy Prussian accent – all this was bad enough. Even worse, he had appointed as his aide-de-camp a Prussian émigré, Colonel Wolzogen, who had not come to

Russia until 1807 and had never served on the General Staff. As Barclay and Wolzogen talked rapidly and fluently in German, the Russians around them suspected every type of treachery. Barclay's natural aloofness turned to frigidity. It was an almost intolerable position for a Minister of War and commander-in-chief.

Barclay and the First Army reached Smolensk on the night of July 31. Two days later he watched impassively from a window as Bagration's carriage drove into the city and the commander of the Second Army hastened up the steps to report to the man whom he insisted on calling 'the Minister.' It could hardly be a warm meeting. Bagration, a proud Georgian prince, had shone with the lustre of victory thirteen years before, a bright star in Suvorov's constellation when Barclay was no more than a painstaking staff officer. Now he had to explain to this former subordinate why he had abandoned Minsk and Mogilev and failed to reach Vitebsk. They greeted each other with formal courtesy and passed into an inner room, away from the inquisitive eyes of émigré Prussians who sought to see significance in every gesture of the two commanders. For a quarter of an hour they talked in private. When they emerged each seemed satisfied, only the dark flashing of Bagration's eyes transmitting the fire that was within him. Perhaps faced by the menace of an invader, they would forego recrimination. The situation was not yet desperate. With the union of the two armies, the Russians could at any rate put 110,000 men into the field against the 170,000 of the Grand Army. There were still grounds for hope.

Co-operation between Barclay and Bagration lasted for barely forty-eight hours. The Georgian found that everyone of Barclay's staff was prepared to listen to his complaints and anything in writing was forwarded by Ermolov to Arakcheyev and the Tsar. His list of grievances multiplied rapidly: there was no fodder for the horses of the Second Army; his men were sent out haphazardly under the scorching sun to look for French outposts which had never been set up; the First Army had requisitioned all the food supplies; he was being deliberately kept in the dark about Barclay's intentions. First he was sent westwards to Katan then due north to Widra, his men trailing aimlessly across the Vitebsk-Smolensk road while Platov's cavalry were in action against Murat thirty miles away. It was exhausting and ineffective. 'I am ordered to stretch my army out like a thread and pull them in all directions,' he wrote to Arakcheyev on August 10, 'For God's sake send me anywhere, if only to command a regiment in Moldavia or the Caucasus.' And on the following day Barclay, weary of fighting this secondary war with Bagration, gave him permission to pull the Second Army back to Smolensk itself when he wished. At times it seemed almost as if the two commanders were playing some strange and dangerous game with each other, in which Russia was no more than a toy tossed by their conceits.

The confusion in the Russian command deepened as Napoleon drew nearer to Smolensk. Did he intend to storm the city or envelop it? Already, to Barclay's surprise, Murat and Ney and Davout had swung to the south of the main road from Vitebsk, almost as if they intended to by-pass the town and press forward towards Moscow. Barclay was perplexed. Ought he to break out to the north, or remain behind the redoubts of the city? Should he, perhaps, send out troops to cover the fords across the Dnieper to his east? Uncertain of his course, he waited for news of action. It reached him on the evening of August 14.

Early that Friday afternoon there was a sharp clash near Krasnoe. Napoleon himself heard the sound of firing and hurried forward to find that Grouchy, whose cavalry was attached to Murat's force, had stumbled into the main Russian rearguard, under Neveroski, and taken several hundred prisoners and seven cannon. Technically the skirmish was a victory for the French, but for the remainder of that day Neveroski was able to slow down the French advance, his men fighting with fanatical courage. The reports arriving at Barclay's headquarters that night were encouraging: Neveroski had checked the French and Bagration had dispatched a corps from the Second Army, under General Raevski, to lend him support. Heartened by this news, Barclay actually considered sending his cavalry and Cossacks out to the north-west of Smolensk early on the Saturday morning, so as to attack Vitebsk and destroy the French depot there while Bagration engaged Napoleon south of the Dnieper. But the harsh reality of the situation soon made this plan of no more than academic interest. Nothing came of it, although Bagration got as far as ordering a small cavalry force to Katan (where it would almost certainly have been destroyed by Junot's Polish lancers, had not their commander – who was having a remarkably bad war – misread the map and sent them down the wrong road.)

By dawn on Sunday (August 16) any prospect of a Russian counter-offensive had gone: the fate of Smolensk itself was in the balance. Most of Raevski's force had by then fallen back to the outskirts of the city, although stragglers from Neveroski's shattered corps were still making their own way along the Dnieper, seeking to avoid the ubiquitous Murat, whose horses were resting only three miles west of Smolensk. At nine o'clock the first French guns opened up on the suburbs. But it was to be a day of movement rather than of bombardment: for Napoleon had decided to assault the town from the south, hoping that at the same time the unfortunate Junot would press on eastwards so as to cut the road to Moscow; and, while Ney's corps was already in position along the Dnieper in the west, it took twelve hours for Davout and Poniatowski to complete their envelopment of the southern suburbs of the city.

Napoleon himself reached the outskirts of Smolensk in the early afternoon and had his tent pitched beside a small copse on the crest of a hillock above the village of Lubnya, only a mile and a half south-west of the citadel where Barclay had his headquarters. It was a good position from which to watch the assaulting troops. Below him a small stream separated his isolated knoll from a lower ridge, whose slopes ran in a semi-circle around the old city of Ivan the Terrible. He could see the ramparts clearly enough, a stone wall thirty feet high and eighteen feet thick, stretching in an arc of two miles with the forts at either end overlooking the Dnieper. Twenty-nine towers, some rectangular and others conical, commanded this defensive line, their brick upper-works covered by wooden roofs. Behind them the guilded cupolas of a dozen churches flashed in the sun against the green and brown of wooded hills, climbing steeply from the north bank of the river. The cathedral of the Dormition, where that day hundreds knelt as priests bore sacred gonfalons and ikons in procession, dominated the skyline, as if in crowning defiance of the enemies of Holy Russia. It was an impressive spectacle for eyes weary of dry and dusty plains.

Through his glass Napoleon could focus on the bridge over the Dnieper, menaced by a French cannonade which crept nearer and nearer. Yet he was puzzled by what he saw: Barclay's army appeared to be crossing the bridge in both directions at the same time for, as Neveroski's tired troops came in from the west, so waggons and caissons were rumbling out eastwards. The sight depressed Napoleon. He had arrived at Smolensk hot in pursuit of the phantom victory which had twice eluded him: 'At last, I hold them in my hands,' he declared. Now it looked as if the Russians were seeking to draw him further still into the interior. He summoned Caulaincourt to his bivouac above Lubnya and asked him if Barclay de Tolly could really be planning to abandon a city which was a mystic symbol to all Russia. But Caulaincourt could offer him no consolation: he had always been convinced that the basic Russian strategy was to tempt the invader to penetrate so deeply into the steppe land that he could be 'shut up amid the ice.' Patiently Napoleon listened as Caulaincourt tendered his reading of the Russian mind. At the end of the conversation Napoleon seemed resigned to a halt in Smolensk. 'We will rest the troops and from this base organize the country and see how Alexander likes that,' he said. Caulaincourt was delighted; he hastened to inform Berthier that the Emperor had seen reason at last. But Berthier, that shrewd old campaigner, had been too long the butt of Napoleon's whims to believe him: cynically, he predicted that such common sense would never survive an entry into Smolensk. Over these matters Berthier was rarely wrong.

Meanwhile, down in the citadel, Barclay conferred that night with Bagration. For once they were in agreement. At daybreak Bagration and the Second Army were to move off towards Dorogobuzh, fifty miles downstream, so that there would be a force astride the road to Moscow whatever happened at Smolensk. It appears, in many respects, a strange decision: Barclay had declined battle at Vitebsk because the two armies were not yet united, but he was now sending Bagration eastwards with 60,000 men on the eve of a major engagement. Writing to Arakcheyev three days later, Bagration maintained that Barclay had given him his word that he would not withdraw from Smolensk: and, as he marched along the Dnieper, Bagration certainly sent couriers back to Barclay entreating him to stand firm. But it is difficult to believe that Bagration, with his knowledge of the Russian position, can ever have expected Barclay to fight anything more than a delaying action. Once the Second Army retired, the Russians in Smolensk were outnumbered by two to one. Bagration's righteous indignation would be more convincing if his record of intrigue to unseat Barclay were less well documented.

Bagration crossed the river and set off towards the hills over which dawn was breaking that Monday morning (August 17). Within a few hours furious skirmishes had begun in the suburbs as Ney and Davout pushed forwards towards the citadel. At ten o'clock Barclay himself watched from the parapet above the Malakhov Gate as the Ufimsky Regiment made bayonet charges against General Friant's infantry division, entrenched in the macabre setting of an old cemetery. The Ufimsky Regiment fought with fanatical determination: was there not an old prophecy that disaster would strike Muscovy once Smolensk fell to an invader? Over to their right, beside the deep chasm of the Dnieper, another fierce action developed as Ney's corps attacked the mound on which the citadel stood: it was in this encounter that the red-headed Marshal was infuriated by a stray bullet which carried away some of the braid from his collar. There was bitter fighting all along the walls: Smolensk was no easy prize for the picking.

Napoleon rode down that morning to the suburb of Roslavl, met General Friant and went on foot eastwards to where Poniatowski's Poles were seeking to break through one of the other gates. He had hoped to launch the main assault at two in the afternoon, but although by noon the Grand Army controlled the approaches to the gates, it had made little impression on the walls, which had stood up to five hours of bombardment by the French twelve-pounders. As the French had no scaling ladders, the infantry actions gradually died away in the early afternoon. At the same time, from opposite banks of the Dnieper each army led its horses down to the river; Lieutenant Lyautey met a Russian officer who, while watering his horse, exchanged greetings in French and some of the men in his battery gave the Russians tobacco. Then, after a lull of some two hours, the duel was resumed and the fraternizers began firing at each other again.

But there was no relaxation for the artillery in the open spaces before the walls. With their cannon hot, the weary gunners continued the bombardment for thirteen hours. In the later part of the day they directed their fire over the ramparts and thereby set fire to many of the wooden houses within the city. If the Russians could not be thrown out, they must be burned out. It was a grim business on that side of the town.

Barclay began evacuating all that he could in the course of the afternoon. The ikon of the Holy Virgin was removed from the cathedral, placed in a carriage and at dusk borne across the bridge over the Dnieper escorted by a battalion of guards who were solemnly ordered to protect it with their lives. The defence of the city meanwhile fell to General Docturov, who all that day was suffering agonies from dysentery. Physically sick and wretched at heart, he withdrew from the citadel to a command-post beside the bridge. All that evening he had to watch as a sad-faced line of refugees sought to cross the river to the new town, away from the choking smoke that bore down upon them, black and orange and grey – for even the wind seemed to come from the French side that night. At eight o'clock the bombardment at last ceased, but with church bells tolling mournfully, tired drummers seeking to rally mutilated regiments, and the walls of burning buildings crashing into the streets, there was no peace in the city.

The men of the Grand Army remembered the fire of Smolensk for the rest of their days: even the terrible sight of Moscow could not wipe it from their minds. Young Henri Beyle – who, as Stendhal, was to become the idol of generations of intellectuals – had not eaten since ten that morning but, at seven in the evening, he was so moved by the spectacle of the burning city that he stood watching it for three hours. Two veteran officers, Bourgoing and Dedem, to whom classical allusions did not come easily, were both independently reminded of their Virgil, and of Aeneas's account of Troy in flames. As darkness fell, each individual fire seemed to jump towards its neighbour, 'forming one vast blaze,' wrote Ségur, 'which, whirling about as it rose, covered Smolensk, and entirely consumed it, with a dismal roaring.' General Mouton, who had ordered the guns to fire into the city when it seemed impossible to breach the walls, watched the long lines of fire across the valley; a hardened professional soldier, generous in heart but unimaginative, he was dismayed at the disaster which he saw sweeping along the horizon. In the small hours, vivid flashes and explosions indicated that the Russians themselves were blowing up such stocks of ammunition as they could not evacuate. It seemed to the watchers on the hills as if there would be little left to them when they entered Smolensk.

Caulaincourt, unable to sleep, sat mournfully staring at burning Smolensk beside a camp-fire outside the Emperor's tent (for the strong wind that was feeding the flames in the town made it a cold night). Napoleon came up to him, with Berthier and Marshal Bessières. All four watched for a while in silence. 'An eruption of Vesuvius!' suddenly exclaimed the Emperor, giving Caulaincourt a hearty clap on the shoulder. 'Is it not a fine sight? . . . Remember, gentlemen, what one of the Roman emperors said: "The corpse of a dead enemy always smells good!"' Caulaincourt and Berthier exchanged glances, 'as men who understand each other without speaking': there would be no halting at Smolensk now.

By five that morning (August 18) Napoleon had learnt from his patrols that Barclay and Docturov had evacuated the town. After reconnoitring the walls, he ordered the army to march in with bands playing. An Italian officer in Eugène's army put his impressions on record: 'To the strains of martial music, proudly and grimly we marched in among the ruins, where the unhappy Russian wounded wallowed in blood and mire. Never since the start of hostilities had we seen such scenes: we were deeply shaken by them.' And Ségur commented icily, 'The army crossed the reeking ruins with its accustomed pomp . . . triumphing over the deserted wreck, and having no other witness of its glory but itself.'

Napoleon installed himself in the Governor's palace which, being built of brick, was hardly damaged by fire. But he spent most of August 18 down by the river, urging Eblé's engineers to complete pontoon bridges so that his troops could cross to the newer parts of the town on the other bank and give chase to Barclay's army, which was still firing on Smolensk from the hills to the north.

Barclay de Tolly began to pull away eastwards at dusk. Half of his men he sent off on a long detour fifteen miles to the north, but the remainder he personally led over rough roads, intending to reach the village of Gorbunovo where there was a bridge over the Kolodnia, a small tributary of the Dnieper. It was a nightmare journey, especially for those in charge of the ammunition waggons.

The drivers were weary and fell asleep. Some caissons and two twelve-pounder guns overturned on the first hill, blocking the route. Moreover, Barclay did not know the country, and does not seem to have found reliable guides, for the whole force, over fifty thousand strong, became lost in the woods. After nine hours of night travel Barclay did indeed find himself, at six in the morning on August 19, entering a village. But it was not Gorbunovo: his army had moved in a half-circle and emerged at Gedeonovo, little more than a mile from where it had set out the night before. And this time, facing them beyond the village, the advance troops of Ney's corps were taking a leisurely breakfast; they had crossed the Dnieper two hours earlier and were waiting for the staff and the other divisions to arrive, believing the Russians by then to be six or seven miles away.

Barclay's army was nearer to destruction on that Wednesday than it had been at any time in the campaign. Yet there seems to have been a failure of intelligence on the part of the French. Ney had no idea that he had stumbled across such a considerable force. He reported to Napoleon that he had met and brushed aside a rearguard; but the Emperor – who had in fact immersed himself in administrative details – was more interested in what was happening lower down the river. There, at eleven in the morning, Davout and Murat encountered a large body of Russian troops between the Kolodnia and another small stream, the Stragan. Some way to the south, at Prudichevo, Junot's corps was at last crossing the Dnieper by a pontoon bridge and moving slowly up towards the confluence of the Stragan and Kolodnia. When the reports reached Napoleon, who had ridden across the Dnieper to inspect Ney's bridgehead, he assumed that contact had been made with Barclay's main army. Ordering Ney forward, he hurried to Davout, who was on a spur of high ground above the Kolodnia known as Valutino Gora, two and a half miles east of Smolensk. Once again the Emperor's spirits rose: he was to have his victory in the field, after all: if Junot came up from the south, the Russians were in a trap.

Napoleon reached Valutino at two-thirty in the afternoon, in time to see Ney force the Russians back across the Stragan. He ordered General Gudin to send his division (four of the best French infantry regiments) to support Ney. He was, however, soon disappointed;

for orderlies informed him that the Russian force was not, as he had supposed, Barclay's main army, but a rearguard under General Tutchkov, supported by some Cossacks and light cavalry. Almost beside himself with irritation, Napoleon turned his horse's head back towards Smolensk, where the business of governing an empire pressed heavily on his hours of soldiering.

But chance had still not finished mocking the Emperor that day. Even before Ney's horse cantered into the smouldering city, he had discovered that the Russians were resisting with sudden determination. By four o'clock the French were indeed in contact with Barclay himself, who had hurried round to the Stragan through Gorbunovo and Lubino, along the route he had failed to find in the darkness of the previous night. Much of his command – three corps of infantry and one of cavalry – was still scattered along the impossible roads, but enough had reached the Stragan to launch counter-attacks on the French. As afternoon turned into evening, so the isolated skirmishes began to look more and more like a battle.

At five o'clock, after an hour's bombardment of the Russian flanks, Ney launched a frontal assault on the Russian line; he crossed the Stragan, but failed to carry the crest beyond it. To derisive jeers from the Russians, Murat's cavalry floundered dismally in marshland below the Russian position. Everything now depended on Junot, whose horses had been seen on the crest of a hillock little more than a mile to the south. Murat personally rode down to Junot's command post and urged him to attack. 'Now finish the business,' he said with his usual fire. 'Glory and a marshal's baton await you!' And, putting himself at the head of the Würtembergers, he galloped towards the Russian line, confident that Junot's men would follow him. But none moved; and the Russian flank remained unassailed. It was a bitter moment for Murat.

Two hours later, with the setting sun blinding the Russian gunners, Ney launched his last assault. General Gudin's division led the attack, but their commander, who was not a good horseman, dismounted at the crossing of the Kolodnia and a cannon-ball carried away both his legs. The division pressed forward with heavy casualties, but darkness had fallen before the French eventually carried the crest. By then it was too late. Barclay and his main army had slipped away down the road towards Lubino. General Tutchkov, who had been wounded, was taken prisoner, but Ney's troops were too exhausted and too badly mauled to continue the pursuit, and Junot, pleading that his orders had limited him to holding the crossing of the Dnieper, refused to take the initiative. It was a sad tale of missed opportunities. Who was the victor, the Russians who had lost 6,000 men and retreated in good order, or the French, whose casualties exceeded 7,000 and who were unable to take up the chase?

When Napoleon sifted the reports that reached him he was furious. Most of the blame he laid on Junot, the old friend who had fought so bravely beside Major Bonaparte at Toulon nineteen years before. 'Junot is losing the campaign for me,' he complained, as he thundered out threats against all cowardly commanders. He would not receive the unfortunate general himself, but despatched Murat to him with a stern message of censure, to which Murat added a stinging phrase of his own: 'You are unworthy to be the last dragoon in Napoleon's army,' he told Junot. It was a reproach which the general found hard to bear. A few months later he went out of his mind and the next year he killed himself.

Yet what had failed at Valutino was not Junot's courage, but the spirit of the Napoleonic Empire. The Würtemberg cavalry remained inactive because they did not see why they should perish in a glorious charge for a cause in which they did not believe. By now there was a disease in the Grand Army more virulent than dysentery; morale had sunk low among the foreign contingents. Napoleon himself sensed it. Back in Smolensk, he remarked to General Sébastiani: 'This army cannot now stop: . . . motion alone keeps it together. One may go forward at the head of it, but neither halt nor go back.' At the moment, the Grand Army could still advance; but it was anyone's guess what would happen once it had to retire.

5

The Two Cities

With the continent divided by war, rumour travelled fast, but news slowly. Hence, although there had been speculation for more than five weeks over the troop concentrations in Prussia and Poland, reliable reports of the opening of the Russian campaign did not reach western Europe until Napoleon was approaching Vitebsk; and this time-lag continued throughout the rest of the year, widening once the ice had enclosed Russia's ports and winter made it hard for couriers to get through by any overland route. Uncertainty led those who were trying to follow the course of events from afar into alternating moods of gloom and elation so that both setbacks and victories were magnified and the drums of war seemed to beat with an oddly irregular rhythm.

In London the first bulletins of the Grand Army and an account of the crossing of the Niemen were printed in *The Times* on Saturday, July 25, and in the *Observer* a day later. Neither paper appears to have rated Russia's chances highly, although both offered their readers the comforting assurance – or pious hope – that the Tsar's armies would fight valiantly in defence of their homeland. Official opinion was, perhaps, a little less sanguine for, to the irritation of Vorontsov, the Russian Ambassador, memories of Austerlitz and Friedland and Tilsit seemed ineradicably fixed in people's minds. Privately he might believe that 'my poor country is lost,' but it was intolerable to be told as much by that omniscient tattler from the Admiralty, Mr Croker. 'We must have the tenacity and perseverance of Peter the Great,' wrote Vorontsov to his son, who was with Bagration. And it was the counsel with which he sought to hearten London.

For some weeks, however, the English press did not even give pride of place to the Russian campaign. It was still amazed that in Washington, five days before the Grand Army entered Russia, President Madison should have had the effrontery – as London saw it – to declare war on Britain. But if American resentment of the high-handedness of the Royal Navy made sour reading that July, there was at any rate good news from the army in the Peninsula, where Wellington had Salamanca in his grasp and the road to Madrid was open at last. Yet by the middle of August, when it was known that three weeks had elapsed without disaster striking the Russians, the newspapers were able to comment favourably on the campaign in Poland and the Baltic lands and to stress the difficulty of protecting long supply lines from Cossack raids. On August 24 *The Times* declared that Wittgenstein's repulse of Oudinot at Polotsk was a triumph for Russian arms; and as London welcomed the news of this first victory, so Lord Liverpool's Government, having formally allied itself with Russia on July 2, began to plan naval co-operation in the Baltic, while at the Foreign Office Lord Castlereagh took on the congenial task of weaving a new coalition against the old enemy. It was good to have a powerful ally once more; but several months were to elapse before the British were convinced that this time the Tsar would not make a shameful peace. There were anxious days ahead for Count Vorontsov; he seems to have avoided Mr Croker as much as possible.

Elsewhere, others too doubted the constancy of Alexander's resolution. His past record and his character were against him, even in his own capital. For the truth was that he had never commanded much respect in St Petersburg society. There was something ridiculous in this ungainly giant, with his round youthful face bent forward in benign affability, deaf ears seeking to catch conversations in which he suspected hidden innuendoes. If bad news reached him, his gentle voice tended to climb to a treble of despair: it was neither impressive nor reassuring. Yet the Tsar was a pathetically unhappy man. Already in 1812, although only thirty-five, he was haunted by eleven years of weakness and vacillation. Later writers have dismissed him as a schizophrenic, but the casual label of the amateur psychologist does less than justice to the turbulence of his inner conflict. He saw himself in those long hours of introspection as a parricide, a voluptuary and a coward: all this his conscience told him, and he believed it to be common talk in the elegant salons along the Voznesensky and Nevsky Prospects. Perhaps it was: but, in his own absence from the capital, his detractors failed to realize that with each day the French penetrated deeper into Russia, so the Tsar's tortured nerves drew from his acute sensibility a new strength of power and of purpose. This time he was determined that there could be no parleying with Bonaparte: the whole principle of autocracy, the only cement in the Russian edifice, forbade it.

These critics in Petersburg had, of course, seen nothing of Alexander since his departure for Vilna in April, and he was not to return until the beginning of August. News of their defeatism had reached him at Drissa, but when he left his army at Polotsk on July 16, he set out first along the road to Moscow, as though he would gain succour from the city which, although no longer the brain of his empire, remained for ever its heart. He travelled with an impressive retinue. General Pfuel accompanied him only as far as Smolensk, where, discredited, he departed from his service (and from the history books). But the Swedish general, Armfeldt, continued with him to Moscow; and so too did Bennigsen, one of the most experienced commanders in Russia, though a Hanoverian by birth. The 'foreign' connections of both men made them for the moment unacceptable to the army in its sudden wave of nationalist fervour. Eventually, on July 23, news reached Moscow that the Tsar was at Perhouskava, less than twenty miles east of the city. At first there was consternation, for people interpreted Alexander's withdrawal from active campaigning as a sign of impending defeat. But the Governor of Moscow, Count Theodore Rostopchin, calmed the alarmists and rode out to welcome his sovereign. He felt it his duty to convince the Tsar that Moscow would live up to its proud tradition and that its Governor, despite a passing resemblance to a doleful bloodhound, possessed the tenacity of a mastiff.

Count Rostopchin is one of the most enigmatic figures in the story of this extraordinary year. He was forty-nine in 1812 but with his sad oval face, deep forehead and heavy eyelids, he looked older. A Muscovite by birth, he had travelled widely in Europe as a young man, and there had been a day in 1788 when he sat in Westminster Hall and listened as Warren Hastings began to face the long agony of impeachment. He seems to have developed a distaste for parliaments, but an admiration for the English landed aristocracy. Back in Russia he tried to apply what he insisted were English agrarian methods to his estate at Voronovo, thirty miles south of Moscow. The experiment was only partially successful and he left for St Petersburg, where people listened to his ideas with tolerant interest and an unshakeable conviction that he was wrong; Catherine the Great, in an excess of heavy-handed endearment, even nicknamed him 'Crazy Theo'. Unfortunately, he incurred her displeasure by an unauthorized marriage with the best-looking of her maids of honour and found it politic to retire to Voronovo, where life was duller, but more predictable, than at the Hermitage or Oranienbaum.

Catherine's death in 1796 brought Rostopchin from the shadows to emerge briefly, under Tsar Paul, as a champion of French alliance. But he was foolish enough to make some ill-considered comments on the conspiracy which brought Alexander to the throne; and Voronovo had its master back again. He would probably have spent the rest of his life as an obscure country gentleman if it had not been for the friendship of the Rostopchins with Alexander's sister, Ekaterina Pavlovna. For, when the governorship of Moscow fell vacant in the spring of 1812, she put forward his name to her brother. It was not well received. 'He's no soldier,' objected Alexander, 'and the Governor of Moscow must bear epaulettes on his shoulders.' 'That,' replied his sister, with the finality of her grandmother, 'is a matter for the tailor': and Rostopchin was appointed.

The Muscovites did not take kindly to their new Governor at first. Like many servants of the state who have waited long for office, he was calculating and ambitious, with a ruthless determination to enforce his will and a partiality for sinuous methods of doing so. On arrival at Moscow, he decided to order the closing of all low cabarets. Vice promptly went underground, but there it was hounded by the Governor himself, who slipped in and out of brothels in disguise, later sending in his police to arrest the malefactors. No doubt it was praiseworthy zeal, but his predecessor, old 'Papa Goudovitch', had been a kindly soul who never bothered about such things. It was tiresome to have a busybody Governor-General.

Yet there is no doubt that the formal social life of Moscow sparkled that spring as it had not done for many years. Foreign actors and singers held the stage of the Petrovsky Theatre and it was fashionable for the nobility and the climbers among the merchants to offer lavish entertainments in the ballrooms of their town houses. Down by the Arbatsky Gate, in the huge wooden ampitheatre which the Muscovites had been calling the *Bolshoi* for the past four years, Adam Gluszkowski had begun to mount ballets in which Russian folk dances were grafted on to the older French tradition. Only the Imperial French Theatre – founded by decree of the Tsar in the season which followed Tilsit – failed to draw an audience: an anti-Bonapartist melodrama, hastily contrived a fortnight before its villain crossed the Niemen in real life, played to empty houses, even though the star attraction was Mademoiselle George, who had once been the First Consul's mistress. But elsewhere, in those last weeks of peace, there was an atmosphere of brittle gaiety through which the new Governor moved, radiating sycophantic goodwill to those who mattered and assuming oracular arrogance before those who did not.

Yet the less attractive sides of Rostopchin's character had a certain merit once the war had started. He possessed a touch of vulgar showmanship which won popular acclaim from the sections of the community he most despised. Poor and ragged French prisoners were exhibited at street-corners with placards round their necks saying, 'See what you are fighting against!' And men heartened by such spectacles could be further titillated by crude caricatures of Napoleon above captions whose obscenities were easily comprehensible to the least sophisticated minds. Then, too, there were extravagantly optimistic broadsheets which fed hatred of foreigners to a people for whom patriotism was a narrowly exclusive virtue. There is no doubt that Rostopchin had a shrewd instinct for primitive propaganda and a gift for discovering the happy phrase. It was, for example, the Governor of Moscow who had sent the proudest of all messages of encouragement to the Tsar in those fateful days at Vilna: 'The Emperor of Russia will always remain formidable at Moscow, terrible at Kazan and invincible at Tobolsk.'

Now, still certain that Russia's salvation lay in her size, this strange representative of the Imperial power, part patriot and part mountebank, went out to Perhouskava to escort the Tsar into the old capital. If he believed that all Moscow was with him, he was probably not far from the truth.

Alexander rode into the city on that Thursday evening (July 23). He was rapturously received, the people kneeling in the streets as he went by, offering them his blessing and looking 'so sad and beautiful,' as one young admirer noted in her diary. He took up residence in the Kremlin palace and that night outside its walls a huge crowd gathered, 'rippling under the moon like the sea in summer' – or so it appeared to the romantic diarist.

This enthusiasm continued for all the eight days the Tsar spent in the city. On Sunday the clergy sang a solemn *Te Deum* for conclusion of peace with Turkey, a negotiated settlement of a war which had dragged on for seven years and which would now free another 60,000 men for service against Napoleon. But although the celebration of the Bucharest Peace cheered the Muscovites, Alexander and Rostopchin were mainly concerned with the war that France had imposed on them. For the Tsar had decided on what was, to him, a revolutionary act: he would appeal to the people for their aid in throwing back the invader.

Rostopchin, whose 'enlightened' views had not outlived the reign of Catherine, was frankly alarmed. Was there, perhaps, a danger that a popular assembly, once summoned, might not disperse? Did Moscow shelter a would-be Bailly waiting to propose a Tennis-Court Oath somewhere behind the Kremlin walls? He began to make inquiries. What he learned did not please him: some merchants hoped to question the Tsar over Russia's military policy. He decided that the representatives of the people must be carefully selected; and, in case of error, he arranged that as they arrived at the palace they should see two carriages waiting 'for those who will be ordered to go.' 'I shall be dismayed,' he said, 'if any evil-minded person violates the peace and forgets himself in the Tsar's presence, for such a person, before concluding his remarks, would find himself setting out on a very long journey indeed.' It was a crude and characteristic way of ensuring that Alexander would find the representatives of the people co-operative; but it was effective.

The Tsar was received by separate assemblies of the merchants and the nobility in the Sloboda Palace on July 27, the Monday on which Napoleon was hoping for his decisive battle in front of Vitebsk. The hour was too critical for anyone to think of writing an account of the meetings at that time, and later versions are qualified by interpolated after-knowledge; but we know enough to follow the general pattern of the day's proceedings. The Tsar began by spending a few minutes with the merchants. Their trade had suffered from the alliance with France and now they were clearly willing to help the State against the author of the Continental System. Rostopchin himself dryly observes in his Memoirs that they wished to 'sacrifice a part of their fortune to save the rest'; but this is perhaps too astringent a comment. Sergei Glinka, who was present, maintains that they were moved by an emotional excess of generosity: 'Sire, take everything: our lives and our property,' they declared. Hurriedly they made a list of their contributions: one small retailer was so affected by the occasion that he wrote 5,000 roubles instead of 500 but even though his original offering was beyond his means and the tears were streaming down his cheeks, his pride insisted that he keep to the figure he had so rashly subscribed. By then, the Tsar had passed to the hall of the gentry and nobility. Here the nominated delegates were prepared, not only to give money, but to allocate serfs to the militia; and some of them undertook to raise and equip whole regiments. The Tsar was well pleased with both assemblies. Rostopchin's fears had been shown to be groundless.

Alexander and his suite set out for St Petersburg on the night of July 31, having honoured Rostopchin with the award of a high decoration. Now the Governor-General was virtually his own master, left to sustain a city which had known no foreign conqueror since the Poles were ejected two centuries before. His first responsibility was to supervise the arming of the militia. This was a difficult task for, although the men were available, weapons were not. Rifles could not be found and most of the militiamen had to be content with pikes. It took nearly a month to muster them, but eventually, on August 26, more than thirty thousand men were ready. That Wednesday they were inspected by the Governor himself and by their commander, Count Markov, a genial country gentleman of Falstaffian girth. Then, blessed by the Metropolitan

Platon and sprinkled with holy water, they set off down the Arbat for the Dorogomilov Bridge and the field of battle, trailing their pikes hopefully as they went and preceded by a moving forest of sacred banners. The poor wretches deserved every consolation that Holy Russia could offer: for twelve days later some ten thousand of them were holding the old Smolensk Road south of Borodino as the sun picked out the crimson breastplates of Poniatowski's lancers advancing through the woods. It proved to be a hard, but uneven, tussle.

Yet Rostopchin had placed his hopes not so much in the sanctified pikemen as in a secret weapon which the Tsar had entrusted to him in June. It is a curious tale. In 1811, a thirty-six-year-old Rhinelander named Leppich (who had once invented a mechanical piano) sought to interest Napoleon in an explosive balloon. He came to Paris, but the French swiftly decided that the versatile inventor was a dangerous crank and promptly deported him. He seems to have resented this indignity for, in the spring of 1812, as the Grand Army moved eastwards, so Leppich travelled ahead of it. Armed with a letter of introduction from Count Ferdinand Zeppelin – whose grandson was to have more success with such things – Leppich was received in audience by the Tsar at Vilna on June 6. Alexander, with his weakness for wild schemes of Germanic inspiration, was fascinated by the potentialities of airborne missiles. He sent Leppich on to Rostopchin with an enthusiastic message; and the Governor of Moscow (ever anxious to please his sovereign) dutifully provided the Rhinelander with an ample supply of money, a hundred labourers and a workshop on Prince Repnin's estate, a few miles from the city. There Leppich – who seems now to have assumed the name of Schmidt, apparently for security reasons – set about designing a balloon which would be 'propelled by revolving blades and steered by a rudder;' it was to be capable of carrying fifty men, or a sufficient quantity of explosive to destroy a whole army corps.

Leppich's researches became one of Moscow's worst-kept secrets. Sunday excursions to the Repnin estate proved a fillip to lagging morale in those ominous weeks of August. If nobody saw any signs of the war-winning device, then at least the precautions along the road around the estate impressed them with its importance. Rostopchin was delighted; he informed the Tsar that he had 'taken to

Leppich as a friend and was cherishing his machine like a child';
more and more roubles were assigned to the enterprise. At last, in the
fourth week of August, one of the Governor's broadsheets promised
the Muscovites that 'tomorrow or the day after,' a small trial balloon
would fly over the city. Hopeful eyes scanned the clear summer sky,
but it was only the tapering towers along the Kremlin walls that
pointed upwards. Neither the experimental balloon nor the big
dirigible ever took to the air.

On September 10 Rostopchin, bitterly disillusioned, wrote to the
Tsar that Leppich was 'a crazy charlatan'; the secret weapon was
making the Governor a laughing stock in Moscow. Yet, strangely
enough, it was not the end of Leppich. As the French drew nearer,
he fled to Nizhni-Novgorod and later he went on to St Petersburg.
There, Alexander, his faith in the balloon unshaken by Rostopchin's
discomfiture, encouraged him to proceed with his experiments all
that autumn. Meanwhile, the Grand Army had occupied the
Repnin estate and found there the remains of his workshop: a huge
wooden sphere, a half-burnt cabin, 180 large jars of vitriol, seventy
casks and six vats. The work on the balloon had been serious
enough, if a little unorthodox. The French, in a characteristic
tribute to the ingenuity of their intractable enemy, decided that
Leppich was a mad English agent; and, while there are no grounds
for this odd assumption, it is still not clear whether he was a common
trickster or an aeronautical seer born a century too soon. He may,
of course, have been both.

There were other foreign residents of far longer standing than
Leppich to trouble Rostopchin. Moscow was by tradition a cosmopolitan city, drawing from both the east and the west; there were
oriental bazaars within its walls and yet, along the Yauza river, the
visitor could see three-storeyed houses with neat rows of trees where
the Dutch and Germans had settled in Peter the Great's reign. But,
for many years now, the French had been the arbiters of good living
for the city. People of distinction spoke the French language more
easily, and wrote it better, than they did Russian; they wore clothes
cut in the French mode, their perfume was French and so was their
wine. They were accustomed to buy luxuries from smart French
shops and to have delicacies prepared for their tables by French
chefs. Their daughters were taught dancing and deportment by

Mademoiselle Lamiral and, until the invasion, Monsieur Adnet and Madame Fusil had frequently delighted them in Racine or Molière. Nor was Gallic influence limited to such temporal pleasures; a French accent evidently held promise of social standing in the next world as well as this. For the most fashionable church in Moscow was certainly Saint-Louis-des-Françaises and the most acceptable churchman was its incumbent, the Abbé Surrugues, who had been head of a theological college at Toulouse before the Revolution and had come to Moscow by way of a seminary in Vilna. Many prominent Muscovites – or more especially their wives – had been received into the Roman Catholic Church by the Abbé, among them Countess Rostopchin. As her daughter later explained with eloquent simplicity, conversion to Catholicism had the advantage of enabling the faithful to make their confessions in French rather than in the language of the common peasantry, and 'of conversing with more elegant and better-educated priests than the simple Russian pastors.' It was, indeed, a strange ascendancy which Paris – or Versailles – had gained over society in Moscow. Yet was it, now that war had come, a dangerous one?

Rostopchin knew that if he harried the French colony in Moscow he would be pandering to a grievance of the unprivileged against the wealthy. It was a cheap way to gain popularity. Perhaps, too, he genuinely believed that these voluntary exiles from France were a potential danger to the security of the city. At all events, in the last week of August he had forty foreign residents, predominantly French, arrested and detained in prison. Two days later they were despatched to Kolomna and thence, by barge, to Nizhni-Novgorod. Before they left Moscow they had to listen to the reading of a message which the Governor appears to have drafted the previous month, informing them that their lives were in danger from the anger of the populace, that they should 'cease to be bad subjects and become good ones' and that they should 'change themselves from French citizens into good Russian bourgeois.' The selection of men and women to be deported seems to have been entirely haphazard, although significantly all the French clergy were allowed to remain. It was a vindictive act; but once again Rostopchin had demonstrated his patriotism before the eyes of all Moscow.

The city needed encouragement that week. On August 22

Rostopchin's daughter had come into his study and found him in deep gloom. Sadly picking up a despatch, he said, 'Take this letter from Barclay to your mother. Smolensk has fallen; soon we shall have the enemy at the gates of Moscow.' Immediately, people began to flee into the country, some men disguising themselves in women's clothes to escape the taunts of the poorer classes, who gathered at the city gates in jeering crowds. Rostopchin's own family remained in Moscow for three more weeks, but long before then most of the nobility had either enlisted in the militia or sought sanctuary in Ryazan or Yaroslavl.

The sadness of autumn hung heavily over Moscow. As the yellow leaves fell from the trees along the river, it seemed almost as if the city itself was withering with them. Strong winds blew clouds of dust through the open squares. Anxiously the townsfolk waited for news and prayed before their ikons. Perhaps the invader would be repulsed even now beyond those hills to the west. But if he were not, then one day his cavalry would raise a dust-storm that would carry with it the hopes of Russia. For only the most sublime fatalists believed that Moscow could perish and Muscovy survive.

Tsar Alexander spent most of these anxious weeks in the stiff dignity of his artificial capital on the Neva, four hundred miles to the north. He arrived in St Petersburg on August 3, elated by the loyal protestations of the nobles and merchants of Moscow. He found the mood in the capital very different. It is true that in Petersburg, too, the trading community had offered two million roubles to the State and the bishops and clergy had raised another million and a half; and the citizens of the capital had dutifully asserted their patriotism by hooting a company of French actors off the stage as soon as they started to play *Phèdre*. But everywhere there remained a marked lack of confidence in victory so long as the command lay in the hands of the 'Scotsman,' Barclay de Tolly, and his horde of German advisers. Three days after the Tsar's return the ceremonial cannon boomed out to celebrate the alleged defeat of Oudinot at Jakabovo; but public rejoicing at the heartening news was muted by the sad reflection that the general who had gained this success, Ludwig Wittgenstein, came from a long line of West-phalian noblemen and was no more a Russian than his adversary. People fired by the novel fancy of nationalism found it galling to laud the triumph of German tenacity.

Yet throughout St Petersburg, and even among his own family, Alexander found the same question being asked: 'Where was a true Russian commander to be found? Where was a man to whom every verst of steppe-land would be as dear as his own blood? Where was the heir of Alexander Nevsky and Dmitry Donskoy, of Dmitry Pozharsky and Alexander Suvorov?' And again and again his interlocutors offered the Tsar the same answer: 'He is here in the capital, commanding the Petersburg militia! Send for Mikhail Illarionovich Kutuzov!' It was a name Alexander hated to hear, for it opened up the trauma of Austerlitz.

Kutuzov was sixty-seven years old in 1812. Thirty-eight years previously, in the autumn in which Napoleon Bonaparte began his studies at the École Militaire in Paris, Kutuzov had been fighting against the Turks at Alushta and an enemy bullet had destroyed his right eye. Seven years later – when Lieutenant Bonaparte, unem-ployed, was contemplating writing a history of Corsica – Kutuzov, under Suvorov's command, was scaling the walls of the fortress of Izmael in the face of heavy Turkish fire. In October 1805, with Suvorov dead for five years, he had led the Russian expeditionary force into Austria and withdrawn it, with masterly skill, from the River Inn to Moravia, despite the constant pressure of Murat and Davout. There, on December 2, he had watched as Tsar Alexander committed the army he had saved to a disastrous battle at Austerlitz against his wishes; it was an experience making a far deeper gulf between the two men than the thirty-two years which separated their births.

There was no doubt that Kutuzov was now an old man. He was so gross that he could not stay in the saddle. He enjoyed the luxuries of life, good food and good wine, the comfort of soft chairs and deep beds. Always attractive to women, he had passed happily enough from a romantic war-hero to a scandalous lecher. Laziness, which as a young man had prevented him studying the theory of war, made him seek rest and tranquillity; and nowadays he spent as much of his day asleep as awake. The shrewdness, which Suvorov had praised twenty years ago, had been formed by habit into slyness: he hated being forced to assess the reports of subordinates; he loathed committing himself to formal orders by the signing of his name. There seemed every reason that summer for regarding him as a spent war-horse put out to grass. And yet he still knew how to get what he wanted out of those he met; he had just returned from Bucharest where, despite all the subtle persuasions of French diplomacy, he had induced the Turks to accept peace. He did not, as yet, possess a marshal's baton, but was it possible those cumbersome gnarled hands could hold the wand of a magician, to charm Barclay and Bagration and Ermolov and Bennigsen into co-operation? Alexander found the idea repugnant; but was there any other pair of hands that could? At heart, the Tsar knew the answer to both questions, but the memory of a bleak December morning in Moravia made him hesitate even now.

The news from the Smolensk front continued to be serious. Its gravity showed through every message that reached St Petersburg. Bagration's censures on Barclay were to be expected, but by the middle of August they were echoed by other voices. On August 12 Count Shuvalov sent Prince Volkonsky to the Tsar with a letter: 'If Your Majesty does not give both armies a single commander, then I am bound to swear, on my honour and in all conscience, that all may be irretrievably lost . . . Even the men in the ranks complain . . . The commander-in-chief is entirely responsible for this state of affairs . . . Another commander is essential, and Your Majesty must appoint him without losing a minute or Russia will be lost.' The Tsar received the letter on Monday, August 17, the day that Mouton's artillery fired Smolensk. That evening Alexander convened a special committee to consider Shuvalov's urgent plea.

For three and a half hours Balashov, Arakcheyev and four other generals wrestled with Alexander's conscience. They knew, as he did, that all the army was demanding the appointment of Kutuzov and that the nobility and the church leaders were at one with the military on this issue. The Tsar agreed that Russia needed a new commander-in-chief, but was there no other candidate but Kutuzov? Personally he seems to have favoured Bennigsen, and even to have hankered after Bernadotte, Napoleon's former Marshal, who was now the Swedish Crown Prince – he, after all, had been on the winning side at Austerlitz and not a witness of the moment when Alexander's nerve had failed, as Kutuzov had been. Yet to appoint either Bennigsen or Bernadotte (had he been willing to accept the post) would merely have fed the flames of xenophobia. At last, the six members of the committee drafted a formal resolution unanimously proposing Kutuzov as commander-in-chief. By then it was half-past ten at night and three hundred and fifty miles to the south, the 'Vesuvius' of Smolensk was erupting: there was no time to lose in protracted debate.

Yet still Alexander hesitated to add his signature to the resolution of the committee. He took the decision in the end only after receiving a letter from Rostopchin in Moscow letting him know that there, too, everyone wished Kutuzov to be given the supreme command. The Tsar's distaste for the step he was taking is clearly shown in the letter he wrote, a month later, to his sister: 'There was nothing that I could do but yield to such general pleading and appoint Kutuzov.' In the shadow of defeat even the narrowest of autocracies cannot sustain itself indefinitely on the personal inclination of the Emperor.

Alexander signed the decree appointing Kutuzov commander-in-chief on August 20 and left immediately for Abo in Finland for a conference with Bernadotte. This meeting gave rise to more than the usual crop of legends: an offer of a Russian command; a suggestion of a marriage link with the Romanovs; a hint that, if Napoleon fell, there was no better candidate for the French throne than the ultra-conservative Gascon, who had once been Minister of War under the Consulate. Although the records of the Abo conference are less dramatic, it is probable that, in moments of private conversation, proposals of this character were, indeed, made by Alexander. His emotional instability always led his mind to flit brightly from one fantastic inspiration to another, and he may have seen nothing incongruous in seeking the co-operation of the Swedish heir-presumptive in a castle which had been a Swedish possession until his own troops seized Finland three years before. The British, too, were anxious to bring Bernadotte into the field against Napoleon, although less devious than the Tsar in their methods; Cathcart, the British Ambassador in St Petersburg, who accompanied Alexander to Abo, was authorized by Castlereagh to draw on a special fund of £500,000 to get Sweden into the war. But neither Alexander's charm nor Cathcart's gold could shift Bernadotte from his original purpose: Sweden sought the acquisition of Norway (which was nominally part of Denmark) and a joint Russo-Swedish raid, with British naval support, on French-held Zealand. With disingenuous amiability, Bernadotte at one time offered to go a little further to meet Russia's needs: he was, he said, willing for the Swedish army to garrison southern Finland and free the Russian forces there for service against Napoleon. Such a proposal could hardly be expected to attract Alexander. The most that he gained from the Abo conference was an assurance of Swedish non-belligerency and the prospect that Sweden might enter the war at a later stage. Bernadotte was far too astute to pit himself against his former master while the fate of Moscow and St Petersburg was in the balance.

Yet the Tsar returned to his capital on September 3 well satisfied with the conference. By the time he reached St Petersburg, Kutuzov had arrived at army headquarters with Bennigsen as his chief of staff. Morale in the capital remained low, none the less. The most cherished treasures were being packed up for removal to distant recesses in the interior, and there was even a plan to transport Falconet's huge equestrian statue of Peter the Great, the 'bronze horseman,' rather than risk its being carried off as a prize by the invader. The distrust which the army felt for the faint hearts in Petersburg increased, rather than diminished, during the Tsar's absence in Finland. There was a general feeling that the Chancellor Rumantzov was too well disposed towards the French and should be dismissed from the court. The Tsar was soon made aware of the army's feelings.

On the very evening of his return, Alexander invited to dinner General Sir Robert Wilson, the unofficial British military representative with the Russian army. Wilson knew more about the Russian military machine than any of his compatriots; he had already written a serious study of the Russians at war in their earlier campaigns against the French – a book which, incidentally, was in

VUE DE LA PARADE ET DU PALAIS IMPÉRIAL DE ST PÉTERSBOURG. AN 1812.

A parade at St Petersburg

The bombardment of Smolensk

Napoleon's library and of which he made frequent use when planning the march into Russia. The British general had been in Smolensk on the eve of its fall and he had come to St Petersburg on an extraordinary mission. For that night, after dinner, Sir Robert gave the Tsar a message from his own officers; they assured him that 'if His Majesty would no longer give his confidence to advisers whose policy they mistrusted, they would testify their allegiance by exertions and sacrifices which would add splendour to the crown and security to the throne under every adversity.'

It was an awkward moment for host and guest. The Tsar went red in the face and stood in silence for a few minutes by the window. He sensed that his sovereign rights were being challenged once more. He had given the army Kutuzov; but now it wanted dismissal of Rumantzov as well. He would never have accepted such a demand from his own officers, as they were well aware when they asked Wilson to act as their spokesman. But at last he assured Wilson that he would give the message sympathetic consideration; and on the following day he sent for him and authorized him to return to the army with the pledge that he would never make peace so long as 'a Frenchman is in arms on this side of the frontier.' 'I would sooner let my beard grow to the waist and eat potatoes in Siberia,' he said. Rumantzov remained Chancellor, for Alexander was too proud to have his choice of ministers dictated by any of his subjects; but henceforth he could be in no doubt that the army commanders would never tolerate negotiations with the French. As he knew well enough, it was always possible for a palace conspiracy to remove a Tsar in whom the officers had no faith.

Uneasily, as the days of September shortened, St Petersburg continued to wait for news. The British Ambassador gave proof of his confidence in victory by taking a three-year lease of his official residence. But others were less sanguine. Alexander himself retired to his villa on the island of Kammionyi and sought comfort from the Bible, opening it at random in the hope that he would find passages to fortify him. And, far to the south, along the road from Smolensk to Moscow, a one-eyed general – so corpulent that he had to inspect his troops in a four-wheeled drosky rather than on horseback – was seeking to vindicate the valour of Russian arms. Time was running short for Russia and for Kutuzov.

6

The Homecoming of
Colonel Davidov

Napoleon had lingered in both Vilna and Vitebsk for more than a fortnight, but he remained in Smolensk for less than a week. Originally he planned otherwise: in Paris, and again in Dresden, he had declared that Smolensk would be the farthest point of advance that summer; if Alexander had not sued for peace when he reached the Dnieper, he would winter behind the solid ramparts of the city and complete the organization of his conquered territories before deciding in the following spring whether to take the road to St Petersburg or the road to Moscow. Now the reeking and smouldering ruins of Smolensk could afford him no sanctuary. For a few hours – perhaps even for a few days – he hesitated: the army, perspiring under shakoes and bearskins, needed a rest; staff officers spoke airily of regrouping; and there were disturbing reports of Russian units still holding out in villages far to the rear. But two facts loomed large in Napoleon's calculations: soon the autumn rains would come, turning the dust-tracks into mud both beyond Smolensk and along his lines of communication; and somewhere ahead of him there remained a Russian army which had still not suffered defeat in a major encounter. The prospect of cornering the elusive enemy spurred him on yet again.

Monday, August 24, was another sweltering day, the temperature climbing to 79° Fahrenheit in the shade. But Napoleon had made up his mind to go forward. Early that morning a report reached him from Murat that made him believe, once more, that he was on the eve of a great battle. About noon on the Sunday fifty miles to the east, a squadron of lancers had emerged from a wood and stumbled across the whole Russian army in defensive positions before the town of Dorogobuzh. It was all Napoleon wanted to hear. Throughout that Monday the orders sped from Smolensk: Eugène must hurry across the Dnieper; Poniatowski must bring up his Poles; the Old Guard was to be put on the alert, ready to march at two in the morning and maintain a good pace 'without, however, exhausting anybody.' A brief letter, mostly commenting on contrasts in the summer weather in Smolensk and Paris, went off to Marie-Louise; a hurried note to Maret told him that the armies were again in contact. Then at one o'clock on Tuesday morning the Emperor's carriage crossed the Dnieper with a small escort and took the Moscow road. So great was his haste that they did not rest their horses until they had covered more than thirty miles.

Events followed the usual melancholy pattern. In the late afternoon Napoleon reached the outskirts of Dorogobuzh. Davout was already there, for his corps had been ordered to replace Ney's in the advance-guard after the heavy fighting on the outskirts of Smolensk. The Emperor reconnoitred the position. The town lay before him intact, for once – but of the enemy there was no sign whatsoever. It was as if Murat's cavalry had seen a mirage: the Russians had slipped away as quietly and efficiently as in front of Vitebsk. Despondently, Napoleon sank into a mood of angry frustration. But there was to be no turning back now. Sooner or later the Russians must give battle before their ancient capital; and Moscow was only fifteen marching days distant from Dorogobuzh.

The Grand Army moved along the Moscow road in three columns. To the north were the cavalry of Eugène Beauharnais and Grouchy and to the south another cavalry corps under Latour-Maubourg, supported by Poniatowski's lancers. Ney, Davout and Murat were in the centre, astride the highway and accompanying Napoleon and the Guard. Relentlessly the advance continued along the Vosmo river to Viasma, which was entered on August 29. At times Murat and the advance-guard would cover thirty miles in a hard day's riding, raking the country in all directions in search of easy laurels: one by one the empty villages passed into French hands, with only an occasional skirmish to remind the invaders that they were in contact with the enemy. But this was no triumphal progress: with the charred corpses in Smolensk, a new bitterness had entered into the campaign. The full bestiality of war gripped both armies: there were no more interludes of fraternization as there had been that morning before Smolensk burned. Now stragglers could expect scant mercy from terrified villagers who emerged from the woods once the army had moved on; and an ashen path marked the route of the retreating Russians. By day distant clouds of smoke showed where they had fired villages and haystacks and at night the French looked out from their bivouacs on a horizon glowing with flames. The Russians sought to deny the French all sustenance.

Yet, curiously enough, the rank and file of the Grand Army fared better in this fortnight than they had done at Vitebsk or Smolensk, or than they were to do at any stage in the retreat. In isolated houses – and sometimes in the towns as well – they found well-stocked cellars and hidden caches of food. Napoleon himself let Marie-Louise know of the vodka which was delighting his troops in Viasma. And Sergeant Bourgogne many years later recalled that his unit of the Guard, which had made do with substitute beer in Vitebsk, graduated to brandy in Viasma. Castellane noted that his batman had obtained white bread and a little coffee for him; and Lieutenant Lyautey, writing to his father on September 1, admitted that the Russians were systematically destroying all the stores, but observed that, nevertheless, 'we see the feathers of chickens and geese in every bivouac.'

But the rigour of a long march in hot weather with no decisive battle was taking its toll. Sickness and (to a lesser extent) desertion accounted for almost one-tenth of the army in the twelve days which followed the departure from Smolensk. Dysentery was rife in some regiments, especially among the Würtembergers. In several units discipline was rapidly evaporating: it was difficult to check pillaging and pilfering (as the Emperor found in Viasma) and there were careless acts of wanton destruction – bad siting of camp-fires reduced Dorogobuzh to a smouldering ruin, and at Slawkovo the Guard inadvertently set fire to the bridge over which they were to move the following morning. Yet, even as the advance continued, the Emperor strove to re-create some of the swagger of earlier campaigns. Each day he would ride on horseback from the headquarters of one corps to another and each day the trumpets would ring out and drums throb as the imperial eagles were lowered in salute. It was as if he sought reassurance in this vast and dismal plateau by catching an echo of Austerlitz or Wagram.

The strain was beginning to tell as well on the senior commanders in the field. Murat's habit of throwing the cavalry recklessly into every chance encounter with the Russians seemed the height of folly to Davout and there is no doubt that casualties were needlessly high, since both men and horses were unduly weary from long days in the saddle. There was an angry scene on August 28 when Murat accused Davout, in the Emperor's presence, of failing to give artillery support to his lancers, while Davout, for his part, complained of Murat's 'thoughtless ardour': 'He pays no attention to the time of day or the nature of the enemy, but dashes up among his skirmishers, dances about in front of the enemy . . . and puts himself in a passion,' he said scathingly. Silently Napoleon listened to his two lieutenants, idly kicking a Russian cannon-ball as they bandied accusations. Common sense was on the side of Davout: it was essential to conserve the army's strength for the decisive battle. But to the young officers Murat, with his astounding uniforms and flaunting contempt for danger, was a demigod. On that very day Castellane noted in his diary, 'It is impossible to envisage a braver man than the king of Naples . . . He exposes himself (in a fight) more than a private . . . It is a miracle that he has still not yet been wounded.' For all his dislike of Murat, Napoleon could not risk a rebuke at this stage of the campaign. Irritated by the whole affair, he urged Davout to subordinate himself to Murat. But there was another quarrel two days later and Murat had to be restrained by General Belliard from hunting out Davout with a drawn sword. The private war of the two marshals smouldered to the gates of Moscow and beyond.

Napoleon's own mood in these days varied from hour to hour. He could still turn on, at will, the charm which had given him such control over men's minds. Conversational asides on the generalship of Alexander the Great or Julius Caesar flattered the younger officers into a sense of comradeship in an epic adventure. He was elated by the news which reached him in Gzatsk on September 1 that Kutuzov had replaced Barclay de Tolly as commander-in-chief; this, he felt, was a sign that the Russians intended to stand and give battle. But, among his closest companions, he had moments of depression and irritability. Trivialities easily jangled his nerves and he would break into angry denunciation both of the men around him and the servants of his empire in the conquered lands. His rage quickly subsided, but it left scars: Berthier was so roundly abused one day in Gzatsk that he declined to take his meals in the Emperor's presence for a whole week. On such occasions Napoleon was an exacting master.

By now autumn had come to Russia – as Napoleon remarked in no less than three letters to Marie-Louise. The first rain had fallen in Viasma on August 29. Three days later there was a storm in Gzatsk and for the remainder of that week the army pitched its tents in sodden fields and the tall poplars along the highway dripped incessantly into mournful pools of mud. The nights were cold and before dawn a clammy mist would add to the general discomfort. Napoleon's spirits seem to have flagged. Marie-Louise had written from Paris telling him of the pleasure she had gained from studying an illustrated account of the Egyptian expedition which her husband had undertaken when she was only five years old. He replied to her from Gzatsk on September 2: 'I am gratified that you find recreation in Denon's drawings of my campaign. You must understand that I have been exposed to endless danger. I have been conducting wars for nineteen years and have fought battles and laid sieges in Europe, in Asia and in Africa. I am going to hurry up and finish this business in order to see you soon and prove to you the emotions with which you inspire me.' Is it, one wonders, the comment of a love-sick husband solicitous for his young wife, or of a veteran general weary of all campaigning?

There is in fact some evidence that the Emperor's own health had given way. He had suffered from irritation of the bladder at earlier moments in his career, particularly during the tensest moments of the Egyptian adventure (which the scribbled note from Paris had brought back to his mind). Now the nervous strain of a long pursuit, the heavy rain driven across the open plain by a strong gale, and the constant jogging up and down in the saddle led to a recurrence of his old complaint. His pulse became irregular; a dryness in the throat made him cough persistently; and his tissues were swollen with fluid from which he could not free himself. It is not certain when the trouble began, for Napoleon had a marked distaste for medical men and avoided consulting them if he could. Probably he was already ill at Gzatsk, where his explosions of irascibility so taxed his companions. At all events, by September 5, he was sufficiently unwell to summon to his tent Dr Mestivier, who had once lived in Moscow and was attached to the Emperor's suite because of his knowledge of Russian conditions. 'You see, Doctor,' remarked Napoleon pathetically on Mestivier's arrival, 'I'm getting old, my legs are swollen and I have difficulty in passing my water; it is no doubt the dampness of these bivouacs, for I depend on my skin for my life.' He needed rest and careful nursing: the fate of war denied him both.

For eleven days the Emperor suffered from acute dysuria. In the early stages it resembled a feverish cold and his personal servants had to wait on him with potions. It is the final irony of the campaign that during those eleven days he was given the battle he had sought for more than ten weeks. Long ago, amid the uncertainties of Brumaire, General Bonaparte had defiantly proclaimed, 'The God of War and the God of Luck are marching alongside me:' had these old comrades in arms at last turned traitor?

Kutuzov reached the headquarters of the First and Second Russian Armies at Tsarevo-Zaimishche on August 29, the day on which the Grand Army entered Viasma, thirty miles to the south-west. His arrival boosted lagging morale; 'A true Russian exorcized the evil genius of the foreigners,' comments Clausewitz dryly. Now there would surely be an end to the retreat and a battle to save the ancient capital. But Kutuzov was cautious. Moscow was still more than a hundred miles away and he was determined not to fight unless he could force Napoleon to challenge him at a point where there was some hope of stemming the advance. Barclay had already taken up positions behind the village of Tsarevo-Zaimishche, but Kutuzov considered that they were dangerously exposed. He was far too wily to be rushed into disaster. Courageously risking his popularity, he ordered the army to resume its retreat, back through Gzatsk and down the road towards Mozhaisk. With Bennigsen as his chief of staff, he did not hesitate to confirm both Barclay de Tolly and Bagration in their army commands for, though he knew how much they loathed each other, he respected their differing qualities. Nor would he curry favour by dismissing the foreign advisers; he needed every experienced soldier who was prepared to serve under him. Showing fine contempt for this fashionable xenophobia, he even appointed one of the most fearless of the German veterans, Colonel Karl von Toll, as his Quartermaster-General (a post he had already held under Barclay). Subsequently, Toll – who was barely thirty years old – became, in effect, Kutuzov's military secretary, collaborating with him in planning each move in the campaign.

It was not easy to find a battlefield in this monotonous ocean of green and grey. There was only one geographical feature which might help Kutuzov: over the centuries the frozen rivers, melting each spring, had cut deep ravines across the face of the Russian plain. The French had already found them an obstacle at Vitebsk and Smolensk and Valutino. Kutuzov had passed just such a place as he travelled from Mozhaisk to Tsarevo-Zaimishche. It was near the monastery of Kolotskoye. He does not appear then to have been aware of its name, but the river was known as the Kalocha, a small stream easily fordable at this time of year.

The Kalocha flowed into the Moskva river some twenty-five miles east of Gzatsk. At the point of confluence there were several dried up tributaries as well as the two main streams and the plain was therefore broken up by a series of ravines and by a shoulder of high ground. A dozen hamlets clustered round the stream, tumbledown houses with sagging roofs, white churches with domes of blue and green, set in fields of grain which lapped the edge of a birch forest. It was a place of little importance, although half a century previously, Tsarina Catherine's engineers, building the New Road from Smolensk to Moscow, had thought it worthwhile to make a detour through the villages, leaving the Old Road south of the hillocks. They were certainly not a formidable natural obstacle, but in this flat and featureless land there was no other point where the defenders could command the main line of advance without being outflanked. Here Kutuzov was resolved to give battle. Leaving General Konovnitsin with a considerable rearguard to delay the advancing French, he hastened back towards the Moskva.

Kutuzov reached the monastery on September 1. He sent Toll forward to inspect the position and ordered the Russians to begin throwing up entrenchments immediately. A detailed directive was despatched to the two Russian armies ordering them to fall back to a three-mile front on the right bank of the Kalocha, straddling the New Road and the Old Road and following the line of high ground above the ravines. Disciplining himself to the uncongenial task of putting pen to paper, Kutuzov wrote confidently to the Tsar informing him that he was awaiting the enemy 'at the twelfth verst from Mozhaisk' in a village called Borodino.

It was a name with which Alexander was no more familiar than his commander-in-chief, although he had passed that way only seven weeks previously. But there was one Russian staff-officer who knew every field and every clump of trees in the neighbourhood. For each mile that he rode eastwards from Gzatsk, Colonel Davidov, Bagration's aide-de-camp over the last five years, was coming home. 'Here I passed the carefree years of childhood and felt the first glow of romance and the dream of glory,' he wrote later. By a curious quirk in the fortunes of war, Davidov was about to fight his first great battle on the edge of a spinney where he had played as a little boy. He arrived in Borodino just in time to see his family house disappearing in the smoke of a camp fire. As a poet he sensed bitterly at that moment the senseless irony of war – but it did not prevent him a few months later from becoming the most daring commander of Russia's guerrillas.

Meanwhile the French too were preparing for battle. The first reports that the Russians were digging in along the Moscow road reached Napoleon in Gzatsk early on September 2. That afternoon, as the corps commanders checked their strength and reported their numbers to Berthier and his staff, the troops were warned that they should prepare for a decisive battle which the Emperor felt was now imminent. The whole French camp throbbed with an air of expectancy. Stores of ammunition were inspected, weapons greased and cleaned, and efforts made to rally stragglers who had fallen out in the surrounding countryside. More ominously, a return was made of the numbers of surgeons and the field dressings which would be available. Everyone assumed that it would be a bloody encounter.

By ten that night Napoleon had all the information he wanted. It was not good. He had crossed the Niemen with 430,000 men. Some had inevitably been despatched to other battle areas – Polotsk, the edge of the Pripet Marshes, the lower Dvina – as well as to garrison the dozen cities which the French had occupied. But battle, skirmishes, disease and desertion had taken a large toll of the rest. On August 24 at Smolensk Napoleon still had 156,000 men; but by September 2 their numbers had fallen to less than 130,000. He was not sure of the Russian numbers, although he knew, from interrogation of prisoners, that Kutuzov had received reinforcements of militiamen and recruits from within the Empire. (Ten thousand militia, indifferently armed, and fifteen thousand fresh troops under General Mikhail Miloradovich had reached Kutuzov's headquarters in the previous week.) In reality, the Russians had at that moment only ten thousand men fewer than Napoleon. The French still had superiority in cavalry but not in artillery (587 guns to the Russians' 640). It was all very different from the type of battle which Napoleon had sought in July, when the Grand Army would have outnumbered Barclay de Tolly's force by three to one.

Napoleon left Gzatsk in the early afternoon of Friday, September 4, riding his charger, Moscow. Despite his illness he spent five hours in the saddle that day. The rain, which had been heavy throughout the Thursday, had stopped but the dampness of autumn hung around the column. Captain Castellane laconically jotted down impressions for his diary: 'Weather cold, road easy going, countryside flat, a few woods, several villages, most of them burnt. They blaze away with muskets and cannon at the advance-guard.' Murat, as ever, was some distance ahead of the main body of troops and at Gridnevo, eleven miles east of Gzatsk, he had a sharp skirmish with Konovnitsin and the Russian rearguard, who withdrew when the French cavalry threatened to turn their flank. Napoleon spent that night at Gridnevo in a bivouac. A forest of birch and fir lay on his left and here, on the Saturday morning, Konovnitsin made another stand at the monastery of Kolotskoye, which had been Kutuzov's headquarters three days previously and which was to serve as the main French hospital after the forthcoming battle. From the belfry tower of the abbey it was possible to see, beyond the woods, a line of seven hillocks – none of them more than 150 feet high – separating the Kalocha from the Moskva river. Spirals of smoke drifted across the woodland: it was there that Kutuzov awaited the French.

A mile ahead of the main Russian defences stood an isolated knoll above the village of Shevardino. On its crest Kutuzov had ordered the construction of field-works and the Russians dragged a dozen heavy guns up the slopes to menace the main route to the village of Borodino. Toll himself insists that this Shevardino redoubt was primarily an outpost to discover the direction in which the French forces were moving; but a number of observers maintain that it was intended to form the key position on the Russian left flank. At all events, Napoleon perceived that so long as the redoubt was in Russian hands, it enabled its defenders to observe all his movements; and that Saturday afternoon he ordered Murat to eject the Russians from the hill.

It was a murderous affair, which raged from four o'clock until after darkness fell six hours later. The assault began with the almost customary gestures of impetuous bravado, the Russians falling back from the exposed village of Doronino as the line of horsemen swept forward. Colonel Méda led his light cavalry, sabre in hand: sixteen years before, as a young gendarme of twenty, he had fired the shot which shattered Robespierre's jaw on the eve of Thermidor; now he would boast of his moment of history no more, for a Russian bullet hit him and he toppled dead from the saddle. This would be no easy victory for Murat. The guns from the Russian battery bounced round-shot over the plain, the Frenchmen pulling up their horses short to avoid the missiles if they were sufficiently quick-sighted to see them coming. Angrily, Murat ordered his horsemen to fall back and sent in General Compans's infantry division, which had been seconded to him by Davout. Compans formed up his men – the 57th and 61st Regiments – in the shelter of a small ravine. The hillside above them was bare and open. They scrambled up it, making directly for the smoking mouths of the guns, or so it seemed to observers watching this isolated action from other slopes. A burst of wild cheering echoed across the valley from the Russian defenders, followed by the whistle of musket-balls and the thud of round-shot. Compans ordered his men to fix bayonets and charge the defences. They wavered, unable in the confusion, to distinguish his orders, and he was forced to lead the 57th Regiment forward personally; he survived, even though a third of the Regiment perished. The Russian gunners made no attempt to flee. When at last the French broke through the entrenchments, they met bayonet with bayonet. By five o'clock the redoubt was in French hands: no prisoners were taken.

Napoleon had watched the attack through a telescope from beyond the Kalocha. So, too, from the main Russian position had Bagration (for the defenders were men of his Second Army). Both commanders knew that the fight was not yet over. Napoleon ordered the 111th Regiment, which had followed Compans up the hill and was relatively unscathed, to form a square, since his military instinct made him expect a counter-attack by Russian cavalry. The afternoon passed into evening and still there was no sign of a Russian move. Then, half an hour before dusk, a brigade of Russian heavy cavalry, swords at the ready and the setting sun reflected from their dark cuirasses, charged the French square, broke through and for a time held the redoubt again. Nansouty's 9th Cavalry Regiment – north Germans, known from the colour of their uniforms and schapskas as the 'Red Lancers of Hamburg' – launched a spectacular counter-attack after dusk. It was a strange encounter. In the gloom the Germans did not see the black cuirasses of the Russians until they met them in what was virtually a head-on collision: metal clashed with metal, but the lances failed to penetrate since they were held at the ready rather than in a thrusting position. Within a few minutes the Germans had fallen back to reform behind the French lines, their faces apparently matching the colour of their uniforms in embarrassment. It seemed impossible to shift the Russian cavalry; but it was no less impossible for the Russian infantry to consolidate the position in the dark. Eventually, fearing an outflanking movement by Ponia-towski, Bagration ordered his cavalry to withdraw and the French were finally left in command of the redoubt. It had cost them over two thousand casualties.

The fanaticism of the Russian defence astounded Napoleon. Ségur describes how he 'fell into a deep meditation' that evening because the French had taken no prisoners. He seems, too, to have been worried by the havoc caused by the twelve Russian cannon and, sensing that an artillery duel was imminent, he sent back orders down the road to Gzatsk to speed up the despatch of guns and ammunition waggons. At the same time, he was afraid that the loss of their outpost might induce the Russians to withdraw, as they had done so many times before. He spent an uneasy night, wondering if the sounds from across the valley indicated that the Russians were pulling out yet again. 'There was a general feeling of exultation,' writes Ségur, 'when the morning sun found the two armies on the same ground where it had left them the evening before.' Borodino would not be another Vitebsk or Dorogobuzh.

There was, however, still another day and another night to pass before the two armies clashed; for the whole of that Sunday was spent in preparation, patrols from each side cautiously reconnoitring each other's positions. At daybreak Napoleon rode with Berthier, Caulaincourt and a handful of officers to the Shevardino redoubt and back down into the ravine, often within easy sight of the Russian outposts. His staff officers were set to work sketching the topography while the Emperor decided on a detailed plan of operations. Again in the afternoon he was in the saddle inspecting the positions where he wished to site the artillery. He could see the Russians strengthening their earthworks and digging entrenchments, slowly and with primitive tools. It was not difficult for him to make up his mind on a general plan of attack.

The main strength of the Russian army was clearly concentrated on the heights above the village of Borodino itself, astride the New Road to Moscow. The centre, on which there was an entrenched battery ('Raevski's redoubt') looked as menacing as the outpost up which Compans's regiments had stormed on the previous afternoon. To the north, Kutuzov's position was helped by the natural lie of the land, for it was there that the Kalocha met the Moskva river in deep, serpentine ravines; a mass of infantry caught in these open gullies would provide the Russian guns with a target upon which they could wreak havoc. As Napoleon looked out on the Russian defensive system from the battered remains of the Shevardino redoubt, it therefore seemed as if this was the natural point from which to launch the main assault, assailing the Russian left flank, forcing it back towards the New Road, perhaps even driving it into the Moskva River in a second Friedland. Yet here, curiously enough, Napoleon's powers of observation misled him: two arrow-shaped parapets – the 'Bagration flèches,' as they became known – stood out clearly as ugly gashes halfway up the hill facing him, 2,000 yards away, and he reckoned that they could be carried by a frontal assault after heavy bombardment; but he did not know that above them, on the crest, was a third redoubt, its guns commanding the southern flank of the hill, but easily capable of lobbing grapeshot down on the attacking troops once they had stormed the two parapets. Moreover, he could not tell how large a reserve the Russians had concentrated, under cover of a birch wood, on the Old Road to the south of the hill. The Bagration flèches were a far more formidable obstacle than they looked.

Napoleon may indeed have had doubts about the development of the battle. Davout proposed a grand enveloping movement through the Utitsa woods and along the Old Road. Napoleon would have none of it: the main force of Kutuzov's army might retreat unscathed along the New Road and it would be another Smolensk without the consolation of winning a city whose name would look impressive in the Imperial Bulletin. This time every regiment and squadron and battery manned by the Russians must be brought to battle and eliminated as opposition. In a brief five-hundred word directive the Emperor outlined his plans for the following morning: a holding attack by Eugène Beauharnais against the Borodino position, while Davout, Ney, Junot and Murat were to go forward against the Bagration defences and Poniatowski test the Russian strength to the south by advancing through Utitsa. But beyond these initial moves he did not commit himself: 'Battle thus being engaged, orders will be given according to the disposition of the enemy,' ran his message to the army commanders. With this somewhat inconclusive instruction, Napoleon tacitly confessed that he could not read Kutuzov's mind. As a guarantee of resounding triumph it lacked conviction.

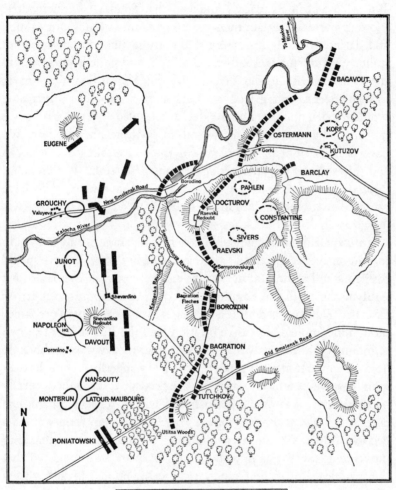

THE BATTLE OF BORODINO

But what *was* in Kutuzov's mind on that Sunday of anticipation? No one knew for certain then and no one knows today, for caution and laziness made him among the most uncommunicative of military commanders. He dictated to Toll, and signed, a despatch to the Tsar describing the defence of the Shevardino redoubt in glowing terms, but giving no indication of what he anticipated would happen on the following day. A scribbled note to his wife was in a similar vein: 'I am, thank God, in good health, my dear. We have been in sight of Napoleon for three days already,' it began and, after describing the action 'on my left flank,' it concludes: 'Our divisions are wonderful, especially the cuirassiers, who have captured five French cannons.' No doubt Madame Kutuzova was duly reassured.

Kutuzov had, in fact, already made his preparations and was ready to wait on events. His troops were stationed in a convex curve spread over four miles and almost equally divided between Barclay's First Army in the north and Bagration's Second Army in the south. It was clear that Kutuzov had three advantages over his enemy: a prepared, though incomplete, defensive position (and the Russians had shown in innumerable actions with the Turks that they would stubbornly hold all entrenchments); numerical artillery superiority and heavier guns (twelve-pounders); and an army which, though woefully inexperienced, was fired by a patriotic will to resist. Kutuzov had taken a gamble, assuming from experience that Napoleon wanted a decisive battle. If the Grand Army attempted an outflanking movement, the Russians would retire (as Napoleon expected that they would). But if the Grand Army were tempted to throw itself against the Russian redoubts in frontal assaults, these could prove so costly that it would cease to be a cohesive machine of war. Then, with its tenuous lines of communication exposed to raids by Cossack horsemen and with the promise of Russian reinforcements coming from the Army of the Danube in Moldavia, the remnant of the invaders would be harassed back to the frontier. As a grand design, this strategy had much to commend it – always assuming of course that the casualties of such a grim battle did not consume the Russian army as well as its adversary. It was a heart-rending prospect.

At midday on that Sunday a slow procession moved along the New Road uphill from the church at Borodino towards the even smaller village of Gorki. With bare heads and arms reversed, the guard battalion which had escorted the ikon of the Holy Virgin from burning Smolensk, led the sacred relic through the assembled troops. As the sunlight flashed on the silver cover of the ikon and its ribbons fluttered in the breeze, the peasant soldiery of Russia knelt and brought their hands across their breasts from right to left, making the sign of the cross in the Orthodox manner. Censers swung with rhythmic dignity and wafts of blue incense drifted across the dusty road. Priests in rich vestments chanted a melancholy litany in the unhurried timelessness of Slavonic plainsong: '*Gospodi pomilui*' – 'Lord have mercy' – responded in unison officers and men.

Across the valley Napoleon and his staff observed and noted this 'extraordinary movement' in the enemy camp. 'Credulous from ignorance, they worshipped their images, fancying themselves devoted by God to the defence of Heaven and their consecrated soil,' wrote Ségur afterwards, with the grudging admiration of a French rationalist. But he was wrong. As Kutuzov lowered his ungainly body to kiss the ikon, he was acknowledging amid the ugliness of war that man had the spiritual power to redeem creation through beauty. The Russians knelt in reverence, not idolatry. They were reminded of God in the way to which they were accustomed: they would have need of Him on the morrow.

When Napoleon rode back to his bivouac beside the village of Valuyevo at six, he found that two visitors had arrived during the afternoon. Colonel Charles Fabvier, aide-de-camp to Marshal Marmont, had set out from Spain a month before to travel sixteen hundred miles with the unpalatable news that Wellington was in Salamanca and the road through the Guadarammas open to Madrid. It seemed a bad omen to some, but the Emperor, whatever he might feel about Spain in later years, was for the moment undismayed:

'The English have their hands full there,' he remarked to Caulain-court with magnificent self-deception. His mind was too obsessed with Moscow to worry about Madrid.

The other guest received a warmer welcome; for Louis de Bausset, a palace official, brought with him a portrait by Gérard of Napoleon's seventeen-month-old son, the King of Rome. Napoleon, tired and racked with discomfiture by his illness, was delighted; the sentimental intrusion from family life kindled his Italianate pride in fatherhood. That evening he personally placed the portrait outside his tent and the veterans of the Old Guard gathered round it in respectful admiration. In one camp, the ikon of Smolensk: in the other, a painting of a child. It is a revealing contrast in attitudes of mind.

The night was an uneasy one. The temperature dropped rapidly after dusk and towards dawn a clammy mist descended on the two armies, now and again blotting out the opposing lines of camp-fires. There was still much activity: Russian engineers were busy strengthening Raevski's redoubt, deepening the trenches and erecting a double palisade so that a dozen heavy guns could be sited on the crest of the hill; the French batteries moved into position; and a group of Russian officers crept forward to the French lines and saw, with awe, a long line of cavalry drawn up, their riders 'as motionless as statues on their horses.' In both camps men were checking their weapons, making bandages, drawing up wills. There was at least one unfinished game of chess (adjourned for four months). Snatches of song came out of the darkness; and here and there men slept as best they could, some exhausted in anticipation and others with complete indifference.

Napoleon himself slept little. His valet says that he had fits of shivering and sustained himself by drinking punch. At times his conversation seems to have rambled on inconsequentially, as if he were in a fever. Constantly he needed reassurance that the Russian army was still there, that his staff could see shadowy figures crouch-ing over the camp-fires. At two o'clock he finished dictating an order of the day which was to be read at dawn:

Soldiers! here is the battle you have so desired! Now victory depends on you. We need it. It will give us abundance, good winter quarters and a speedy return to the homeland. Carry yourselves as you did at Austerlitz, at Friedland, at Vitebsk, at Smolensk, so that the remotest posterity speaks with pride of your conduct on this day. Let them say of you, 'He was in that great battle under the walls of Moscow.'

Although geographically misleading, for the walls were over seventy miles away, it was a stirring proclamation: an amended version, merely promising 'to open the gates of the Russian capital,' was read to some units, but the original appeared in the *Moniteur* for home consumption three weeks later.

At half-past five in the morning Napoleon reached the crest of the hill above Shevardino up which Compans's division had stormed thirty-six hours ago and from which he intended to observe the day's events. Soon after he arrived there the sun rose, shining through the mist as it had done at another battle seven years before. The parallel pleased him: 'It is the sun of Austerlitz!' he declared for the sake of the generals around him (and no doubt for remotest posterity as well). No one in his entourage seems to have noticed that it was a phrase he had used once already in this campaign; but perhaps it would have been tactless at that moment to have recalled the disappointment of Vitebsk.

7

'The Most Terrible of all my Battles'

At six in the morning of September 7 more than a hundred guns on
the French right flank opened up on the Bagration flèches almost
a mile ahead of them. It was an impressive overture to the battle,
but, after such meticulous siting, disquietingly ineffective; for the
receding fog made the atmosphere heavy and the shots fell short of
their target, dropping harmlessly into the soft grass of the slope.
Hurriedly the gun teams sweated to advance their batteries, while
nearly two miles to the north Eugène Beauharnais's artillery began
to hurl roundshot into the village of Borodino. Shortly afterwards
in the French centre Ney's guns, too, fired on the Russian positions
facing them, so that the whole shoulder of high ground shuddered
with the impact of bombardment. As the Russian cannon answered
back, seeking to pick off the massed French troops before they could
move forward, the smoke of explosives mingled with the rising
mist and drifted through the ravines in a reeking cloud. For eight
hours the thunder of a thousand guns was to be so deafening that the
crackle of musketry became inaudible; regiments were forced to
respond, not to the verbal order or the bugle call, but to the flash of
coloured rockets in the sky or to arms upraised in theatrical gesticu-
lation. There had been nothing like it in the other Napoleonic
battles.

On the extreme right of the French, Poniatowski's horsemen
became heavily entangled in brushwood as they moved towards
Utitsa and his corps made a late entry on the scene. It was therefore
in the centre that the first infantry moved forward, the divisions of
Compans and Dessaix in Davout's corps advancing around the edge

of a birch wood towards the flèches. As they broke cover, three batteries of Russian guns turned on them and they also met a withering fire from a regiment of Russian grenadiers. Solid iron shot fell among the leading officers, striking them down like skittles in an alley. Compans was hit by a musket-ball which penetrated his right shoulder: his successor, General Rapp, who already bore the scars of eighteen wounds, received four more in the course of a single hour. Dessaix, too, was hit. It seemed an almost impenetrable line of fire and, for a moment, the troops wavered: should they fall back for the cover of the woods? Davout, close behind them, galloped forward and led the 57th Regiment on the foremost Russian guns with fixed bayonets. But the Marshal, with the high prow of his cocked hat tantalizingly conspicuous, proved an irresistible target for the sharpshooters. The muskets fired, his horse fell dead under him, and Davout was thrown on his head. As he lay ominously still on the ground, an orderly hastened to Napoleon on the Shevardino mound. But Davout was only stunned; regaining consciousness he stiffly declined to leave his men. Another horse was sent for; but he was, in reality, too badly bruised and shaken to lead the shattered division forward, though he managed to stay in the saddle; and in due course his troops merged with the Westphalian regiments in Ney's corps.

Over on the French left, Eugène's corps had met with initial success. The Delzons division found Borodino itself held by light infantry of the Russian Imperial Guard, already severely shaken by the preliminary bombardment. They were dislodged without much difficulty and, to his surprise, Delzons found the bridge over the Kalocha intact. Elated, Delzons sent his leading regiment, the 106th, sweeping over the river and up the steep cutting along the road to Gorki (and Kutuzov's headquarters). But, on either flank, the Russians opened fire on the dense column, which faltered and turned in confusion. Delzons himself fell dead and so did most of his officers; the regiment was overwhelmed. The French stood fast in the shattered and smouldering houses of the village, but the Russians recovered the right bank of the river; and this time they saw to it that the wooden slats of the bridge went up in smoke. For the remainder of the day a thousand-yard No Man's Land, littered with dead and dying, separated the two armies along the New Road.

This savage contest around the bridge of Borodino was fought out beyond the range of Napoleon's vision. From the banks above Shevardino the village was hidden by the swelling rib of land on which the Russians had constructed Raevski's redoubt, but he had a good view of the Russian centre where Ney was hurrying to the support of Davout's hard-pressed divisions. Anxiously, with Berthier by his side, the Emperor paced up and down in his grey greatcoat, arms behind his back, or sat on a special stool seeking to piece together the scraps of conflicting information which the orderlies brought to him and occasionally peering through his telescope at the mêlée, as if expecting to discern from some magnified detail a significant shift in the fortunes of the battle. But throughout the morning as the early mist gave way to sweltering sunshine, all he could see was a confused mass of attack and counter-attack, horses rearing and falling, the glint of swords and bayonets, the orange flame of smoking cannon, broken limbs tumbling obscenely into the dust. Close above him, the dark mass of the Old Guard was drawn up as on parade. Somewhere a regimental band played the marches of an earlier campaign: '*Allons, enfants de la patrie!*', rang out the stirring brass, '*Le jour de Gloire est arrivé!*' And so for many it had: but not as yet for the Guard, it would appear. Impassively, in battle order, they awaited the will of their sovereign commander; and he was determined to preserve them to the end as the one inviolate unit of his dwindling army.

It is hardly surprising that when later the survivors came to look back on that day, the general pattern of Borodino escaped them, although they remembered vividly the details of action. With thousands close to oblivion, all passage of time becomes irrelevant, so that hours are telescoped into minutes, while the mind tortures seconds of apprehension into an eternity. No one knows precisely when Marshal Ney, standing out at the head of his men 'like a captain of grenadiers,' waved them forward on to the Bagration flèches. It cannot have been later than eight o'clock, and yet already the approaches to the parapets were choked with dead soldiers and horses. They stumbled into the first two entrenchments and up to the third, which they had not seen as they waited to go into action. Russian twelve-pounders fired grapeshot down on them and there was no shelter on the slope. Before nine o'clock the Russian cuirassiers had come up, toppling the lightly armed Würtembergers from their horses in a charge down the hill; and the entrenchments were once more in Russian hands. Only the prompt action of Murat and the arrival of a squadron of Polish lancers checked the cuirassiers. It was half-past nine and the French commanders had gained only a few hundred yards; and from the north another Russian corps was coming to Bagration's assistance.

For perhaps twenty minutes horsemen and artillery paused along the spur of land. But the gunners were never silent, finding new targets in the columns of reinforcements hastening to the aid of both sides. Then the Grand Army swept forward again, over the front line of Russian defenders and into the flèches once more. Desperately the Russian drivers forced their teams of horses to drag the heavy guns away from the oncoming army, but as they hastened back over the brow of the hill, they passed through the Russian Second Corps, which had marched south from the New Road and was now charging down to dislodge Ney's men before they could establish themselves in the defences. Weary from the grim attack, the troops of the Grand Army proved no more able to withstand this onslaught than they had been an hour before. For a third time they were thrown back to the edge of the woods.

From the Shevardino mound Napoleon sent a horseman forward to order more batteries to be turned on the Russian position. Perhaps as many as four hundred guns were now concentrated on this one knoll. Bagration himself – an inspiring leader in close combat, like Ney in his fearlessness – saw that another effort would soon be made to storm the flèches. This time he was determined to take the initiative; and, shortly before eleven o'clock he sent his whole left wing down on the French position, the infantry moving forward with fixed bayonets behind the light cavalry.

For the first hundred yards the French held their fire as the relentless tide swept down on them. Then, levelling their muskets, they fired a volley into the advancing line and rushed into a counter-attack. Bayonet met bayonet as in some grotesque and deadly fencing match. Bagration, astride his horse within the entrenchments, exclaimed 'Bravo!' in admiration of the courage of both sides; but at that moment a French battery raked the flèches with grapeshot. A splinter struck Bagration in the leg. It was not, at first glance, a mortal wound, and Bagration with supreme self-control remained imperturbably in the saddle, for he sensed that his presence among them gave the defenders the will to resist. But blood began to stream down his horse's flank and those around him saw his face go white beneath the thick patches of gunpowder with which it was smeared. Slowly, as though wrestling with an inner reluctance, his body began to slip off his horse. His adjutant caught him, and, still conscious, he was carried on a stretcher to the shelter of the far side of the hill. There he was lifted into a drosky which bore him back up the valley and off the battle. As it sped painfully across the uneven ground, gloom descended on the Russian soldiery for, although their commander lingered on for another seventeen days, they believed him already dead. 'The soul itself had gone from the whole of the left wing,' wrote one of his officers later. A stray splinter of grapeshot had virtually won the morning for Napoleon. In these minutes of consternation Ney finally seized the flèches and this time the weary Russian survivors were driven back and into the dried up creek on the far side of the hill. Only the exhaustion of the attackers prevented a complete breakthrough.

The fighting around the flèches had been so critical that the Russians poured in most of their reserves to strengthen Bagration's position. This had enabled Poniatowski, to the south, to clear the village of Utitsa (where the Moscow militia made their valiant stand) but the French and the Poles were unable to exploit their success because they too were concentrating all their efforts on gaining the flèches. With their capture, the crucial point in the battle shifted 1,200 yards to the north, across another deep ravine to the hill above the burning village of Semenovskoye where Raevski's redoubt commanded the centre of the French line.

Eugène's corps had been assigned the task of storming the Raevski position. His engineers constructed pontoon bridges across the Kalocha and by half-past nine the infantry divisions of Morand and Broussier were on the right bank of the river, although Montbrun's cavalry was held up by heavy brushwood. The odds were heavily in favour of the French. Raevski had only sixteen battalions of infantry to hold the hill as he had already sent two regiments to Bagration. His redoubt was incomplete and the actual area of fortification was small; he decided to concentrate his guns in the redoubt, trusting in the infantry to halt a French attack until reserve divisions could reach him. A hundred and twenty-five yards ahead of the protective parapets his men had dug a long line of man-traps concealed in the heavy grass. Raevski himself had been injured a few days before the battle – 'Through my own carelessness a bayonet projecting from a waggon had pierced my calf,' he wrote – and was forced to spend most of the day dismounted, behind the parapets. The prospect for him was a poor one; and yet he was supremely confident.

Broussier's division made an exploratory thrust towards the redoubt soon after ten o'clock, but heavy fire from the cannon and the constant whirr of musket-balls from the slopes on their flank made the men fall back to wait for cavalry and artillery support. An hour later General Bonnamy, of Morand's division, led the 30th Regiment forward up the slope. Among those who followed him were Colonel Fabvier, who had arrived from Spain on the previous day and who seems to have regarded himself as the custodian of the honour of Marmont's army, and Captain François, who was generally known as the 'Dromedary of Egypt,' having dined out for years on tall stories of his experiences as a Sergeant in the Army of the Orient in 1798-99. 'I have never found myself in such a bloody encounter,' he was to write after this day's action.

As Bonnamy's men reached the crest of the ravine in front of the redoubt, round shot ricocheted among them. From above, a dozen twelve-pounders in the Russian battery fired a salvo of grapeshot at them. Hastily the Russian gun teams re-loaded and sent down a second salvo at short range. Some of the attackers stumbled into the man traps. A reeking cloud of gunpowder drifted down the hill, so that the Frenchmen moved forward as though under a smokescreen. 'We could not see the enemy,' complained Raevski afterwards. Suddenly an ordnance officer on Raevski's left gave a warning shout, 'Excellency, save yourself!' Spinning round, Raevski saw fifteen feet ahead of him French grenadiers hacking through the palisade. With difficulty and hampered by his injured leg, he forced a way through to the left wing of his defenders, seized a horse and painfully galloped off to the opposite hill to rally his supporting infantry for a counter-charge.

For a moment it seemed as if the redoubt was lost to the Russians. Amid the guns the defenders seized ram-rods and wheeled at the French. Captain François flailed about himself with his sword; a Russian hacked off the tails of the captain's uniform jacket, but missed his body. Then suddenly Raevski's infantry were on them, forcing them back, out of the redoubt. At that moment, General Ermolov with a column of chasseurs was on his way southwards to help Bagration's men. The chasseurs turned their horses and guns on the approaches to the redoubt and a shower of grapeshot prevented the French from making a further attack. The 30th Regiment virtually ceased to exist. Fifteen hundred Frenchmen were left wounded or dead on the hill. Colonel Fabvier, seriously wounded, dragged himself back to the French lines. So too did Captain François, fainting from loss of blood as he reached the relative safety of the slope before the river. General Morand, cut on the chin by grapeshot, was beside him; but of General Bonnamy there was no sign.

Yet Bonnamy, by remarkable presence of mind, had saved himself. Caught by the infantry when they stormed back into the redoubt, he lay motionless on the ground with fifteen bayonet wounds in his body. As a Russian soldier prepared to administer the coup de grâce, Bonnamy called out 'I am the King.' There was only one 'king' whom the Russians respected, grudgingly believing that he had super-natural powers – the King of Naples, Marshal Murat. The Russian, believing that he had captured Murat, dragged the general to a superior officer (who promptly made him a sergeant and awarded him the Cross of St George for his meritorious service). At once wild elation surged down the lines. Everyone on the hill heard the good news. A major with an elegant lisp rode excitedly among the troops yelling at the top of his voice, 'Little Bwuvvers, Moowat's taken!' It was the only moment of light relief on that grim morning. Incredibly, Bonnamy survived and returned to France after two years as a prisoner of war; but the Russians were to see the genuine King of Naples that very afternoon and none could claim him as their captive.

By now it was noon. The guns had been thundering out for six hours, and, where they could, the survivors of the morning's ordeal snatched some food. Up on the Shevardino mound Napoleon refused his luncheon; heavily taxed by his feverish illness, he had already taken a glass of punch and he accepted some Chambertin, but he would not eat while the issue of the battle was in doubt. Two and a half miles away, at his headquarters above Gorki, Kutuzov knew – as perhaps Napoleon feared – that at any moment a Russian diversion would throw the immediate plans of the French awry and force them to think of their own defences. A raid on the French flank would give the defenders of Raevski's redoubt time to re-organize, if nothing more.

So far, the seven thousand Cossack horsemen in the Russian Army had taken little part in the battle. Detachments had jousted with Poniatowski's lancers in the abortive fighting around Utitsa, but the main force had sat their horses inactive beside the Moskva river, more than three miles from the carnage above the Kalocha. This inactivity had been far from the liking of their commander, Matvei Ivanovich Platov. Before eleven o'clock he obtained permission from Kutuzov to make a daring raid with the bulk of his horsemen, supported by thirty-two squadrons of the regular cavalry reserve under General Uvarov. In all, some seven or eight thousand horse-men began to move down on the left flank of the French position shortly before midday.

Fording the Kalocha a couple of miles downstream from Boro-dino, the two columns remained hidden from the scouts of Eugène's corps by a ridge of sharply rising hills. The first warning that the Grand Army had of their presence was a sombre and apparently endless line of horsemen coming over the crest of land facing them, sabres and helmets flashing in the sun as if they were a legion of reinforcements arriving on the battlefield to decide the issue. Eugène's men, mostly at this point Italians and Croats, promptly fell back towards Borodino, sending an orderly to alert Eugène, who was beyond the Kalocha in front of Raevski's redoubt. But Platov's irregulars bore down on them in a wild gallop, descending on the Italian infantry before it could form the customary defensive square, and there were some minutes of wild panic.

It was a critical moment for the Grand Army. Uvarov, however, was by nature more cautious than Platov and his hesitancy gave Eugène the chance to counter-march with Grouchy's cavalry so as to cover the approaches to Borodino itself. Faced by resolute squares, with French horsemen lined up behind them, the Russians were effectively checked. Had Uvarov been a Bagration or a Raevski, he would have charged the French position, but, conscious that he was without support, he hesitated and the opportunity for turning the French defences was lost. Perhaps, too, looking at the wild antics of Platov's horsemen with the jaundiced eye of the professional soldier, he feared the impetuosity of the Cossacks. At all events, the raid came to nothing. For over two hours the opposing forces eyed each other suspiciously – for, while the Russians were uncertain of the strength facing them, Eugène for his part could not be sure that Uvarov and Platov were not the vanguard of some massive counter-attack. Then, shortly before three o'clock, the Russians turned and disappeared behind the screens of the hill. Eugène and the cavalry had already returned to their former positions across the Kalocha; and the Croats and Italians evidently thought it prudent not to pursue the retreating Russian host.

Nevertheless, the Russian incursion had given the troops on Raevski's redoubt their respite; Kutuzov and Barclay were able to send Ostermann's division, which had so far seen little action, to stiffen the defence. Yet, before the assault was renewed, Napoleon ordered up all his remaining guns, so that a savage concentration of roundshot and grapeshot fell among the Russian troops, grouped tightly together on a narrow front. Their will to resist was fast ebbing away; but the French, too, were exhausted after more than eight hours of fighting in the heat which, on that day at any rate, was as sweltering as their comrades in Marmont's army were experiencing in Spain. By the early afternoon the constant thundering of guns, the parching, blinding dust and the sheer horror of the carnage had engendered throughout both armies moral weariness more terrifying than physical fatigue. For the rest of the day officers and men could only stumble forward like soulless machines, almost cracking under the strain of what was expected of them and yet paradoxically achieving more than anyone could have asked. Years later Napoleon looked back on Borodino from the lonely silence of St Helena: 'The most terrible of all my battles,' he declared, 'was the one in front of Moscow. The French showed themselves worthy of victory and the Russians of being invincible.'

But at two o'clock on that Monday afternoon it was still not certain which of the hollow-eyed armies would end the day victorious. Neither side had as yet committed its last reserves: the cavalry of the Imperial Russian Guard remained with Kutuzov on the road beyond Gorki; the twenty thousand men of the Old Guard and the Young Guard were drawn up on the slopes above Napoleon. Three times Murat had requested the Emperor to send in units of the Guard, but so far the only section to come into action had been the artillery of the Young Guard. Now, for a fourth time, he sent one of his generals to ask for 'the cavalry of the Guard, with whose assistance he could turn the entrenched heights.' This time Napoleon seemed to relent: Marshal Bessières should lead the horseguards down to Murat's position. But where was Bessières? No one in the Emperor's entourage could find him: it was an absurd situation. Then it was remembered that Napoleon himself had sent him off to report on the battle as it appeared from another vantage-point. By the time he returned it was too late for the horseguards to go forward.

Eugène, meanwhile, was conferring with Murat and Ney. Although irritated by the Emperor's reluctance to part with the Guard, they still had one corps of cavalry which had survived the morning almost unscathed. For Montbrun's heavy cuirassiers had sustained only one serious blow – the loss of Montbrun himself, killed by a stray cannonball as he was marshalling his troops. To succeed him, Napoleon had despatched one of his aides-de-camp, General Auguste de Caulaincourt, the brother of Armand de Caulaincourt (who was the Emperor's Master of the Horse and a former ambassador to Russia). Now it seemed as if Auguste de Caulaincourt was to give the cuirassiers a chance to avenge their commander's death. From the plain beside the Kalocha Murat pointed out to him the fresh troops of Ostermann, waiting on the southern slopes of Raevski's redoubt. So long as they covered the entrenchments a frontal assault would prove as costly and abortive as it had before noon; but if Caulaincourt could break through Ostermann's corps and take the redoubt from the rear, Broussier's infantry could advance up the hill, scale the parapets and hold the position once it had been taken. The project was a daring one, characteristic of the marshal who proposed it.

Slowly two battalions of infantry, with a covering screen of light cavalry, began to move forward. Beside them were the 5th Cuirassiers, massive horses bearing heavily built men, their powder-tarnished helmets gleaming dully as they advanced at a steady trot. At their head rode Auguste Caulaincourt, gradually quickening the pace. Fain, Napoleon's secretary, watched the whole charge from above Shevardino, where spectators leaned forward excitedly as if they were in Paris witnessing some colourful manœuvre from the Imperial dais in the Champ de Mars. With the whole incident fresh in his mind, Fain recorded their impressions in glowing prose. They clearly saw the cavalry dashing ahead towards Ostermann's line, horses' tails streaming behind them, riders bending forwards as they increased their gallop over the thickly matted grass. Through the Russian troops they passed, beyond the redoubt. Suddenly they wheeled to the left, 'disappearing in a cloud of dust and smoke.' Behind them, in a flurry of yellow and black, charged a Saxon cavalry regiment, the Zastrow Cuirassiers. At the same time, the bayonets of Broussier's infantry glittered as they crossed the man-traps and advanced on the parapet. 'Assailed on every side,' writes Fain, 'the volcano thunders, flashes and sends forth torrents of fire that are redoubled and then suddenly extinguished.' The spectators realized that the redoubt, which had defied them for so long, was firmly in French hands.

Auguste de Caulaincourt reined in his horse, turned and broke into a gallop once more, as he saw the Russians beginning to reform in the valley beyond the hill. But, as he emerged from the redoubt, a musket-ball hit him and he dropped forward, shot through the heart, his horse falling with him. Lieutenant Wolbert, his personal aide, rode wretchedly back to the group of onlookers to inform the Emperor and break the news of his brother's death to Armand de Caulaincourt, who was at the Emperor's side. He declined the

Emperor's offer to permit him, in his grief, to withdraw from the field. Together they rode down the slope and through the ruins of Shevardino village to meet Murat in front of what was left of Raevski's redoubt. It was just three o'clock and all that remained to the Russians were some outer fieldworks.

The battle was not yet over. But to Napoleon, descending into the cauldron for the first time, it seemed as if the moment had come to turn the Russian withdrawal into a rout. He informed Murat that he was prepared to send the Young Guard against these last Russian positions. Berthier was against such a move and Murat, for once, uncertain. To get a clearer idea of the situation he galloped up to the fallen redoubt – where he had allegedly been seized four hours before – and saw across the valley that the Russians were still in good order and preparing for a counter-attack. He rode down to Napoleon and added his objections to those of Berthier: only if Napoleon was prepared to risk the Old Guard as well as the Young Guard would it be possible to mount another charge against the Russian lines. The Emperor hesitated. All that day he had refused to throw in the ultimate reserve and he stood by his earlier decision: 'I will not have my Guard destroyed eight hundred leagues from Paris,' he declared irrevocably. The Grand Army would advance no farther that day.

For another hour the French and their allies had to beat off desperate Russian attacks. Kutuzov had sent forward the Imperial Guard and Barclay de Tolly himself led them in a fierce charge on the ridge at Semenovskoye. But Eugène and Murat brought up eighty guns and the Russian guardsmen wavered and broke under the impact of one last heavy cannonade. By four o'clock the Russians had established a new line of defence one thousand yards behind the positions they had held when the guns first opened up, ten hours before. Late in the afternoon there was a skirmish between a French infantry battalion and the Finnish rearguard, while the Poles were still in contact in the woods around Utitsa and opposing batteries occasionally lobbed roundshot at one another; but otherwise the great battle died inconclusively away. The sky clouded over and a gentle drizzle wept over the crumpled corpses. As dusk fell they were shrouded in mist: at least Nature could observe the decencies.

That night the French bivouacs were silent; there was no singing or swapping of stories – everywhere, writes Ségur, a 'gloomy taciturnity.' As Napoleon rode back to his tent there had been a few ragged cheers of 'Vive l'Empereur,' but no elation. Most of the officers believed that Borodino would be another Wagram, when failure on the first day had been redeemed by victory on the next. The line of Russian camp-fires flickering intermittently through the mist reminded them that they had still not broken the enemy. But on this night Napoleon felt no need to send out orderlies to reassure himself of the Russian presence. With a great fire burning in front of his tent and in the centre of a square formed by his Guard, the Emperor slept in utter exhaustion.

The day had seen the completion of a change in the character of warfare. Gradually in each successive battle of the Empire, artillery had taken over the task of clearing a way for attacking columns from the old infantry skirmishers. There had been moments when the guns dominated the battlefield at both Friedland in 1807 and Wagram in 1809, but never to such an extent that the horsemen and infantry had become mere adjuncts of the artillery. Yet this was what they were at Borodino. Perhaps it was the inevitable consequence of filling the ranks with virtually untrained conscripts and of recruiting cavalry from the subject states: massed formations were a sign of declining quality. This, however, had been a development in the Grand Army and dictated by Napoleon himself (who was, after all, the supreme artilleryman of his epoch). The staggering shock of the day's fighting was the fire-power with which the Russians had answered the French bombardment. The age of cannon-fodder had come, although more than a century was to elapse before it reached its peak of tragic futility in the fields of France and Flanders.

The full significance of what had happened eluded the survivors of the battle. Yet as they clustered round fires, the raw damp biting into their over-taxed muscles, the veterans sensed that it had been both a horrible and a strange battle: few prisoners, no trophies, only a line of hillocks above some ruined villages. Then, too, there had been the high casualty rate among the senior commanders – ten generals killed, thirty-nine wounded, and the colonels had fared almost as badly (ten dead, twenty-seven others incapacitated).

The Battle of Borodino

The Conference at Fili

'Each moment,' writes Sergeant Bourgogne, with pardonable hyperbole, 'a message was sent to the Emperor, "Sire, such and such a General is killed or wounded," and his place had to be filled on the spot.' The loss of these officers was in some peculiar way proof of the bitterness of the contest. And the men were puzzled, too, by the behaviour of the Emperor. Few knew that he was ill, and, to those who had been with him in other campaigns, it seemed strange that he had remained for so long on the Shevardino mound rather than riding down to fire the enthusiasm of the attackers at some point where the enemy's resistance had been prolonged. It had been Murat and Ney who had willed victory that day by their example; you could not miss the white plumes and flowing cloak of the one, nor indeed the red hair and red face of the other. Yet the Imperial Eagles seemed almost to have had their wings clipped: it had been no Austerlitz.

Above Gorki, Kutuzov was seeking to assess the reports which reached him from the various commanders. That evening, surprised perhaps to find himself still holding the New Road, he had genuinely considered renewing the battle on the following day and had dictated a despatch to Alexander claiming a Russian victory. But, as estimates of the casualties came in, he realized that he could not afford another action. The earliest figures painted an even grimmer picture than the reality: 58,000 men were said to have been lost, or almost half of his effective strength. (He had, in fact, lost 43,000 men – one-third of his army.) Early on Tuesday morning he decided to pull back towards Moscow. The retreat was on once again: Platov and the Cossacks were left as a rearguard.

Fog hung over the battlefield until well after dawn that Tuesday. When it lifted, Napoleon could see that the Russian Army had pulled away. He ordered Murat to follow it with as many squadrons of cavalry as he could muster. The Emperor rode several times over the battlefields, inspecting the remains of the redoubts and supervising, as best he could, the primitive medical services which were still seeking to save some of the wounded. 'There are five dead Russians for every Frenchman,' he remarked with horrible satisfaction to an officer who accompanied him. ('I suppose he took Germans for Russians,' the French colonel wrote coldly in a letter home.) Then, leaving the unfortunate Junot to guard the hospital at Kolotskoye and clear the battlefield, he rode with the Old Guard to the gutted village of Ukarino, only two miles from the town of Mozhaisk.

A courier was already speeding towards Paris with a letter for Marie-Louise: 'I write to you from the battlefield of Borodino. Yesterday I beat the Russians; their whole army, 120,000 strong was there. The battle was a hot one: victory was ours at two in the afternoon. I took several thousand prisoners and sixty cannons. Their losses can be estimated at 30,000 men. I lost many killed and wounded . . . My health is good, the weather a little fresh.' As so often in his letters to the Empress, he conveniently juggled the facts – he had only taken 700 prisoners and had lost more than 30,000 men himself – but it is significant that he had not realized the extent of the Russian casualties.

Next day, from somewhere beyond Mozhaisk, Kutuzov too found time to write to his wife: 'My dear, I am thank God in good health and I have not been beaten; and I won the battle with Bonaparte.' It was a magnificently laconic verdict on Borodino; and yet, in the end, was it really so far from the truth?

8

Fili

Three hundred and fifty miles to the north, St Petersburg was still without news of the battle four days after it had been fought. To the foreign residents the city seemed austerely beautiful that autumn, a façade of imported elegance under the pale northern skies. From opposite banks of the Neva the twin gilded spires of the Admiralty and of St Peter and St Paul tapered gracefully like minatory fingers towards the heavens; down the quays a long line of ornamental statuary breathed the last enchantments of rococo fancy, while behind them, the romanesque dome of the Kazan Cathedral threw in majestic shadow a colonnade of which Bernini would have been proud. It was the eve of St Alexander Nevsky's Day and the air was heavy with accumulated patriotism; for the young capital, which had as yet so little history of its own, appropriated the legends of ancient Vladimir with the same avid eclecticism as it filched styles of architecture. The people of St Petersburg knew that a battle was imminent at some outlandish village near Mozhaisk; anxiously they waited for another courier to arrive. If Kutuzov had defeated Napoleon, then it was fitting that the city should rejoice on the festival of the prince who had earned the epithet 'Nevsky' by routing foreign marauders along this very river six centuries before. If Kutuzov had lost, then Holy Russia needed the intercession of the warrior saint for her salvation.

That Friday Kutuzov's bulletin reached the Tsar. 'At night we remained masters of the field of battle,' it said. True, it mentioned a strategic withdrawal of six versts towards Mozhaisk, but there was no need to make that public; such subtleties were beyond the general understanding. It was enough that Russia appeared triumphant and Moscow saved. Traditionally, the Imperial family heard mass that day in the monastery of Alexander Nevsky. There, in the church dedicated to his patron saint, the Tsar announced the victory. It was an hour of great emotion.

The news spread rapidly through the city. Salvoes from the fortress broadcast the tidings across the steel-grey waters of the gulf; the clamour of bells rocked the multi-coloured cupolas; and the diplomatic corps were summoned to a solemn *Te Deum* in the great cathedral. Honours flowed in an almost boundless largesse: a marshal's baton and a hundred thousand silver roubles for Kutuzov; bounties for the other officers according to their rank; the Tsar's portrait for Madame Kutuzova; and five whole roubles each for the common soldiers. Wild rumours filled the streets: When would the Cossacks free Smolensk? Had peace already been concluded? When would the cage bearing the prisoner Bonaparte reach the city? Fireworks and chains of lanterns made gay the night sky, as citizens and peasantry surpassed each other in drunken celebration. It was as if the Butter Week revels, which preceded Lent, had come out of season.

But by the following evening disturbing reports were circulating through the capital. Mozhaisk, it seemed, was in the hands of the French and Kutuzov was still falling back towards the low hills around Moscow. How, then, could Borodino be claimed as a victory? The people of St Petersburg were puzzled and alarmed. It required too much logistical ingenuity to prove that the Russians could afford their losses – terrible although they had been – while the Grand Army could not. On the map, Napoleon's advance through Vitebsk and Smolensk to Mozhaisk looked like a long arrow piercing the heart of Russia: no one could see that after Borodino the arrow would be so blunt that it would fall broken from its target. As the endless lists of dead and wounded arrived in St Petersburg, depression settled once more on the city and the faint hearts in the Imperial family – the Dowager Empress and the Grand Duke Constantine – began to urge the Tsar to make peace while there was still something to save: no other army in Europe had ever sustained such casualties; it was imperative that terms be sought. Yet the Tsar, although bitterly angry, was obdurate: he would not parley so long as the French were on Russian soil, even if they held Moscow. But of this his subjects could not be certain.

A fortnight after the festival of Alexander Nevsky there was another solemn moment in the Russian Orthodox calendar – the anniversary of Tsar Alexander's coronation. The contrast between the two occasions showed how low the Tsar's stock had fallen. He would not risk riding on horseback through the streets to the Kazan Cathedral, as he had done in other years. Instead, he drove in the Tsarina's closed carriage with hundreds of onlookers staring at him, sullenly hostile. As he mounted the granite stairway, climbing slowly towards the massive portico, there were no cheers; the foot-steps of the Tsar and his attendants resounded round the colonnade in a hush so profound that it seemed as if no other creature in the whole vastness of Russia dared break the silence of mourning and disil-lusionment. The mood of the people of St Petersburg was fickle – but so too were the whims of history.

Moscow realized sooner than St Petersburg that Borodino had not halted Napoleon's advance. There, too, at first a *Te Deum* had been sung in gratitude for victory. But, only two days after the battle, watchers on the hills west of the city saw the ominous glow of camp-fires in the night sky some twenty-five miles away; and, on the following day, Governor Rostopchin issued a bulletin announcing the fall of Mozhaisk but confirming that Kutuzov had declared he would 'defend Moscow to the last drop of my blood.' That, it was felt, was as it should be – for Holy Moscow, 'the third Rome' to the faithful, was no mean city.

Rostopchin, himself never the most stable of men, was almost hysterical in urging the Muscovites to rally to the defence of their heritage. A proud proclamation was plastered on the walls and gates of the town:

We must aid our soldiers to save our capital, our cradle and our refuge. Arm yourselves now, take bread for three days and assemble on the Three Hills, the banners of our Holy Saints in your hand. I will gather there with you and we will destroy the enemy. Heavenly Glory to those who do not stay behind. Immortal Glory to those who die in battle; but Damnation until Doomsday for those who refuse to come.

The words were magnificently defiant and they had their effect. While St Petersburg was still celebrating the victory of Borodino, thousands of peasants and townsfolk flocked out of Moscow and gathered on the three Sparrow Hills above the road to Mozhaisk. They brought with them pitchforks, staves and hatchets; but the sacred banners remained in the city – and so too did Governor Rostopchin. Urgent business detained him in his official residence along the Lubianka. After waiting all day for him, the men who had responded to his call were sent back to their families at dusk. Perhaps Rostopchin had never expected them to come, for the people of the city paid little attention to the pronouncements of their Governor after the folly of the Leppich balloon; but this fresh deception only increased their bitterness and that night they began to leave Moscow by the hundred, hour after hour, the numbers increasing as the new day dawned.

Ever since the news of the fall of Smolensk had reached the city on August 22 there had been a steady movement of women and children from the wealthier families to Nizhni-Novgorod and other distant cities, but it was nothing to the mass flight eastwards which started on September 12 and continued until the Grand Army arrived at the town barriers. Long columns of sad-faced refugees trudged towards Yaroslavl and Vladimir and Ryazan. Most were on foot, poor peasants clinging pathetically to their little world (as others were to do in so many parts of Europe more than a century later). The more fortunate had vehicles of one sort or another. Carts and waggons, droskies and troikas moved slowly forwards through the grey dust in a dismal cavalcade of horses, goats and cows. Occasionally, a carriage would try to thread its way along the road as some aristocrat sought the sanctuary of his country estate; in one of them Rostopchin's wife and three daughters fretted impatiently as the horses crawled towards Yaroslavl. Tumbrils and litters bore the wounded of Borodino away from the city, although many remained in Moscow, too ill to be moved. Somewhere along the road to

Vladimir a detachment of grenadiers faithfully carried Bagration on his last journey, dying but still conscious of the tragedy around him. That weekend over two hundred thousand Muscovites evacuated the old capital; and there was little food to succour the famished horde. Grimly they moved on eastwards.

Behind them, and still west of Moscow, other columns were also moving eastwards, a dozen miles a day. Ever since he had pulled away from the village of Gorki, Kutuzov had been in retreat with Murat and the French cavalry hard on his heels. To those around him, Kutuzov continued to speak of another battle to defend Moscow: it was expected of him. But Kutuzov, the 'old fox of the North,' as Napoleon had dubbed him, was above all a realist. He knew that he had barely 70,000 men, of whom a fifth were poorly armed and inexperienced militia. A second Borodino meant virtual destruction and would not save Moscow. He seems to have thought, at one time, that Miloradovich and the rearguard might make 'a show of battle' before the walls of the city; but it hardly made sense to sacrifice lives for a gesture of honour. The steppe-lands rolled on for hundreds of miles beyond Moscow, a sea of open country lapping the Urals. Geography and not sentiment must dictate strategy. This was no ordinary land campaign with armies disputing every ridge in some compact State: it could almost have been a naval war where a fleet commander manœuvres a rival admiral away from his bases so as to destroy his puny vessels on the great emptiness of an ocean. Surely the right policy was to preserve the army intact and wait for the coming of winter? It would be a hard decision.

That Sunday morning (September 13), while thousands were leaving the eastern gates of the city, the Russian High Command reached the village of Fili. Today it is a Moscow suburb, with a Metro station close to the place where Kutuzov passed these anxious hours. But then Fili was in the country, a pleasant retreat on hills outside the city as Hampstead was to London or Georgetown became to Washington. Peter the Great's uncle, Prince Naryshkin, had built a baroque church of red-brick and white stone on an eminence above the village and from its octagon lantern the towers of the Kremlin could be clearly seen less than five miles away, across the Moskva river. It was easy enough for Rostopchin to ride out to confer with Kutuzov. He reached Fili at ten that morning.

Rostopchin found Kutuzov seated in front of a fire and warming himself, for the weather had turned colder. The two men talked together in private for half an hour. Kutuzov, distrustful as ever of the written word, left no record of the conversation, but from Rostopchin we have two accounts: one is a letter to his wife, written under stress eleven hours later; and the other is a passage in his memoirs, written many years afterwards. To his wife, he wrote simply: 'He asked my opinion and I said that, being with his army seven versts from Moscow, he ought to give battle and, if he lost, place himself on the road to Kaluga so as to close the interior [*le midi*] to the enemy and to gain supplies and reinforcements. He agreed with me in everything.'

The later version shows interesting variations. 'He told me he had decided to give battle to Napoleon in the very place we then found ourselves. I said to him that the land behind our position sloped down rapidly almost to the town and that if our line fell back, it would be thrown against the walls of Moscow . . . and that he risked losing the whole army in this way. However Kutuzov continued to assure me that he would not be forced out of this position.' If Kutuzov *did* fall back, he was thinking of a retreat northwards so as to cover the road to St Petersburg. It was Rostopchin himself who persuaded him that it would be wiser to turn south towards Kaluga, whence reinforcements from the Black Sea could reach him. Rostopchin adds that there was confusion among the generals and that Kutuzov requested the despatch from Moscow of two miraculous ikons – and a dozen bottles of wine. 'That conversation showed me the baseness, timidity and irresolution of this head of the army, who received the title "Saviour of Russia" even though he did nothing to merit it.'

It is a tendentious account, full of jealous rancour. The truth, of course, eludes us still; but Kutuzov rarely wasted his words and it is probable that confronted with this ridiculously self-important Governor, the old Brer Fox 'lay low,' like Tar-Baby 'sayin' nothin'.'

He had sounded Rostopchin's opinion and received an answer from the heart rather than the head. Now it was for the officers of his staff to convince him of the need to fight: for the moment he kept the heavy thoughts troubling his own mind to himself.

Five hours after Rostopchin rode back from Fili, Kutuzov summoned a military council. All his leading staff officers attended, except for Miloradovich, who was still actively resisting the enemy advance. The meeting took place in a peasant's wooden cottage (which has survived to the present day) and the scene was later to be enshrined on patriotic canvas by Kivchenko. The artist faithfully captured the tension of the moment. Eight generals (and Colonel Toll) are gathered round a teak table. At the far end, leaning aggressively forward, Ermolov stands glowering at Kutuzov. The bullet-headed Bennigsen shows an impassive profile; opposite him, Raevski looks alertly ready, fingers interlocked on the table top. In the far corner, beneath a simple ikon with a small lamp, is Barclay de Tolly, an expression of resigned acceptance on his face. All are listening to Kutuzov, who sits beside them in the only arm-chair, old and grey, an unbuttoned jacket hanging loosely over his gross frame. An aide stands behind him, taking notes. There are maps on the table, but nobody notices them; everyone watches the septuagenarian Marshal as he raises his left hand in a gesture of weary emphasis.

Perhaps it was not like that at all and Kivchenko's imagination may have given to the scene a unity and orderliness it never possessed. Certainly, if any officer did keep written minutes, they were later lost, for we depend once more on the memoirs of those who were present at Fili. Yet such records as we have confirm the essential truth of the painting. Kivchenko was right to emphasize the dominance of Kutuzov: the generals may have argued, but, in the end, the decision had to be his alone. In that tired hand rests the fate of far more than his army.

It is clear that Kutuzov opened the meeting by a statement of general policy: his main objective was to preserve his men; if they were broken in battle, 'Moscow and Russia would perish.' Bennigsen and Ermolov favoured an immediate attack upon the French before they could concentrate in a strong position against them. Barclay, who was still Minister of War, thought a decisive victory beyond the resources of the present Russian Army; despite his grievance against the man who had superseded him, he favoured a retreat and he was supported by Raevski, Toll and Ostermann-Tolstoy. But should they retreat to the Volga, as Barclay proposed, or towards Kaluga, as Toll suggested? Or should they, as the majority still wished, stand along these very hills and fight the battle that sentiment demanded? Suddenly, after an hour, Kutuzov cut all arguments short: 'You are afraid of falling back through Moscow,' he declared, 'but I consider it a providential way of saving the army. Napoleon is a torrent which as yet we are unable to stem. Moscow will be the sponge that will suck him dry . . . I order a retreat.' He left the room: the council was over. Perhaps none could see the meaning of his metaphor – but they were to remember it later.

That night the officers and soldiers heard of the decision with sorrow and stupefaction. A letter was sent to Rostopchin at seven in the evening informing him that Moscow would be abandoned: 'My blood froze in my veins, I believe I will die from sorrow,' he wrote to his wife. In a long report – which only reached St Petersburg after considerable delay, since the officer bearing it lost his way – Kutuzov explained to the Tsar how he had decided that, with his troops still weak from the losses of Borodino, he could not risk a battle before Moscow. 'I dare humbly to submit that the entry of the enemy into Moscow is still far from entailing the fall of Russia . . . The loss of Moscow can be atoned: it does not imply the loss of the country.' Behind the repeated assurances, lay an unspoken plea not to conclude a dishonourable peace.

By eleven o'clock the first Russian troops had begun to defile through the dark and deserted streets of Moscow.

While the momentous council was in session at Fili, Napoleon himself was a dozen miles back along the Mozhaisk road, in the village of Borowska. He had entered the town of Mozhaisk on the previous Wednesday, so ill that he had lost his voice and his secretaries had been reduced to the hair-raising task of deciphering his handwriting instead of drafting his despatches from dictation. He spent three days in Mozhaisk, nursing his illness, and by the Sunday he was able to write to Marie-Louise, 'My cold (*sic*) is over.' At Borowska he had gone into residence at Prince Galitzin's country estate – 'The only genuine château we have seen since entering Russia,' declared Castellane in his diary. Now every battalion in the army was eager to reach Moscow, where 'abundance and good winter quarters' awaited them.

Napoleon still expected the Russians to fight before Moscow and he feared that they might trap the Grand Army as it pressed rapidly forward. At Borowska he halted every column until he had received news of Kutuzov's movements. His own cavalry was so exhausted that reconnaissance was limited to the immediate vicinity of the main line of advance, although he had already sent Poniatowski south, in case the Russians attempted an outflanking movement. That Sunday evening he learnt with surprise and relief that Murat's scouts could discover no signs of a Russian defensive position. If the Russians would not give battle in the approaches to their Holy City, then he argued that their army must have been so badly mauled at Borodino – or 'the Moskva', as he preferred to call it – that they would be incapable of offering further resistance that year. 'The conclusion of peace awaits me at the gates of Moscow,' he had said in Vitebsk. Tomorrow he would pass through those gates. And then – ?

At dawn on Monday the whole army moved forward through one last forest towards the Moskva river. By noon the vanguard had left the trees behind and was climbing the slopes of the Sparrow Hills. At that moment the sun came out, so that men remembered later in the comfort of reminiscence that they had reached the great city on 'a beautiful summer's day.' For they were now almost there. Suddenly, as they topped the crest of the ridge, all Moscow was spread out below them – bright rays flashing on golden cupolas, silver crosses sparkling over roofs of red and black, with the grey façade down the long roads broken here and there by green foliage and the river winding in a sharp bend under the walls of the Kremlin. Veterans who had seen Vienna and Berlin and Madrid found the spectacle infinitely more exciting. The Byzantine magic of the city fired the imagination: only the capture of Constantinople could surpass it. Men broke ranks, waving and cheering, and there were shouts of 'Moscow! Moscow!' as though they had until now hardly credited its existence. Then, discipline asserting itself, they were ordered into parade uniforms and, as a band struck up, the fantasy dissolved in the familiar banality of a regimental march.

Napoleon, who had not risked the saddle since leaving Borodino, descended from his berlin at the foot of the Sparrow Hills and mounted his favourite grey, Emir. On the crest, he reined in the horse and looked down on Moscow, deeply moved. His Marshals hustled around him, 'drunk with the enthusiasm of glory' (says Ségur) and they lavished compliments on the Emperor who had led them across Europe. 'Here, at last, is the famous city!' he exclaimed; and then, as though vexatious memories clouded his thoughts, he added, 'It is high time!' Eighty-two days had elapsed since he crossed the Niemen, five hundred miles to the west. Now he was on the Poklonnaya Gora, the 'Hill of Salutation', where over the centuries travellers seeing Holy Moscow for the first time had knelt in reverence. Here he would await a deputation of city dignitaries, for the surrender of an ancient capital demanded ritual obsequies. Murat had already gone forward to the town barriers; no doubt he would soon return with some men of eminence: a town of this size could hardly be empty. What was delaying him?

By now Moscow, was, indeed, almost deserted. Kutuzov had gone: anxious to escape attention in the main streets, he had been led through six miles of twisting alleys by a staff officer who knew the city like the back of his hand. Rostopchin had gone: before leaving, he had opened the prisons and ordered the public execution of an alleged traitor to appease a mob clamouring for his own blood. Bennigsen, Barclay and all the other military counsellors had gone: their regiments had struggled through streets blocked by over-laden carts, past drunkards breaking into unguarded cellars. There remained some fifteen thousand citizens (mostly foreigners) and the desperately wounded. When Napoleon reached the Poklonnaya Gora there was only one person of authority in the whole city, General Mikhail Miloradovich, and he was supervising the retirement of his rearguard. As Murat approached the town, Miloradovich still had two corps of cavalry and ten regiments of Cossacks within the walls. He sent envoys to Murat under a white flag and begged for a truce. They met at the main entrance to the city.

Murat seems to have enjoyed that afternoon. Ever since Tilsit he had known that his legendary valour and eccentricities of dress made him a figure of awe and amazement to the Cossacks. He was delighted to be received at the gates of Moscow by a Cossack escort. The Russian officer who had been entrusted with seeking a truce offered flattering compliments to Murat. The Cossack riders openly admired the elegant embroidery on his uniform and the long feathered plumes in his Polish cap. Murat was pleased: such an appreciative enemy deserved chivalrous treatment. In a characteristic gesture, he decided to distribute gifts to Miloradovich's emissaries. His own watch he passed to the Cossack commander. But clearly this personal liberality was not enough: his orderly officer, General Gourgaud, was induced to hand over his own repeater, a particularly fine piece of jewelry, 'received from an illustrious hand,' says Baron Denniée (who knew him well). And eventually the whole of Murat's suite parted with trinkets for the benefit of the other Cossack officers: bandits could not have fared better. The Cossacks withdrew and Miloradovich obtained his truce. Apart from some isolated skirmishers around the Kremlin, no one resisted the French occupation. The Russian rearguard set off down the road to Ryazan unmolested – and the richer by a handful of watches and jewels. Until seven o'clock on the following morning (Tuesday, September 15) the main body of the French army would remain outside the city barriers; and any Russian soldier found in Moscow up to that hour would be allowed to pass freely out of the town.

Napoleon approved of the truce, for he did not want Moscow destroyed by savage fighting as Smolensk had been. But, up on the Poklonnaya Gora, he was growing restless. At five o'clock he went in his carriage down to the Dorogomilov Gate, twelve hundred yards west of the Moskva river. Impatiently, he remounted Emir and rode down to the river bank anxiously eyeing the line of buildings across the water. A peasant, whom they assumed by his clothes to be a Polish Jew, volunteered in formation to the Emperor and his companions about places of interest. But Napoleon's mood did not lend itself to tourist chatter. The Dorogomilov Bridge had been cut by the retreating Russians: he ordered engineers to ford the stream and have pontoons in place within the hour. Then, appointing General Durosnel to be Governor of Moscow, he sent him forward with a strong escort to take over the administrative functions of the city and to find the deputation of Moscow worthies who appeared to have eluded Murat.

Two hours later Napoleon was still waiting for the deputation to arrive. Such a delay was intolerable. Orderly officers told him that Moscow was empty: he refused to believe it. Count Daru, the Minister of War, was beside him at the Gate and Napoleon now decided to send him into the city with a third detachment of troops to see for himself what was happening. As he gave Daru his instructions, Napoleon seems to have tried to remember a collective noun which would embrace the Russian governing class; suddenly, from his desultory reading of Russian history, it came to him: 'Bring me' he told Daru, 'Bring me the Boyars!' There had been no Boyars in Moscow for a century – they were liquidated by Peter the Great – but Daru dutifully set off on his mission.

Soon Daru reported back to Napoleon: Moscow was virtually deserted. Stubbornly, Napoleon waited; there had to be someone to surrender the city. At last Durosnel returned with half a dozen Russian labourers and a tutor in French, who had hailed him as he rode into the town. Only then would Napoleon accept the truth: the city that lay before him was a fibrous skeleton, its empty palaces absorbent pores.

The sun had set by now and leaden clouds were rolling up from the east. To ride into the city under such conditions would have been a dismal anticlimax. The Emperor surveyed the formless cluster of buildings by the river: they looked uninviting. But three hundred yards from the Dorogomilov Gate was a wooden house, under construction; Fain describes it as a large inn and Caulaincourt as a low tavern; it was certainly no place for an emperor, but it would serve well enough for the headquarters of a general on the march. Gloomily, General Bonaparte resigned himself to spending the night there: tomorrow the Emperor Napoleon would enter the Kremlin.

Most of the army remained outside Moscow that night. The artillery of the Imperial Guard stayed on the Poklonnaya Gora. A heavy thunderstorm broke over the hills. As the water streamed down the folds of their tents, the officers of the Guard fortified themselves with hot punch and listened to reports from sutlers who had already slipped into the city and returned with tales of soft living; outside, the gunners wrapped themselves in long cloaks to pass one last night in damp discomfort. It poured continuously for several hours but spirits were high. A week before, they had been promised 'abundance and good winter quarters.' Now the long trek was over.

Some regiments had already entered the city, despite the formal truce. Poles, Prussians, Saxons, Italians, Croats, French – all made their way through the empty streets. Somewhere the band of the Old Guard played 'Victory is Ours': no one looked out on them. General de Ségur and Baron de Bausset rode into the Kremlin to prepare the state rooms for the coming of the Emperor. Everywhere there was chaos and confusion. They were tired and little could be done that night. Bausset threw himself into an armchair but he could sleep only fitfully. Soon after midnight he abandoned the attempt, and crossed to the window: 'Some distance away, in whatever direction I looked, there were flames leaping up,' he wrote later. It was an ominous development.

9

The Flames of Moscow

Sergeant François Bourgogne, of the Imperial Guard, had passed through six tedious months since leaving Portugal in March. He had seen little fighting, but long days under a parching sun had been followed by cold and hungry nights and the strain of the advance was wearing down even the most hardened veterans. Life was not so bad for the Guard as for less fashionable regiments, for they received rations with far greater regularity, but it was good to see at last a great city on the horizon and Bourgogne was pleased to be among the first troops to enter Moscow that Monday afternoon.

It took Bourgogne and his company an hour to reach the centre of Moscow. They followed the regimental band through silent streets, past the closed shutters of the Arbat and under the eccentric towers of the Kremlin to a square at the southern end of Lubianka Street. They halted, at four o'clock, in front of what had been until that very morning the official residence of Governor-General Rostopchin. Since the Emperor was anxious to avoid indiscriminate pillaging, strict orders were given that no member of the Guard should leave the square once they broke ranks. Yet by five o'clock, when the column reformed, there was a choice selection of wines and delicacies beside the knapsacks; 'We went to the houses in the square to ask for food and drink,' Bourgogne explains disarmingly, 'but as we found nobody in them we helped ourselves.' Such a pragmatic approach to victualling hardly made for good discipline; but it was a way of life which was to spread rapidly through the Grand Army in the next few weeks.

For the moment more urgent matters pressed for attention. To

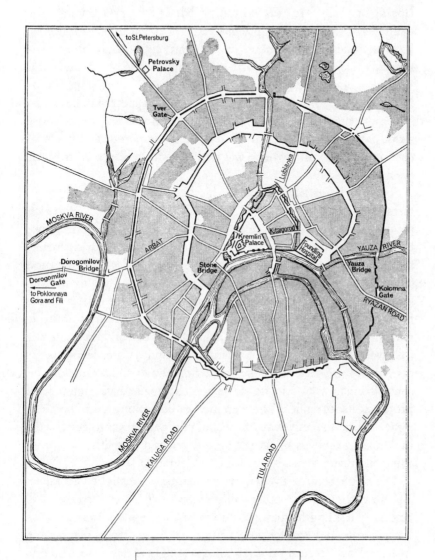

FIRE OF MOSCOW
1812

Shaded areas are those destroyed by fire

his right, Bourgogne noticed a spiral of thick smoke with flames lapping its base. He was not surprised; it was easy enough for marauders ravaging an empty city to set wooden houses on fire by accident: one drunken looter casually waving a candle in a well-stocked cellar could start a blaze. It had happened in other towns and villages along the route and there was every reason to expect it in Moscow as well. But two hours later the flames appeared to be jumping nearer; the Guard commander could see that the fire was far more serious and he despatched patrols to hunt for pumps and hoses to contain the blaze. Bourgogne was sent off with fifteen men towards the flames.

For seven hours Bourgogne and his men forced their way through the streets of central Moscow. Deserted Italianate palaces with rich paintings and tapestries were menaced with immediate destruction, but ahead of them lay another world almost Oriental in character, for they were moving into the bazaars and arcades of Kitaigorod (Chinatown). There jutting stories jostled each other in narrow alleys and thin wooden walls flared up like eucalyptus trees in the bush. To these veteran soldiers it was an experience more terrible than any battle. Every now and again the roar of an explosion was followed by the crash of a falling roof and a cascade of sparks carried the fire farther to the west. Sometimes shots rang out, as some Russians who had stayed in the city made a vain gesture of protest at its surrender. There seemed to be nothing with which to fight the fire: the only way of checking the flames was to destroy the buildings in their path. As yet no one realized that this was something far greater than any ordinary conflagration.

The scene became even more grotesque once night had fallen. By now there were others in the burning streets: patrols still anxiously hunting for pumps and hoses; and fugitive Russians 'with long beards and sinister faces' hurrying away from the blazing quarter. Since, even at midnight, it was as light as day, it seemed odd that the Russians should be carrying flaming torches in their hands, but, says Bourgogne naïvely, 'we let them pass us quietly.' Only when his patrol found some Russians actually firing a church did they take action. It was two o'clock in the morning when Bourgogne reported back to his colonel outside Rostopchin's residence. 'Our soldiers were clothed as Kalmucks, Chinese, Cossacks, Tartars,

Persians and Turks, and many of them were covered with splendid furs,' he wrote later. Lawlessness had already taken over.

Out at the inn by the Dorogomilov Gate Napoleon's staff heard details of the fire by eleven o'clock. But they had no idea of its extent, nor indeed of the anarchy which it carried with it. There was little alarm at headquarters, even when it was learned that two houses were in flames not far from their own position and well away from the main blaze. It was felt that the Russians would hardly have chosen to burn their own Holy City. Probably there had been careless siting of camp-fires once more, as at Slawkovo and Dorogobuzh. A routine reprimand was dispatched to the commanders of units in central Moscow. No one bothered to wake the Emperor.

By Tuesday morning the fire did, indeed, appear to be under control and there was nothing to suggest that Moscow was faced with imminent disaster. Soon after six o'clock, Napoleon mounted his grey, Emir, and rode down the deserted streets to the Red Square and into the Kremlin. It was hardly a triumphant entry, but he was satisfied. 'Here I am, then, at last in Moscow, in the ancient palace of the Tsars, in the Kremlin!' he remarked to his companions with almost pathetic self-congratulation. He climbed the massive red stairs leading to the Tsar's apartments and hung the portrait of the King of Rome, which Bausset had brought to him at Borodino, on the wall. That afternoon he ascended the belfry tower of Ivan Veliki, which stands on the highest ground in the city and from where he could see the whole of Moscow. Apart from the thin spiral of smoke from the smouldering ruins of the bazaars and the marching lines of his own troops, the city lay motionless below him. Back in his apartments he despatched some administrative orders and then rode for half a mile along the river, from the Stone Bridge to the Foundling Hospital, and returned to the Kremlin. Almost certainly he wrote to Marie-Louise – although the letter has not survived – but there was no pressing business and he retired to bed early. So, too, did Caulaincourt and most of his suite. It had been no day of glory.

It was, however, the night which remained in men's minds, their recollections so confused as to blur at times the line between experience and invention. At half-past ten a valet awoke Caulaincourt with the news that the centre of the city was in flames. 'I had only to open my eyes,' he wrote later, 'to realize that this was so, for the fire was spreading so fiercely that it was light enough to read in the middle of my room.' But as yet the Kremlin itself was in no danger and Caulaincourt, like the officers at the inn on the previous night, decided not to disturb the Emperor, for his staff knew well enough that he was a tired and sick man.

Caulaincourt himself rode out into the streets to make certain that the troops were under arms. By now a strong north wind had sprung up and was driving the flames towards the river. Shortly after midnight, fire broke out at two new points and patrols began to bring in captured incendiarists. Curiously enough Caulaincourt does not appear to have heard of the fire-raisers caught on the previous night. Only now did the terrible truth begin to dawn on the French High Command – that Moscow was being deliberately transformed into a flaming Hell. The arrested men confirmed that there were no fire-pumps or hoses because Rostopchin had ordered them to be sent out of the city with the retreating army. Reports came in of explosive fuses found in palaces north of the district menaced by the fire. There could be little doubt that someone had drawn up a cold-blooded plan to reduce the whole of Moscow to cinders and ashes.

The Emperor was called at four o'clock on Wednesday morning. With the wind veering round from the north to the west, it seemed as if nothing could save the city from destruction. But Napoleon was still inclined to attribute the fire to chance. He was convinced only after witnessing the interrogation of two incendiarists in police uniform. Momentarily the news almost shattered him: 'A demon inspires these people!' he declared, 'They are Scythians! This is a war of extermination. What a people! What a people!'

Throughout the morning the fiery gale swept remorselessly across the city. Napoleon remained in the Kremlin, watching the smoke and flames jumping nearer. The Guard seized buckets and soaked the roofs of houses in the path of the fire. But the real danger came from sparks which were carried a considerable distance in the high wind. At one time the Kremlin stables were alight; beyond them lay the Arsenal and the ammunition waggons of the French artillery. The Emperor himself went across to the Arsenal to encourage the fire-fighters. His presence in a critical moment of a battle had worked miracles. But now he found himself an embarrassment. With the probability that an explosion would destroy the Emperor as well as themselves, the gunners almost lost their heads; and the General in command of the Guard had to beg him to withdraw from the danger area. The ammunition waggons were saved.

The Guard commander was not the only one worried by the Emperor's presence. His staff wished him to evacuate the Kremlin entirely. But the fortress had become a talisman of victory for Napoleon: withdrawal implied recognition of disaster; obstinately he continued to pace through the Kremlin rooms, stopping at every window, smiling disdainfully at the alarm of his attendants. At last, Berthier, resourceful as ever, pointed out that by remaining in the Kremlin, the Emperor was placing himself militarily at a disadvantage; if the Russians should seize the opportunity of the fire to attack the French outposts, Napoleon would have no means of communicating with his troops, for the flames had cut across the direct routes out of the city. The strategic argument succeeded where common sense had failed. At four o'clock in the afternoon Napoleon reluctantly gave orders for central Moscow to be evacuated, apart from the troops seeking to contain the fire. He would set up his headquarters in the Petrovsky Palace, a couple of miles beyond the walls of the city along the road to St Petersburg.

The order came almost too late. Heat was already cracking the glass of the Kremlin windows and Caulaincourt noticed that the fur edging on the grenadiers' shakoes was singed. If the Emperor delayed much longer, sparks would fire the narrow wooden bridge which provided the only route to the Moskva esplanade where his horse was waiting. Slowly Napoleon descended the red stairs and, leaning on Caulaincourt's arm, crossed the bridge and reached a small gate opening on the quay. 'Flying sparks and tongues of flame scorched the air,' wrote Ségur. 'We almost choked from the smoke.' At the Stone Bridge Napoleon mounted Tauris; but immediately he was faced by a new problem. General Boulart saw the Emperor hesitate: how was a way to be found through the ruined streets? A Russian police official, suspected of incendiarism, was offered his life if he could guide the Emperor's party to safety. He did his best, but the landmarks were gone. It was a painfully slow progress.

'We were forced to protect our cheeks, hands and eyes with handkerchiefs and headgear, turning up the collars of our uniforms,' wrote Montesquiou, who was a member of the party. Flames seemed to meet in a vault above their heads; the horses hobbled over cinders, men and beasts gasping as their lungs struggled for air. Keeping as close to the river as possible, they at last reached the Mozhaisk road and stumbled out into the suburbs, past the inn where Napoleon had spent the Monday night. It was not the way to the Petrovsky Palace but, at least, it took them away from the flames. Several miles outside the city they re-crossed the river and, after a long detour, turned northwards and reached the Palace, exhausted, at half-past seven. Napoleon, deep in thought, was silent. That day he had suffered a defeat; but who had vanquished him? The name on everyone's lips was Rostopchin.

A mile of fire continued to light the evening sky. Even at the Palace it was possible to read from the glare of the flames. It could be seen from far off in the country. Miserable clusters of refugees stood weeping as they watched the glow growing brighter in the night sky: 'Mother Moscow is burning,' they cried. Twelve miles away, at Panki on the road to Ryazan, Theodore Rostopchin too saw the reflection of the blaze and knew his work was accomplished.

Rostopchin's behaviour in these feverish days baffled contemporaries and puzzles historians, not least because of inconsistencies in his own chronicle of events. In later years he was prepared to deny that he had ever ordered the burning of Moscow: it was, it seems, all the work of the French and their allies. Unfortunately for Rostopchin's reputation this explanation does not stand up to close scrutiny, as even his own family perceived. Some fires were certainly started by the carelessness of the invading army and the devastation was made far worse by a strong gale which no one could have foreseen, but there is no doubt that the Governor-General himself must bear the responsibility for the destruction of three-quarters of the buildings in the city entrusted to him by the Tsar.

It is impossible to determine the precise date at which Rostopchin decided that Moscow should be put to the flames. As early as August 24, with news of the burning of Smolensk fresh in his mind, he wrote to Bagration hinting in the obscurity of fine writing that the city might be set ablaze if the invader entered its gates; and a number of people of rank later recalled that he had spoken to them in similar terms. Threats of this kind were in character and it is probable that no one who knew the Governor-General took him seriously. It was not until he had heard of Kutuzov's decision, taken at the Fili conference, to abandon Moscow without a further stand, that he took positive action. That night he summoned to his official residence the chief of police, Ivashkin, and gave him orders which would make it impossible for the invading army to combat a great fire: all mobile pumps were to be camouflaged with netting and evacuated down the road to Riazan with an escort of dragoons, and more than two thousand firemen and police were to go with them; any fire-fighting equipment which could not be removed was to be destroyed; the fire-floats along the Moskva river were to be scuttled. The following night Colonel Ludwig von Wolzogen, a Prussian officer on Barclay's staff, noticed the strange convoy of fire-engines under escort down the road to Kolomna while he was riding beside Rostopchin himself. He asked Rostopchin why they had been withdrawn from Moscow – and received the enigmatic reply that there were good reasons for doing so.

Removal of the fire-fighting equipment is not, of course, proof of organized incendiarism. But Rostopchin had more drastic measures in mind. Even before receiving Ivashkin he had written to the Tsar: 'Bonaparte will find Moscow as empty as Smolensk. Everything has been carried away. Moscow in his hands will be a desert, if Fire does not consume it – and it could become his tomb.' Arson could not be left to chance; now it was essential to lay trails of combustible materials and to see that explosive fuses were left in the principal buildings. For this task, too, Rostopchin relied on his police officials. At five o'clock in the morning of September 14 he sent for one of Ivashkin's deputies, Voronenko, and ordered him to go to the arcades in the Kitaigorod and to start fires there when French troops entered the city. Voronenko was able to carry out these instructions until ten o'clock that night; and he appears to have had the help of a number of subordinates.

Although Voronenko is the only fire-raiser to have given an explicit account of Rostopchin's designs *after* the occupation of Moscow had ended, there is evidence from the French side that other police agents were at work, possibly on the instructions of Ivashkin and Voronenko rather than of Rostopchin himself. Napoleon subsequently ordered the creation of military commissions to investigate the activities of captured incendiarists; and they certainly believed in a general plan of destruction instigated by Rostopchin himself. Fuses and trails discovered in houses untouched by the flames seem to provide further proof of organized arson. They can hardly have been supplied without the connivance of the municipal authorities and the police; many indeed were believed to have been brought into Moscow from the Leppich workshop. It is hardly surprising that the French began to assume that the whole of central Moscow was one monstrous infernal machine, a giant booby-trap planted by Rostopchin and sprung by his associates.

Rostopchin undoubtedly knew that Moscow would be set ablaze before he fled the city. In a sad letter to his wife, despatched as he was about to leave the Lubianka and join the column of refugees, he declared that all was ready for the city to be burnt to the ground. And as he left for his country estate that Monday morning, he halted on a hill outside Moscow, turned to his son and said, 'Take a good look at the city. You are seeing it for the last time. In a few hours Moscow will be no more than dust and ashes.' So precise a statement must be more than intuitive prophecy.

There remains, of course, one great uncertainty. Moscow was the treasure-house of Tsardom. It had been spared the horrors of bombardment. Why then did its Governor-General order the city to be destroyed?

At the time, French cartoonists saw events with horrifying clarity. Sometimes they depicted Rostopchin as a pyromaniac dashing across Moscow with a flaming torch in his hands; and sometimes he was shown despatching bands of villainous Tartars to fire elegant mansions, despite the entreaties of women and children living in them; but always they made his eyes dilated and contorted his face with insane fury. These impressions of Rostopchin are, of course, grossly exaggerated, but since good caricature is fantasy projected from reality, there remains sufficient substance behind the image for it to be recognizable. In the five months since he had become Governor-General of Moscow, 'crazy Theo' consistently radiated authority, not from some inner compulsion of personality, but by means of a series of extravagant gestures – bombastic proclamations, braggart bullying, lying bulletins, the great nonsense of the Leppich balloon. To such a man, the common sense of Kutuzov at the Fili conference was completely antipathetic. The loss of Moscow seemed to him a historical climacteric, a second fall of Byzantium; a tragedy of these dimensions demanded a dramatic sacrifice. Perhaps he even believed that, in some mysterious way, he was expressing the General Will of the Russian people – and there were those who would have agreed with him. It was unthinkable that the French and their allies should desecrate the sanctuary of Moscow. The myth of Ragnarök, mutual destruction of the Holy One and the power of Evil in order to achieve a nobler society, is far older than Wagner and broader in its appeal than Scandinavian folk-lore. It was as much in character for Rostopchin to plan the immolation of his city as for Hitler and Gœbbels in more recent times to seek 'a world-historical end' for the Third Reich in beleagured Berlin. Devastation of the familiar serves as the ultimate irrationality for hysterical romanticism.

Four years later, in a private letter, Rostopchin looked back on this awful September with greater calmness of mind. 'In the past,' he wrote, 'I overstretched the duties of a loyal subject and acted as though I were a demon or an Asiatic drugged with opium.' As a self-analysis it came remarkably close to the French caricatures.

Moscow continued to burn for four days. The strong winds at last gave way to heavy rain, which did as much to quench the fires as the efforts of the French and their allies. Napoleon remained for two nights at the Petrovsky Palace and the bulk of his army was in camp around him. At times he would stand silently by the windows looking out on the long line of smoke and flame. Once he was heard to mutter, almost to himself, 'This foreshadows great misfortunes for us!' But for most of this period he was strangely inactive, withdrawn from a disaster which he had never anticipated. Only Berthier was constantly at his side.

The Petrovsky Palace had been built some thirty-five years earlier by Tsarina Catherine to celebrate victory in the Turkish wars; and it was a flamboyant exercise in neo-classicism. Young Castellane found it 'very attractive.' 'It is set behind high brick walls flanked by towers in the style of the Orthodox churches and has a truly romantic appearance,' he noted in his journal. Closer acquaintance dispelled such illusions. The great rooms, externally so self-assured, had been emptied of their fittings. There were no chairs or tables. The palace had to be furnished with hasty improvisation by Eugène's staff. Camp-beds littered each salon and there was an odd profusion of foot-stools. Nor were the grounds spared. Around the palace was a so-called 'English' garden – clipped hedges, grottoes, mock pagodas, acacias and lime trees. But now the invading army had made nonsense of all this landscaped orderliness. Generals had headquarters in Chinese pavilions, while their staffs were housed in leafy arbours or ornate kiosks. Through the mud soldiers slithered in clothes looted from bazaars and arcades – Persian hats, Cossack cloaks, fur caps. From time to time charred paper fluttered down on the bivouacs of the men, and when the wind veered to the south the bitter smell of burning timber hung heavily over the whole camp as if to scorn its absurdities. To Captain Labaume, a cavalry officer in Eugène's corps, it seemed as if the Petrovsky Palace had suddenly been given over to a carnival. These were days of hideous unreality.

Yet in the palace grounds there was at least some semblance of discipline; within the city all was anarchy. Each day officers were detailed to go back into Moscow from the Petrovsky Palace in order to save some priceless treasures. Thus on Thursday evening (September 17) Castellane accompanied General Narbonne to the Yellow Palace. But there was little that they could do. It was difficult to get through the streets; it was even harder to make the French patrols respond. Pathetic groups of Russians who had refused to leave the city in the mass evacuation were now trundling their possessions away on hand-carts – and were openly robbed by the French soldiers

as they did so. By Friday looting had become general. Even Castellane, who had tried on the previous day to give the civilians some
protection, seems to have accepted it as inevitable. 'I secured several
fur-lined cloaks,' he wrote in his diary for that day. 'If you want
anything, you buy it from one of the soldiers. The troops seize
everything from the path of the fire and in some way this makes
pillaging legal.' At that same time, Bourgogne's captain was
despatching details of ten men in various directions to hunt for
'provisions.' 'Our soldiers called the pillage of the town "The Fair of
Moscow",' adds Bourgogne unashamedly in a footnote to his
account of these events.

Russian eye-witnesses paint, of course, an even grimmer picture
of the sack of the city. They were especially shocked by the dese-
cration of the churches and the drunkenness that spread through the
occupying armies as they burst into well-stocked cellars. The
Russians themselves took a fair share of loot and some of the soldiery
used this as an excuse for searching any civilians whom they found
and confiscating anything of value. At times this activity was taken
to ridiculous lengths. The great Russian man of letters, Alexander
Herzen, was then a babe a few months old. In his memoirs he
recounts how his nurse had told him that he was carried through the
burning streets of the city and snatched from her arms by a soldier
who insisted on unfastening his napkin in order to see if it concealed hidden jewellery. But at least the invaders were not so depraved
as to murder the child; later, one of the soldiers even gave him some
soggy bread.

For the four days of the fire the French authorities seem to have
done little to keep order in the city. Courts-martial interrogated and
condemned captured incendiarists and left their bodies strung up
from the charred stumps of trees along the main avenues. But it was
not until the second week that they began to take action against their
own demoralized troops. Looting was officially made punishable by
death and a number of offenders were shot. But most of the rank and
file kept their 'purchases,' many sending home enthusiastic letters to
their wives assuring them of the prizes they would bring back from
the wars in due course. Sound discipline was never completely re-
established, especially among the troops from the subordinate states
of the Empire.

By Friday morning, September 18, the fire had died down sufficiently for Napoleon to leave the Petrovsky Palace. At nine in the morning he mounted one of his horses – it was the grey called Moscow, on which he had entered Kaunas twelve weeks before – and returned to the Kremlin. As the Tsar's apartments were undamaged, Napoleon was able to take up residence once more in the rooms he had been forced so hurriedly to evacuate.

That afternoon he rode through the smouldering ruins of the city, past the ashes of the Bolshoi theatre, down to the Stone Bridge, along the walls of the Foundling Hospital (which had survived) to the Kolomna Gate and back to the Kremlin by following the outer moat to the Yellow Palace. 'At intervals,' writes Ségur, who appears to have accompanied the Emperor, 'fragments of walls or half de-molished pillars were now the only vestiges which marked the site of streets . . . His progress was impeded by a long file of marauders searching for booty, or returning with it, and by noisy gatherings of soldiery grouped around the entrances of cellars or the doors to palaces and shops and churches which the fire had nearly reached.' It was the first clear indication to Napoleon of the extent of disorder among his troops – and it filled him with apprehension. He insisted on firm measures to restore discipline, especially in the Guard regiments. At the same time, he dictated a note for Berthier, ordering him to set aside a stone-built house near the Kremlin for those members of the French colony who still remained in Moscow; they at least would receive some protection and be assured of regular rations.

Some of the French officers were deeply affected by the horror of the city: 'Happy are they who never saw that terrible spectacle, that picture of destruction!' Caulaincourt declares. Before the fire, central Moscow had contained some six thousand houses built of stone and another three thousand of wood; nearly seven thousand homes had been destroyed in the blaze, apart from the market area and many of the public buildings. Some of the larger churches which stood detached in squares had escaped the fire (but not the epidemic of feverish looting). The north-western suburbs and the Kremlin had suffered little damage, partly because the wind had changed on the third day, blowing the fire back to the east. Estimates of the total destruction vary; the Abbé Surrugues (whose church of Saint-Louis-des-Françaises had been saved) reckoned that four-fifths of the city had been devastated, and this would appear to be an accurate figure. The actual loss of life is hard to determine: nobody knows how many Russians remained in the city after the general evacuation. Many of the wounded from Borodino must have perished when the two hospitals went up in flames, although Rostopchin claims that he succeeded in getting twenty thousand of the sick away from the city before the arrival of the French. There must also have been casualties among the occupying soldiery: some were killed by Russian civilians desperately trying to save their homes from being looted; and even more appear to have been caught in a drunken stupor by the flames. Yet direct loss of life was small compared to the suffering caused in Moscow during the following winter by the devastation.

The Emperor was determined to minimize the significance of the disaster for the French. Back in the Kremlin that Friday evening he wrote to Marie-Louise: 'You will have received the news from Moscow. Today I visited every district. The town is a fine one. In burning it the Russians have sustained a great loss; only a third of the houses remain. The soldiers have plenty of goods and provisions, they have ample stores and a considerable amount of French liquor. My health is good.' The letter rang, perhaps a little hollowly, with all his customary optimism. No hint here of the doubts and hesitations in his mind: the urgency with which he hoped the Russians would make peace; the fear that their 'decisiveness' in firing the city showed a determination to continue the war; the great problem of whether or not to withdraw at once from the smouldering city. As so often with the young Empress, Napoleon was sheltering from reality behind the comfort of illusion.

Yet, in one sense at least, his words were not so far from the truth. The material effects of the fire on the French proved less drastic than Rostopchin and the Russians believed. Each day new caches of food were discovered in the cellars of houses damaged or even destroyed by the fire. The incorrigible Bourgogne acquired for his company several hams ('having found a shop full of them'), much salt fish, two barrels of suet, some sacks of flour, a hundred packets of sugar, some port, five hundred bottles of rum and seven large cases of champagne; his men also found and killed a wandering cow in order to have fresh meat. Such gustatory eccentricity may not, of course, have been general and it was moreover only the product of the early days of looting, but so long as the army was in Moscow there was no shortage of food, nor indeed of fodder for the horses. At times, wheat and fresh meat became scarce, but detachments of men were detailed to round up cattle from the neighbouring estates and bring them into the city, where strict rationing was imposed once order had been re-established.

Count Daru, the Minister responsible for supplies, believed that there was even enough food in Moscow for the army to winter there. At Vitebsk he had urged Napoleon to call a halt and the Emperor, knowing that he had dealt with problems of the commissariat for ten years, at least accorded him a respectful hearing. Now other experienced staff officers agreed with him; and it was inevitable that their views should carry considerable weight with the Emperor. Caulaincourt, for his part, set about mobilizing the resources of the fields around Moscow which had been spared the ravages of war; transport waggons were sent under escort to bring in potatoes, cabbages and hay from the surrounding countryside. Hence, although the grain stores had been among the places first fired by the incendiarists, new reserves were swiftly established in improvised depots. It is nevertheless probable that Daru and his colleagues had miscalculated, judging the situation from parallels with western Europe and making insufficient allowance for the demands that would have been made by a Russian winter. The quality of the food brought in was particularly low and, of course, the sources of supply were swiftly used up. At heart Daru seems to have preferred the security offered by a city – even one in ruins – to the uncertainties of supply waggons in the bleak steppe-land.

Other stores, apart from food and liquor, were found within the walls of the Kremlin citadel. Rostopchin had failed to evacuate a considerable quantity of ammunition and saltpetre, probably hoping that the fire would ignite the arsenal and cause a devastating explosion. Napoleon himself drew up an inventory of the military material left by the Russians in the city: 150 field guns, 60,000 new rifles, 1,600,000 cartridges, 4,000 hundredweight of powder, 3,000 hundredweight of saltpetre. It afforded valuable replenishment to the Grand Army; and the Emperor took particular pleasure in letting the Russians know that it had fallen into his hands.

But, despite the loot and the chance discoveries, the fruits of victory in Moscow proved bitter-sweet. The order of the day which the Emperor had issued on the eve of Borodino had assured his troops 'abundance, good winter quarters and a speedy return to the homeland.' The incendiarists had seen to it that the Grand Army was denied two of these promises. Now, more than ever, Napoleon was anxious for peace in order to fulfil the third of his obligations. Contact had to be established at once with the Tsar; he must learn of the perfidy of the man to whom he had entrusted the ancient capital. It was unthinkable for the world to believe that the French had fired Moscow. But who could communicate with the Russian Imperial family? Napoleon was informed that one senior Russian officer had chosen to remain in the city; the Director of the Foundling Hospital, Major General Tutolmin, thought that his first duty was to his charges and refused to join in the mass evacuation. On Friday, while fires were still burning in the suburbs, Tutolmin was summoned to the Emperor's presence in the Kremlin. Perhaps even now Napoleon could gain the peace which he had assured his officers awaited them in Moscow.

The Great Fire of Moscow had a curious epilogue, played out some twelve days later at Voronovo, Rostopchin's estate thirty miles from the ruined city. On October 1 the Governor-General was at Voronovo with Bennigsen, Ermolov and the Englishman, Sir Robert Wilson, as his guests. The situation was dangerous. Patrols from Murat's army were in the neighbourhood and Rostopchin had already permitted his serfs to leave the estate and set out for the east. It would have been disastrous for Rostopchin to be captured by the French; his departure could not long be delayed. But suddenly he announced to his guests that he was going to fire his mansion rather than allow it to fall into enemy hands. It was a beautiful building and they pleaded with him not to make such a sacrifice. But, writes Wilson in his chronicle of the campaign, 'All discussion was useless; his resolve was inflexible.'

His guests gathered outside the house. Each was handed a burning torch and followed Rostopchin up the grand staircase. Then, as if following some solemn ritual, the party proceeded around the house systematically igniting each apartment. Once Rostopchin hesitated: he could not bring himself to set fire to his own marriage bed; this task he entrusted to General Wilson. Within fifteen minutes flames were shooting up from the whole building. Outside the stables, which Rostopchin had also fired, host and guests stood watching as the walls and roof fell in. Then they mounted their horses and rode off towards Ryazan and the headquarters of the Russian army.

Later that day one of Murat's officers reached Voronovo. Attached to a pillar he found a message written by Rostopchin:

For eight years I have improved this estate, and I have lived happily here in the bosom of my family. The dwellers on this property, numbering seventeen hundred and twenty people, left it at your approach and, of my own will, I set fire to my mansion rather than let it be polluted by your presence. Frenchmen, I abandoned to you my two residences in Moscow, with furniture worth half a million roubles. Here you will find only ashes!

This defiant proclamation, which was so much nobler than those which had preceded it, was brought to Napoleon in Moscow. He treated it as a ridiculous gesture and ordered it to be sent to Paris as proof of Rostopchin's instability. But, adds Caulaincourt frankly, 'It had a profound effect on every thinking man; the sacrifice of his own house, irrespective of what others did, won for the Governor more admirers than critics.' Yet would he, one wonders, have made so dramatic an exit from his estate had there been less eminent witnesses of his departure?

General Kutuzov

Napoleon
by Vereschagin

Rostopchin, Governor of Moscow

10

Two Candles by the Window

General Ivan Tutolmin, a veteran of Suvorov's wars and a councillor of state, was essentially a man of peace. As Director of the Foundling Hospital, he was dedicated to the service of the orphans entrusted to him by the Dowager Empress Maria Feodorovna, the Tsar's mother and patron of all imperial charities. It was difficult in the feverish uncertainties of Rostopchin's city for a retired soldier in his seventieth year to safeguard what had already become recognized as the cradle of Moscow's ballet, but this was the task which Tutolmin set himself. As the enemy approached the city, he had ordered all children over twelve to be evacuated to Kazan, but it had not been possible to get the younger ones away and he insisted on remaining with them in the orphanage. During the second night of fire a crescent of flame swept down on the hospital from the north, but, with buildings burning less than two hundred yards away, a change of wind saved the orphanage and Tutolmin found himself left with the care of several hundred boys and girls in a devastated city given over to looting. If Napoleon was eager to make contact with a responsible Russian official, Tutolmin for his part was no less anxious to secure the protection of the French Emperor for his orphans.

Napoleon, who had admired and possibly coveted the solid stone mass of the hospital on his rides through the city, received Tutolmin in the Kremlin on September 18. With the King of Rome simpering beatifically from Gérard's portrait on the wall above, Napoleon was in his most gracious and expansive mood, even though the window was lit up from time to time by new spurts of flame as the wind continued to fan the smouldering ashes beyond the Kremlin. The Emperor was glad to hear that the children were already learning to play with French soldiers; he would be pleased to station guards at the hospital and ensure their welfare. He was, he said, not accustomed to wage wars of such savagery: Vienna and Berlin had remained unmolested by his armies and so it should have been with Moscow. But now the criminal activities of Governor-General Rostopchin had destroyed the work of centuries. Such devastation was alien to the traditions of the French army. Russian generals he would meet on the field of battle, according to the laws of war, and Tsar Alexander was his 'dear brother'; but for Rostopchin he felt nothing but bitter hatred. It was as well for Tutolmin to understand this.

Was there, the Emperor asked, anything more that Tutolmin wanted? The Russian sought permission to write to Maria Feodorovna informing her of the 'miraculous escape' of the Foundling Hospital and praising the efforts of the French to save the city. Napoleon was delighted. He would do all he could to see that Tutolmin's letter was safely despatched. Indeed, he even suggested that Tutolmin might include a postscript assuring the Dowager Empress of Napoleon's goodwill: he was convinced that it would soon be possible to restore the old friendship between Alexander and himself 'if no one sought to prevent it'; this would be a sure way to end 'all our misfortunes.' The letter was written and a member of Tutolmin's staff was escorted through the French outposts and sent along the road to St Petersburg. The General himself returned to the Foundling Hospital full of praise for the French (although he was wise enough subsequently to decline to serve as Mayor of Moscow in a puppet administration).

It was a strange episode. Napoleon had made no formal proposal for peace, nor even suggested an armistice. All he had done was to authorize a Russian state councillor to remind the Tsar's mother that there had been a bond of friendship between the French and Russian sovereigns. The inference, however, was clear enough: if Alexander could rid himself of Napoleon's personal enemies, then neither the blood of Borodino nor the ashes of Moscow need stand between them; a brotherly hand was held out to the Tsar, as it had been after Friedland.

Napoleon, of course, knew all too well the Tsar's record of inconsistency and he calculated, accurately enough, that Maria Feodorovna could have no liking for the men around her son. Tutolmin's message was thus a subtle way of making mischief within the Romanov family, and in earlier years it would no doubt have achieved its purpose. But Napoleon failed to understand that the weakling of Tilsit and Erfurt was by now almost as much a figure of the past as General Bonaparte. There were still moments of despair, but never of collapse. Even Maria Feodorovna, although temporarily inclined to tearful scenes of panic, proudly declared, 'Oh this splendid people! It has shown plainly enough what it really is!' No doubt she was gratified to learn that the Foundling Hospital was safe; but no response was ever made to Tutolmin's report of Napoleon's sentiments and there is no evidence that it reached the Tsar. Moreover, it would have needed far more than these insidious blandishments to incline the Imperial family to peace. 'The flames of Moscow lit up my soul' Alexander was to assert in later years.

It is probable that Napoleon, at heart, had little confidence in this tentative overture. For on the day after his meeting with Tutolmin, he was prepared to receive in audience in the Throne Room of the Kremlin a second Russian notable who had been found in the city, Ivan Alexeyevich Yakovlev (the natural father of the six-month-old baby who became Alexander Herzen). While Tutolmin had stayed in Moscow from a sense of duty, Yakovlev remained there through his own natural procrastination and ineptitude. He had intended to flee with the other great landowners, but on the eve of his departure he entered into a long argument with his brother-in-law over preparations for the journey and, in consequence, his carriage was still standing in front of the house when French dragoons came down the street. But Yakovlev was lucky. He had once visited Paris and met Marshal Mortier. Now, as the fires died down, he hunted out Mortier, who knew that he had influential contacts at the Russian court and brought him to Napoleon.

Yakovlev, a slightly ridiculous bumbler, does not appear to have impressed Napoleon and at first he refused to give him a pass to leave the city. But the Emperor was, once again, anxious to clear his reputation and he repeated much of what he had said to Tutolmin: Rostopchin's savage vandalism was denounced; his own love of peace was known to the world and would readily have been appreciated by Tsar Alexander had he not surrounded himself by stupid advisers. Yakovlev suggested that it was for the conqueror to offer terms of peace and obstinately persisted in pressing his personal problem of getting away from Moscow. Napoleon thereupon appeared to change his mind: Yakovlev could go to St Petersburg on condition that he undertook to do all in his power to deliver a personal letter from Napoleon to the Tsar. Yakovlev claims to have warned Napoleon that he should not expect any response from Alexander, but he agreed to undertake the mission. He was promised a temporary lodging for his family – their home had gone up in smoke – and a safe conduct through the French lines.

Early next morning an aide-de-camp escorted him to Napoleon's study. The Emperor was pacing up and down in a dressing-gown, snuff-box in hand. There was no doubt of the importance he attached to Yakovlev's mission, for his mood was sombre as he handed him the letter. Once more he stressed the need for it to reach the Tsar personally. And then, like Tutolmin's messenger two days before, Yakovlev and his family were led out along the Petersburg road and despatched on their way north.

It was twelve weeks since Napoleon had sent Balashov off from Vilna with his last letter to Alexander. Since then the Grand Army had marched into Minsk, Vitebsk, Smolensk and Moscow itself, the ravines of Borodino had echoed to the thunder of battle, and a desolate trail of charred towns and villages lay smouldering across the Russian plains. And yet, even so, Napoleon hardly changed the tone in which he addressed the Tsar. At Vilna he had blamed the Russian ministers for the deterioration in relations with France, and stressed the warmth of his personal feelings for Alexander. From Moscow he vilified Rostopchin for destroying 'the proud and magnificent city,' listed the military booty captured in the Kremlin, and blandly assured the Tsar that he was waging war against him 'without animosity.' 'A single note from Your Majesty,' he declared, 'would have stopped my campaign, either before or after the last battle.' Once again, no peace proposals were made, but every phrase showed that the Emperor wished, more than anything else, for news of a Russian emissary. The war had gone on long enough: other enemies and fronts called for attention. It was time for the conquering general to show magnanimity; but how could he, if the conquered refused to acknowledge defeat?

Hopefully, Napoleon remained in the Kremlin waiting for news from St Petersburg. Marshal Mortier was appointed Governor of Moscow and given the unenviable task of restraining the troops from plunder and, at the same time, organizing the resources of the city. The Emperor himself spent much time within his study; for a whole week, from September 23 to September 29, he never even left the Kremlin walls. Honours were distributed with great ceremony at elaborate investitures. Favoured officers dined within the state apartments of the Tsars. But for the first fortnight that he spent in Moscow, Napoleon rarely went among the troops. He was, however, determined that they should be aware of his presence. Each evening a valet was instructed to light two candles by the window of his study, so that soldiers passing through the square below might glance up and say, 'Look! The Emperor sleeps neither by day nor by night! He is working continuously!' Castellane, who records this characteristic ruse, admits that Napoleon worked for long hours, but adds that he was accustomed to sleep for part of each day (a habit commended by another war leader in more recent times).

Kutuzov, by contrast, spent most of the night and much of the day in sleep, eighteen hours of the twenty-four, said his critics. Yet in his waking moments he was as wily as ever. Napoleon and Murat had expected the main Russian army to concentrate on the road to St Petersburg. Had Barclay de Tolly remained in command, this was, indeed, what would have happened; it was a natural defensive move. But Kutuzov favoured the plan proposed by Colonel von Toll. He withdrew, not to the north, but to the south-east, along the Moskva river and towards Ryazan. Then, with considerable audacity, he swung westwards towards the fertile area around Kaluga, so that his cavalry patrols threatened Napoleon's communications through Mozhaisk. Moreover, far to the south-west in the Ukraine, another Russian force, the so-called 'Army of Moldavia', was moving northward from the old Turkish front. From Kaluga it would be easier to make contact with this force (34,000 strong) and mount a serious offensive against the French from the south.

The Russian withdrawal at first successfully deceived Murat who, as usual, had been entrusted by Napoleon with the advance-guard. As he scoured the country east of Moscow, his reports to Napoleon were filled with optimism: there was no longer a Russian army; it had melted away. It was not until Murat's patrols turned southward that Napoleon began to suspect Kutuzov had out-manœuvred his adversaries. On September 21 the Emperor instructed Berthier to order Marshal Bessières to swing to the west with a strong 'corps of observation' and advance on Podolsk. There, at last, contact was renewed with Kutuzov; but it was September 26 before Napoleon received a clear picture of the Russian movements.

Kutuzov wanted to reorganize his army and wait for a favourable opportunity to take the initiative. Once he discovered that Bessières and Poniatowski were advancing on Podolsk, he proposed a further withdrawal. By now he was as much at loggerheads with his staff as Barclay had been, and at one point he even offered to hand over the command to Bennigsen if he could find a favourable position from which to offer battle with the enemy. But in the end, complaining and scheming with casual irresponsibility, they followed the old warrior back towards the river Nara. There, at the village of Tarutino, fifty-five miles south-west of Moscow, the main Russian army took up defensive positions on September 29. Kutuzov himself set up headquarters in another village, Letacheva, three miles beyond Tarutino. He was prepared to wait through those autumn days for a favourable moment to attack the French. Reinforcements would reach him from Kaluga and Orel and Kiev, while sixty miles to his south the ordnance factories of Tula turned out more and more cannon.

With Napoleon in the Kremlin and Kutuzov ambling slowly back to Tarutino, the character of the whole campaign changed once more. From Smolensk to Moscow the full bitterness of the war had separated the rival armies; there had been needless savagery on both sides. But now, with only the advance-guards in contact, a mutual disinclination for action lulled them into a tacit truce. Murat had been sweetened by the honeyed words of the Cossacks when they received him in Moscow, and Russian officers continued to visit him after the occupation of the city; he was impressed by their air of respect and accepted their assurances of goodwill. The Emperor was duly informed that the Russian, and especially the Cossacks, wanted peace and were only waiting news from St Petersburg. Murat could easily believe that the war was over. Agreements were even made between his staff and individual Cossack commanders whereby the Russians would evacuate villages in Murat's path without setting fire to any of the houses. The Cossacks showed great courtesy, especially so long as Murat was advancing in the wrong direction, away from Kutuzov's line of retreat.

At first Napoleon regarded Murat's flirtation with the enemy as an unimportant irrelevancy, and he seems to have been amused when an unaccommodating Cossack band so far forgot itself as to seize some of Murat's horses and transport. But the habit spread from Murat to other commanders, notably General Sébastiani and Marshal Bessières (who held conversations with the Russians under formal flags of truce). Napoleon became alarmed by what he heard: although the Russians often stressed their desire for peace, they also spread alarm among the French by emphasizing how far the army had come from its homeland and how grim the Russian winter could be. Strong reprimands went out from Berthier to both Sébastiani and Bessières: the Emperor 'decrees the penalty of death for any officer who shall talk under the flag of truce with the enemy's outposts without authority to do so.' But although the Imperial thunder might disturb the corps commanders, it had no effect on Murat, who continued to parley with the Cossacks and blithely passed on to the Emperor the information with which they fed him. And although Napoleon kept asserting that Murat was allowing himself to be duped, the persistence with which the Russians spoke of their desire for peace was not displeasing to him. For, unwilling to accept the finality of Alexander's silence, he continued until the end of the month to hope for a reply to the Tutolmin letter and the Yakovlev mission, although it seemed increasingly improbable that either communication had reached the Tsar.

Napoleon was intrigued, although hardly alarmed, by Kutuzov's inactivity along the river Nara. The real danger, as he knew perfectly well, lay elsewhere. He was acutely conscious of his own exposed position in Moscow. On the map, the Grand Army appeared as an arrow embedded in the heart of Russia. Yet the blow had not, as yet, proved mortal and an arrow is a slender instrument: it seemed all too easy to snap off the shaft. Already individual units were raiding the rear: thus on September 25 eighty dragoons of the Guard were surrounded and captured by Davidov's band of Cossacks and hussars near Malo-Viayma. This was, in itself, ominous; but, even worse, the Russians were slowly massing two considerable armies on the French flanks. Ultimately these movements could constitute a really dangerous threat.

The Russians were well placed, on paper, for a counter-offensive against the French communications and there were many in St Petersburg who favoured it. A Russian corps, some 40,000 strong, remained under Wittgenstein's command on the Drissa, north-west of Vitebsk; and an entirely independent Russian army under Tormassov was south of the Pripet Marshes and in a position to move in an arc on Minsk. Both groups were receiving reinforcement: 12,000 Swedes under General Steingell reached Riga from Finland on September 20, so as to strengthen the northern flank; and Chichagov's Army of Moldavia linked up with Tormassov on the river Styr during the night of September 22–23.

This double threat from Wittgenstein and Tormassov had momentarily troubled Napoleon earlier in the campaign, while he was at Vitebsk: Wittgenstein had defeated Oudinot at Jakabovo on July 30 but Napoleon had sent one of his ablest field commanders, Gouvion Saint-Cyr, to the Drissa and repelled with little difficulty an assault which Wittgenstein imprudently made on Polotsk (August 17); and similarly Schwarzenberg and the main Austrian contingent were well placed to take care of Tormassov. Nevertheless, the knowledge that these two Russian armies flanked his communications and were receiving fresh troops continued to worry Napoleon.

So far all was well; but potentially there was an even greater danger. Napoleon relied heavily for support on two reluctant allies, his father-in-law, the Emperor of Austria, and the unfortunate King of Prussia, for whom he had never troubled to disguise his feelings of contempt. Could he be certain that if the Russians launched a counter-offensive against his communications, his brother sovereigns would afford him the support which he expected from them? The main Prussian contingent was theoretically co-operating with Marshal Macdonald in front of Riga, but relations between the Marshal and the Prussian officers had never been good and were daily becoming more and more strained. Nor did Napoleon trust the general evolution of Austrian policy. He had a high regard for the personal loyalty of Schwarzenberg, but few illusions about Metter-nich. The amiable façade of the Dresden meeting seemed, after the passage of four months, disturbingly brittle.

It was, in fact, from Schwarzenberg that the first warning came of possible defection; guarded phrases in a letter which reached Berthier in Moscow alerted the Emperor. 'The Austrians and the Prussians are our enemies in the rear,' he declared. The alarm was, of course, premature but it prompted swift action in the Kremlin. Messages were dispatched to both Berlin and Vienna emphasizing the need for reinforcements and reminding each government of its obligations. Even the Empress Marie-Louise was enjoined by her husband to write frequently to her father, to keep him posted with all the news and to suggest that he send more men to serve under Schwarzenberg, 'of whom he should be proud.'

At the same time, Napoleon issued a directive which was intended to strengthen French control over Lithuania and the occupied territories of White Russia. Political administration had rested with Maret, the foreign minister, who was in constant touch with the Emperor from Vilna. Early in October, Napoleon placed all responsibility for the rearguard and for the isolated garrisons in Vitebsk and Smolensk in the hands of Marshal Victor. On paper Victor had, at that time, nearly 40,000 men and they were rapidly being strengthened by new levies sent eastwards from France. This army of Victor's was to constitute a central reserve under the direct authority of Napoleon. If, however, any attack was made from the flank against Vitebsk or Minsk or Vilna, Marshal Victor was ordered to act on his own initiative. In his directive, Napoleon gave Victor clear warning of the danger to his right rear from the combined army of Tormassov and Chichagov, but he considerably underestimated its size. For the moment this did not matter, since the threat was not an immediate one, but ultimately it inclined Victor to pay greater attention to Wittgenstein in the north than Chichagov. Had Chichagov been an experienced General, rather than an Admiral in command of an army through a chance whim of the Tsar, Napoleon's miscalculation could have proved disastrous. But, as it was, Marshal Victor had the opportunity to see that adequate supplies were accumulated at Minsk and Vilna. Even in ruined Smolensk, where Victor established his headquarters in the last days of September, it was possible to achieve some sort of order. ('The French are at present working frantically to make this place capable of defence,' wrote a Hessian captain on arriving in Smolensk at this time.) Victor was a hard task-master and permitted excesses against the unfortunate peasantry which have blackened his name, but without his dispositions the subsequent plight of the Grand Army would have been even grimmer.

In the Kremlin, with candles at his window, Napoleon was seen to be governing his Empire, wrestling with the problems of a continent at war from his distant eyrie on its easternmost fringe. Administrative efficiency was, of course, severely taxed. Despatches for the Emperor were brought back from Paris to Moscow in fifteen or sixteen days and the return journey took as long. A courier would leave Paris in the early morning. Post-horses stood by to carry him across the continent in a succession of relays, most of them covering a distance of about fifteen miles. After travelling by day and night for a week and a half, he would stop at Vilna for despatches from Maret and pass speedily on into Russia through a succession of fortified post-houses. Occasionally, Russian patrols threatened the route from Smolensk and the courier had to move circumspectly, but during the whole month in which the French were at Moscow only two couriers were captured, one travelling in each direction. It was a surprisingly reliable daily service, although at times minor accidents caused the courier to reach Moscow in the evening rather than the small hours of the morning. Caulaincourt, who had organized the system of communications, was justly proud of his achievement: 'It was as easy to travel from Paris to Moscow as from Paris to Marseilles,' he declared in his Memoirs.

Yet government from afar posed problems of its own. If administrative matters had to be referred from a senior civil servant to the Emperor, there was a delay of more than a month before his decision was known. Sometimes the question was comparatively trivial – a detailed policy ruling for the Minister of the Interior over censorship of a historical work, for example – but other issues had greater urgency: the appointment of a new commander for the Army of Portugal; the wisdom of maintaining infantry units among fever swamps on the island of Walcheren. And there was a similar delay if the Emperor sought information: what news was there from America? Why had Maret sent him no reports from Vienna or from Constantinople? Even exchanges of this character with the Foreign Minister in Vilna took a fortnight, and Vilna lacked the resources of the Quai d'Orsay. It was fortunate for the French that during these weeks in Moscow Napoleon was never faced with a critical emergency in the west. He knew quite well that it would be impossible to govern the Empire by such time-consuming methods once winter had cut the roads; he could not wait indefinitely for peace proposals from St Petersburg.

When a fortnight had passed with no response to either Tutolmin's message or Yakovlev's mission, Napoleon summoned a conference of his marshals and principal advisers. According to Ségur, they waited on him, during the morning of October 3, after he had spent 'a night of restlessness and irritation'; he proposed a march on St Petersburg by way of Tver, but encountered strong opposition from Daru and Davout, partly because it was late in the year and also because of the marshes through which it would have been necessary to advance. Caulaincourt, too, writes of a project for moving against St Petersburg, although he does not think that the Emperor seriously contemplated such an enterprise with winter approaching. Ségur's dramatic account of a stormy session round the conference table must be treated with reservation.

There is, however, convincing evidence that Napoleon had in mind a far more elaborate plan. During the first days of October, he dictated a memorandum in which he made an accurate assessment of the situation and outlined a possible course of action. It was clear to him that he would soon have to leave Moscow. He was not, however, prepared to risk the loss of prestige which would be bound to follow a retreat; he therefore favoured a movement which would permit him to remain in contact with Paris, making use of his accumulated supplies and of the reinforcements moving eastwards, while at the same time offering a serious strategic menace to the Russians, should the Tsar be so unwise as to reject his friendly overture. Accordingly, he proposed that the main body of the Grand Army, including the Guard, should withdraw obliquely to the north-west, so as to concentrate 40,000 men around the town of Velizh. Marshal Victor and Marshal Saint-Cyr should unite their forces on the Drissa, give battle to Wittgenstein's army, and advance to Velikje Luki, sixty miles north of Velizh, with another 70,000 men. Meanwhile, Murat, and Ney would retire through Smolensk and take up a position around Rudnya, so as to keep Kutuzov south of the Dnieper, while the striking-force of the Grand Army was pointing directly towards the Russian capital. 'St Petersburg being thus menaced,' Napoleon declared, with optimistic finality, 'one must believe that the enemy will make peace, but if the circumstances of the enemy movements do not allow us to advance, we will remain at Velikje Luki.'

This memorandum is an interesting document, but, at least in the form in which it has been preserved, ambiguous and possibly incomplete. Little attention is given to the imminent arrival of Chichagov's Army of Moldavia and no allowance made for the poor quality of Victor's men, raw and ill-equipped. It is hard to believe that anyone could regard St Petersburg as seriously threatened by a weary army which, at Velikje Luki, would still have been more than two hundred miles from the Russian capital. Presumably, unless the Tsar had sued for peace, the Grand Army would have wintered in the region around Velikje Luki and waited until the following spring before advancing on St Petersburg; but it would have been difficult under such circumstances to have presented the re-deployment of Napoleon's troops as anything short of a retreat. Moscow, as the Emperor himself was fond of saying, was 'a political position;' Velikje Luki was no more than a name on the map. Moreover, north of Velikje Luki were the endless marshes around Lake Ilmen, the fenland which had sheltered Alexander Nevsky, with the primeval city of Novgorod forming a watery redoubt lapped by soggy reeds and mud-flats. Such country was almost impenetrable in mid-summer (as Hitler's army was to find in 1942); an advance in winter or during a spring in which the rivers were swollen with melting snow would have been virtually impossible.

If, as seems likely, this plan was discussed at the conference on October 3, it is hardly surprising that the marshals sought to dissuade the Emperor. Yet the alternatives were not attractive: to remain in Moscow throughout the winter meant isolation from France, even assuming that supplies would be adequate; to fall back along the direct route to Smolensk would imply a political reverse and involve the army in a retreat through devastated country; a thrust south-wards towards Kaluga and the arms works of Tula would have taken the army into a fertile region, but away from its main objectives and the tenuous chain of communication with Paris. More and more it became clear that the only way to avoid humiliation was to dictate peace to the Russians from the vantage point of the Kremlin. Napoleon saw that he must make a further effort to persuade the Tsar to accept a settlement.

On that same Saturday (October 3) Napoleon sent for Caulaincourt. For four years he had served as ambassador in the Russian capital: few Frenchmen had ever won such respect there; and he had, moreover, attained a level of personal friendship with the Tsar. To Napoleon his duty now seemed self-evident. Bluntly the Emperor asked him: 'Will you go to Petersburg? You would see the Tsar Alexander. I would entrust you with a letter and you would make peace.'

Caulaincourt, however, was a man of strong character; he was convinced that no good could come of such a mission and he declined to undertake it. Napoleon persisted: he was certain that the nobles wanted peace, that the Tsar lacked the confidence of his generals, and that everyone at court feared a French advance northwards from Moscow. Still Caulaincourt refused. He argued, with some justification, that the arrival of a personal emissary from Napoleon would harden Alexander's resolve to continue the struggle, for it must reveal the essential weakness of the French position. Napoleon

173

modified his proposal: if he would not go to St Petersburg, then would he seek out Kutuzov at Russian headquarters? But it was no use. Nothing could persuade Caulaincourt to act as peacemaker under such conditions.

Caulaincourt would not go, but his successor as ambassador, General Lauriston, was at hand and Napoleon sent for him. But Lauriston, too, considered the proposal ill-advised: he preferred to decline the mission. The Emperor had had enough. He ordered Lauriston to set out for Kutuzov's headquarters and seek a safe-conduct to journey to St Petersburg. 'I wish for peace. I must have it. I need it at all costs, except my honour,' he declared. An almost hysterical sense of urgency had begun to dominate Napoleon's calculations.

So anxious was Napoleon for Lauriston to be received by Kutuzov that he instructed Berthier to send a note to Murat asking him to inform the Russians in advance that an emissary from the Emperor was on his way to their headquarters. But Lauriston early ran into difficulties. Soon after dawn on October 5 he reached the Russian outposts on an escarpment over a small stream, the Chernitchnaya, a tributary of the Nara. There he was met by Prince Volkonsky, aide-de-camp to the Tsar, and by General Bennigsen. Both wished to know his business, but he refused to speak to anyone except Kutuzov and returned to Murat at Winkovo, a few miles north of the stream. He was too experienced in these matters to compromise his instructions at so early a stage; patient determination merely enhanced the importance of his mission.

While Lauriston waited, a confused debate was going on in the Russian camp. The possibility that the French might seek an accommodation with Kutuzov brought to the surface all the latent suspicion and mistrust. Kutuzov himself was fully prepared to receive Lauriston and curious to evaluate the purpose of his visit, but the British observer, Sir Robert Wilson, and two relatives by marriage of the Tsar (the Duke of Oldenburg and the Grand-Duke of Würtemberg) insisted on being present as witnesses: a demand to which Kutuzov, understandably, had no intention of acceding. For some time it looked as if the meeting with Lauriston was off. Bennigsen, meanwhile, acting on his own initiative, returned to the advance-posts, sought out the loquacious Murat and exchanged views with him; both commanders spoke freely of their desire to end the fighting. Thus, for a few hours, it seemed almost as if the undeclared war was giving way to an undeclared peace.

Back at Kutuzov's headquarters in Letacheva, agreement was eventually reached between the commander-in-chief and the three unsolicited guardians of his honour. He would receive Lauriston alone, but they could remain within call. At midnight Lauriston was persuaded, with a proper show of reluctance, to cross the Chernitchnaya again and ride out to Letacheva; and, as he entered Kutuzov's study, he duly noticed Wilson and the royal dukes waiting in an adjoining room. The significance of their presence did not escape him.

Both Lauriston and Kutuzov were professional soldiers, long accustomed to the menacingly gentle exchanges of the diplomatic game. Each understood the other well enough: only the eavesdropping amateurs remained uncertain of the tenor of their conversation. Lauriston began by assuring Kutuzov of Napoleon's goodwill and of his wish to end for all time the conflict between the two 'great and generous nations.' 'Need this strange and unparalleled war drag on interminably?' Lauriston asked. He brought with him, as evidence of his Emperor's sentiments, a personal letter (which has never been found) from Napoleon to the Tsar. With dignity, Kutuzov replied that when he had taken up his appointment there had been no mention of peace and he could not comment on such matters; but he undertook to inform the Tsar of Napoleon's wishes: nothing appears to have been said of Lauriston himself proceeding to Petersburg. Lauriston carried the conversation a stage further: he asked for an armistice while awaiting news from St Petersburg and began, with some restlessness, to calculate how long it would take for messengers to reach the Tsar and convey his reply back to headquarters. But Kutuzov would not commit himself; he refused a formal armistice (although the French understood him to have agreed to a cease-fire between the advance posts on the Chernitchnaya and the Nara) and Lauriston returned to Winkovo and duly took his carriage back to Moscow.

All this Kutuzov faithfully reported to the Tsar in a long letter which was borne to St Petersburg by Prince Volkonsky, together with a copy of Napoleon's message, although Kutuzov retained the original, presumably because he had no wish to appear as an intermediary for direct communication between the rival sovereigns. But much of the conversation with Lauriston never found its way into Kutuzov's report. The Frenchman had complained of the barbarous behaviour of the peasantry towards invaders who fell into their hands: Kutuzov replied that the Russian people regarded the French as little different from the Tartars who had swept into the country under Genghis Khan. Lauriston denied that the French were in desperate straits and emphasized that the Russians should not overrate the setback suffered in Spain, 'where Madrid is temporarily occupied by the English.' But Kutuzov, shrewd old fox that he was, could sense the discomfiture of the French in everything that Lauriston had to say. Scarcely three weeks had passed since he had taken the momentous decision at Fili to abandon the city: already the sponge of Moscow was beginning to suck in the Napoleonic torrent. Kutuzov was content to wait upon events.

When Lauriston arrived back at the Kremlin on October 6 and Napoleon heard that Volkonsky was bearing his message to the Tsar, he was triumphant. Nothing else mattered, not even Lauriston's failure to get farther into Russia than advanced headquarters; he was convinced that this time there would be a reply, although there had been no response to his earlier overtures. He knew the Russians, he declared: peace would be theirs within a fortnight. Ségur records his saying to the marshals, 'On receipt of my letter Petersburg will celebrate with bonfires.' Hence, like Kutuzov, he too was prepared to wait. He had no fear of the Russian winter; it was all a bogey which Caulaincourt had conjured up to frighten the children.

Outwardly Napoleon was in higher spirits than at any time since the start of the campaign. Two years before, he had spent all October at Fontainebleau, a happy month of autumn sunshine, beside the young Empress, with plenty of hunting and plays staged on three evenings each week by actors from Paris. Now, within a few hours of Lauriston's return, he scribbled off a note to Marie-

Louise, 'The weather here is splendid, as fine as in Paris, it is a regular Fontainebleau day'; and the Fontainebleau allusion figured time and again in his small talk that week. Junior officers, too, were infected by the contagious air of elation. 'Lauriston has been well received by Generals Kutuzov and Bennigsen,' noted Castellane in his diary for October 6, and on the two following days he duly commented on the 'superb weather': 'The natives are saying "God must be pleased with you, it is usually much colder," ' he added on October 8.

By now, the Emperor could afford to relax, even though his officers knew that uncertainties continued to trouble his mind. He lingered over meals and spent less time in his study and more in the saddle. There was a succession of spectacular reviews, the line swinging past impeccably in the great square of the Kremlin. On Tuesday, October 6, it was the infantry of the Old Guard; on Wednesday, Roguet's division; on Saturday, Compans's; on Sunday, Gérard's; and so on, day after day. One afternoon he visited the Kremlin churches with all the curiosity of a tourist, and several times he would ride out of the town down one of the roads towards Kaluga (which, Castellane noted, he tended to call 'Caligula'). In the evening his candles burned far less over maps and military directives. As at Vitebsk, an urgent message for 'good new books' had gone off to the harassed Imperial Librarian in Paris, but until they reached him, Napoleon had a number of books which he insisted on keeping beside him for moments of leisure; his personal servant claims to have noticed him reading Voltaire's *Charles XII* in the Kremlin but, if so, he can hardly have found it comforting; and Ségur unkindly censures him for 'passing whole hours, half reclined, with a novel in his hand.' Gossip commented archly on the visits of Madame Marie-Rose Aubert, a thirty-year-old Lorrainer, who owned a milliner's shop off the Lubianka and was said to have been a French spy for several years; but scandal could attach to her nothing more damning than an improbable claim to have prevented the Emperor from emancipating the Russian serfs. But other distractions were certainly less compromising. The Italian tenor, Tarquinio, twice sang for the Emperor and a young pianist named Martini gave a private recital. Moreover, the Emperor spent three evenings in re-drafting the constitution of the state theatre of France, the *Comédie Française,* sending back to Paris a decree which regulated its composition in minute detail. Was this, one wonders, prompted by a sentimental reminiscence of those carefree nights in the calm of Fontainebleau?

It was, in fact, on that Wednesday (October 7) that the 'French Theatre in Moscow' gave its first performance. Most of the company of the Tsar's Imperial French Theatre had chosen to stay in the city at the approach of their compatriots. When the fires began, they sought protection at the Petrovsky Palace. Napoleon proposed that they should mount plays for the men of the Grand Army and instructed Louis de Bausset, his senior palace official, to supervise arrangements for the production. With much difficulty Bausset found some costumes, stored for safe-keeping in a fourteenth-century church, and requisitioned a private theatre in one of the few elegant town-houses to be spared the flames, the Pozniakov Mansion. The company opened with Marivaux's three-act comedy, *Le Jeu de l'Amour et de l'Hasard,* preceded by a curtain-raiser by Ceron. Eleven performances were given in all; the repertoire was varied, although always light in character, and included some ballet (which pleased Bausset, even though he adds ambiguously, that the dances 'were truly Russian in style and not at all as performed at the Paris Opera'). The Emperor himself never visited the Pozniakov Theatre, but the imaginative originality of his idea for entertaining the troops made such an impression that the productions are mentioned in many letters and most memoirs of the time. Not everyone, of course, was satisfied – Castellane wrote ruefully on October 10, 'You only get two actresses for your money' – but in a modest way the 'French Theatre' was an effective antidote to the boredom of inactivity.

Yet, despite the panache of the daily parades and the ripple of theatrical comedy, Moscow remained little more than a grotesque skeleton hollowly mocking its past. The smell of charred wood penetrated everywhere, and the gaunt smoke-grimed walls of roofless palaces towered over French bivouacs and improvised huts where the spawn of the dead city sought refuge. The ordered existence of a civilized people had perished in the flames. Inevitably, prostitution flourished, although at various levels of sophistication and according to a graded scale of social euphemism: Count Narbonne, who was born in the Paris of the Pompadour, found shelter for a thirty-five-year-old courtesan who enjoyed playing the harp; Bourgogne and his Sergeant-Major discovered two 'Dulcineas' with a taste for Danzig gin, who were prepared to wash and mend for them in return for pretty clothes filched from the general loot; but for the ordinary, coarse rankers there remained as always ordinary, coarse harlots, who had declined to flee from the city in anticipation of good business. It was in the streets and around the watch-fires that life was at its ugliest: many women of good character were forced to sell themselves for want and hunger; and animal bestiality was never far below the surface. They were harsh days. Once clouds had blotted out the late sunshine, a raw miasma settled over the huts and rubble, and the relic of a city was cruel with the menace of winter.

It is not possible to assign a precise date to the moment when Napoleon made up his mind to quit Moscow. Perhaps, in a sense, there never was such a time, for doubt and indecision continued to plague the expedition as they had done for more than three months. Yet at the end of the second week of October the army sensed that it would soon be on the move once more. The weather was treacherous: by Tuesday, October 13 – a week after the Emperor had been cheered by the 'Fontainebleau' sunshine – snow was falling, although as yet it did not lie in the streets and the following days were mild again. But it was a warning that winter could speedily march in from Siberia: someone heard the Emperor say, 'We must hurry. In eight days we should be in winter quarters.' Significantly on Wednesday the 14th Berthier was told to have all reinforcements of artillery and cavalry halted at Smolensk. At the same time, the evacuation of the wounded, which had begun four days earlier, was speeded up. And yet, among the rank and file, there continued to be talk of India and of the womenfolk of central Asia.

There was once more a general bustle of activity. At the lowest level this implied a renewed outburst of frenetic plundering. The Emperor, too, sought his share of loot, a triumphant trophy to set in Paris beside the winged lion with the agate eyes from the Venice Piazzetta and the collections of foreign masters enriching the

Musée Napoléon at the Louvre. This time he coveted the huge iron cross surmounting the highest tower in Moscow, the church of Ivan Veliki in the Kremlin; it would, he felt, look well above the gilded dome of the Invalides. On October 16 engineers from the Guard fastened a cable to the cross and began to lower it from the cupola; the weight was too much, a cable snapped, scaffolding collapsed, the Sappers ran for their lives and the cross lay broken in three pieces on the ground. But Napoleon had his trophy. The broken cross was placed in a waggon with other holy relics and attached to the Emperor's baggage-train.

By that Friday (October 16) plans were well-advanced for leaving the city. Maret in Vilna was notified that the Emperor intended to set out from Moscow on October 19, give battle to Kutuzov on the road to Kaluga and, if the weather held out, advance on Tula before wintering in Smolensk and Minsk. On the same day Napoleon himself wrote to his Minister of Police: 'Soon I shall move from here, enter winter quarters and prepare my operations for the coming year.' But his actions were less decisive than his words. He was still reluctant to withdraw from the city without a response from St Petersburg to his overtures for peace. It remained inconceivable to him that Alexander should persist in dragging out the war. Once more he sent for Lauriston.

On Friday Lauriston set out again for Murat's headquarters at Winkovo. He carried a letter from Berthier to Kutuzov: it did not ask if a reply had been received from the Tsar, but the unformed question could be read behind the vague sentiments of every phrase – 'General Lauriston has been charged to prepare arrangements for giving the conflict a character conformable to established rules of warfare and ensuring measures minimising the evils the country must suffer to those inevitable in a state of war.' But Lauriston had little heart in his mission; there was no sense in inviting a rebuff by a further interview with Kutuzov. At Winkovo he arranged with Murat for the letter to be taken through the advance posts and across the Russian lines by one of his aides, Colonel Barthemy, who would discover if there was any prospect of renewing the negotiations. Lauriston himself returned to the Kremlin on the Saturday evening; by doing so he missed by a few hours the first sharp action since Borodino.

For at five o'clock on Sunday morning Russian cavalry suddenly swept on General Sébastiani's camp five miles west of Winkovo, capturing more than thirty guns and a large quantity of baggage. Totally surprised, relying on the unofficial truce, and with many men out foraging, the French line broke in disorder, and for some hours it seemed as if the Russians would gain a striking victory. Murat, however, threw his carabineers into a bold charge (which, as usual, he led personally) and the Russian advance was checked, but not until it had cost the French and their Polish neighbours in the line more than 2,500 casualties. Then, with Kutuzov reluctant to send up reinforcements, both sides withdrew from the banks of the Nara, as if shocked that the even tenor of their relations should be disturbed by such a flash of violence.

The battle of Winkovo, as it was called, was hardly more than a skirmish, but it convinced the Emperor that he must leave Moscow without waiting for an answer to Berthier's letter. While commending Murat's courage, he was furious with him for allowing such slackness to spread among the French outposts. He was informed of the Russian attack while reviewing Ney's corps at noon on the Sunday, and he immediately decided to take the field against Kutuzov. The final preparations were hurried forward. Marshal Mortier was instructed to hold Moscow with some 8,000 men: he was to concentrate them within the Kremlin walls and announce that the Emperor would soon return to the city; when eventually he too had to leave Moscow, he was to blow up the Kremlin, the Arsenal and any other public buildings that might be of service to the Russians. Mines and fuses were made available to him in abundance.

Everything was ready for Napoleon to leave the city that Sunday evening, but, though his escort was already waiting, it was announced that the Emperor had changed his mind. He would spend one last night in the Tsar's apartments and set out the following morning.

Once again, a long procession of men and vehicles made for the gates of the city. Carriages, carts, waggons, droskies, kibitkas, horsemen and pedestrians converged on the roads to Kaluga from two in the morning until late on Monday afternoon. More than a hundred thousand troops with a horde of refugees and camp-followers passed slowly across the city, hampered by the clutter of booty they had accumulated in the past weeks. About noon, the Emperor, too, crossed the Moskva river and moved off to the south-west. The sky was bright and clear, as it had been five weeks ago to the day, when he stood awed by the sight of Moscow from the Poklonnaya Gora. Now the mood of his officers was sombre: 'It is late,' said General Rapp, 'and winter may overtake us on the way.' But the Emperor was not downcast: pointing upwards, he said, 'In that brilliant sun do you not recognize my star?' His faith in the talisman of Austerlitz remained undiminished, but this time he faced westwards; it was the setting sun that lit his path and the Empire seemed weary in its afterglow.

11

Maloyaroslavets

Tsar Alexander spent most of September outside St Petersburg. After his dangerously sullen reception in the Kazan Cathedral, he visited the Winter Palace only rarely that month, preferring to stay on Kammionyi Island, isolated behind the six-columned portico of the villa Bazhenov had designed for his father (a building which closely resembled James Hoban's White House in Washington). There, from the simple dignity of an oval salon, he could look out across the garden front to the reedy shallows of the gulf and seek from their pallid stillness a mental peace which eluded him within the city.

They were sad days. His mood varied from hour to hour as he fought against the melancholic despair that was natural to his temperament. In a public manifesto he urged his subjects to wage a holy war against the tyrant, beseeching the Almighty 'to look mercifully on His Sacred Church and redeem the liberty and independence of nations and kings.' Yet, for all the fine sentiment, it was hard to keep faith with one's own conscience when every message spoke of disaster and the saviours imposed by popular will remained inactive on the far side of Moscow. 'Make no peace of any kind!' demanded Ekaterina Pavlovna imperiously from her refuge in Yaroslavl on September 15; and three days later, 'You are being accused of having lost your country's honour and your own.' These were cruel words from a favourite sister; only the Tsarina seemed confident of her husband's resolution and only his Bible afforded him comfort. It was in these desperate weeks on Kammionyi Island that the Tsar discovered the inner strength of that mysticism which was to puzzle and confound foreign observers in later years, sanctifying Russian egoism by a unique revelation of Providence.

All this, of course, lay in the future. Yet, by the end of September and before he had heard of Napoleon's assurances of goodwill, the Tsar had finally won the struggle with his own inconstancy. On September 30 he was able to write firmly to his sister at Yaroslavl, 'You can be certain that my determination to go on fighting is more unshakeable than ever. I would rather cease to be what I am than compromise with a monster who is the misfortune of the whole world.' And, as if to confirm his resolution, he took up residence once more in the long palace beside the Neva, with its memories of his grandmother and the triumphant roll of Suvorov's victories.

It was there at the end of the second week in October that Alexander received Prince Volkonsky. The Tsar already knew of Napoleon's peace feelers: he was informed of Yakovlev's mission by General Wintzingerode, who had him arrested as soon as he entered the Russian lines and sent under escort to Arakcheyev; and he had also read sharp letters from General Wilson complaining of Kutuzov's apparent willingness to fraternize with the French emissary. Hence he had had an opportunity to decide in advance what he would say to Volkonsky. Carefully he read Kutuzov's letter, with its account of Lauriston's visit and its copy of the message from Napoleon, and then he turned to Volkonsky and exclaimed, 'Peace? But we have still not made war. My campaign is only just beginning!' A crushing rebuke was despatched to Kutuzov on October 21: the commander-in-chief must know that it had always been his will that there should be no peace talks with the French. He was particularly displeased to hear that Bennigsen had met Murat: strong action must be taken against any other generals who made friendly contact with the enemy. He would not deign to reply to Napoleon.

Help was beginning to reach Russia; 50,000 English rifles were landed in St Petersburg early in October and other supplies would follow. Slowly, painfully slowly, the alliance which Pitt had sought and Castlereagh cherished was becoming a reality and the Tsar's Empire was moving into Europe. It was seventy-four weeks since Alexander had bade Caulaincourt farewell on his recall as ambassador, with the warning that a war between France and Russia would be long and desperate, but that he 'would not be the first to sheath the sword'; in another seventy-four weeks this same Alexander, standing in gilded stirrups, and with gold epaulettes and a gold collar, would be received by Talleyrand in the Rue St Florentin as conqueror of the city of Paris. His proud words to Volkonsky were more than empty bombast.

Meanwhile, in Tarutino and Letacheva life at Kutuzov's headquarters followed a similar pattern of mistrust and intrigue. The commander-in-chief himself was a silent observer of much that went on; he certainly had a strategic plan in which he himself believed, but there seemed no purpose in discussing its details with generals who regarded him as an old dotard to whom they owed little loyalty. Before Borodino, even the most ambitious were prepared to accept as commander a man who would lead the Russian regiments into battle; but after Fili and the abandonment of the historic capital they saw him as scarcely better than a traitor. There were some who were in Kutuzov's confidence. 'I will play for time, lull Napoleon as much as possible and not disturb him in Moscow,' he explained to the young Prince Golitsin. 'Every device which contributes to this object is preferable to the empty pursuit of glory.'

It was wise counsel, but hardly popular at that moment; for there was no reason why imaginations thrilled by noble gestures and pounding cavalry should derive satisfaction from the tedious common sense of a war of attrition. When both Bennigsen and Miloradovich sought out Murat behind the French lines they were, at any rate, in the company of a warrior they could understand and admire, although they accepted the inevitability of regarding him as an enemy. In due course, Madame de Staël was to write of Kutuzov as the new Fabius Cunctator, and it was a title well-deserved; but even the ancient Romans had at first preferred the swashbuckling cavalryman, Minucius, as their commander against Hannibal. Caution in war has won plaudits only when time and victory cast it to the winds.

In this atmosphere of frustration it was easy for frayed tempers to

strain friendship and twist rivalry into a bitter vendetta. Coolness
for a time separated Toll from Kutuzov, and at one moment the
commander-in-chief was so angry with General Ermolov that he
threatened to have him cashiered from the army. Odd echoes
lingered on of old disputes, for although Bagration was dead, his
champions continued to intrigue against Barclay (still nominally the
Minister of War) and his 'Germans'. It was all sadly dispiriting. Yet
other feuds seemed gentlemanly compared with the mutual hatred
which divided Bennigsen and Kutuzov; each contemptuously
dismissed the other as a coward and delighted in petty insults.
'Where is that imbecile, that red-headed one?' demanded Kutuzov
during the Winkovo skirmish, pretending that he could not
remember his Chief of Staff's name. And Bennigsen, furious that
Kutuzov should have failed to support him that day, reported on the
action in a masterpiece of sustained vituperation: 'His Majesty's
armies,' he concluded, 'achieved this victory with precision and
order such as are seen only at exercises. It is regrettable, very regrettable, that Your Serene Highness should have been too far from
the arena of conflict to gain a complete view of the beautiful
spectacle of this battle.' Such venomous exchanges hardly made for
unity in command; and the tittle-tattle of camp gossip was reported
readily enough to St Petersburg by the Tsar's relatives and General
Wilson.

While Kutuzov and his chief of staff insulted each other, Colonel
Barthemy waited to deliver the letter from Berthier which had
originally been entrusted to Lauriston. At last he was admitted to
Kutuzov's study, but the meeting was brief: there was little to be
said on either side. But Kutuzov despatched a reply in French on
October 21 (curiously enough, the same day on which the Tsar,
four hundred miles away, was dictating the letter which rebuked
him for having received overtures from the French). It was a
dignified indication that there could be no talk of peace and an
explanation of why the campaign did not appear to follow 'the
established rules of warfare' for which Napoleon had made his
self-righteous plea: 'However much one may desire to do so,' wrote
Kutuzov, 'it is hard to stop a people angered by what it has seen . . .
and unable to distinguish between what is accepted and what is not
accepted in ordinary wars.' Barthemy, still not knowing for certain

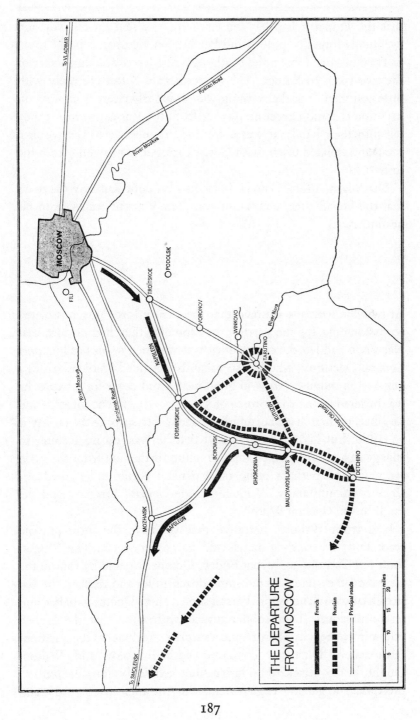

THE DEPARTURE
FROM MOSCOW

French
Russian
Principal roads

miles
5   10   15   20

that the Emperor had left the Kremlin, was sent on his way and
eventually found Napoleon and Berthier on October 22 in the town
of Forminskoie, forty miles south-west of Moscow on the shorter of
the two roads to Kaluga. The Emperor read Kutuzov's reply with
little comment, but the warning was ominously clear: from now on
his soldiers could expect no quarter from the Russian people if they
fell into their hands. It was a comfortless message to receive in a
small and isolated town, with Cossack irregulars prowling from the
east.

That night, a lone Cossack horseman brought Kutuzov the news
that the French were at Forminskoie, barely twenty miles from his
headquarters.

At first the Russians assumed that the enemy force was an isolated
corps foraging for the garrison in Moscow; they had no idea that
Napoleon had left the city. Kutuzov summoned to his headquarters
General Docturov, who had so valiantly defended Smolensk from a
sick-bed in August. Now, in good health and eager for a battle, he
was ordered to marshal a force of 3,000 cavalry, 12,000 infantry and
84 guns and march on Forminskoie. He was to surprise the enemy if
he could, but his orders stipulated that he was 'on no account to
engage in a combat which might require further aid from the main
army . . . and perhaps bring on a general battle under disadvan-
tageous circumstances.' With him rode General Ermolov and the
Englishman, General Wilson.

It is from Wilson's narrative that we have the most graphic
account of Docturov's march and its consequences. The Russian
force left Tarutino early that Friday, October 23, and by four in the
afternoon they had covered some dozen miles and reached the last
stretch of woodland before Forminskoie. There Docturov halted and
sent out scouts. They soon returned with news that the French
position was heavily guarded and a surprise attack out of the question.
Immediately Docturov conferred with Ermolov and Wilson.
Ought he to attack? His instructions explicitly forbade him to
precipitate a general engagement, but his men were ready and

thirsting for a fight; what, he asked Wilson, would an English commander do? Wilson had little doubt of the answer: wait on the alert and organize reconnaissance parties; and the Russians agreed with him.

But it proved hardly necessary to make a long reconnaissance. That evening the Cossacks came with momentous news: the French had left Forminskoie and were moving southwards on Borowsk in considerable force; this was no foraging party; Docturov had stumbled against the main body of the Grand Army. Nor was this all. Outriders brought in a French prisoner who declared that Moscow was evacuated and the Emperor himself with the columns on the Kaluga road. There was no time to lose. Messengers were sent to Kutuzov and the maps spread out. No one on Docturov's staff knew the region, but it was not difficult to see what should be done. There was one strong position which any commander would seek to hold, a town which had sprung up above a river-crossing and on which five roads converged. Its name was Maloyaroslavets; and by seven o'clock that evening Docturov's corps was on its way there.

The Russians marched throughout the night. Although Maloyaroslavets was only twelve miles away by the direct route, it was hard going, for Docturov, anxious to conceal his presence, kept his troops well away from the road, pushing onward through scattered woodland and across flat meadows heavy with loam. Often the men could see the lights of enemy waggons as they trundled southwards unaware of the Russian force observing them a few thousand yards to the left. All the previous day it had rained and the flooded streams and ditches slowed the passage of the artillery, with every rivulet requiring an improvised pontoon, so that cannon tottered drunkenly in the darkness as the gunners hauled them painfully forward. Yet, before dawn, the town was at last ahead of them, its wooden houses sleeping and the bridge still in shadows between the hills. All seemed quiet and Docturov allowed his men to rest after their weary march. Then, as day broke, rattling wheels echoed through the market-place, the ravines caught up the crack of musketry, and a column of troops swept Maloyaroslavets sadly into history.

It was a typical Russian town with a population of about ten thousand. Like so many others, it was built on a hill above a river, the Lutza, which cut a winding course through a succession of ravines. But here the escarpment ran some distance back from the right bank of the stream, so that there was a broad open space between the last buildings in the town itself and the cluster of houses and a church which lay beside the bridge. It was these few hundred yards of wasteland which were to be the scene of most of the fighting that Saturday, although the battle swung backwards and forwards through the narrow streets as one or other of the contending armies appeared to have victory in its grasp. The town changed hands no less than seven times before dusk.

The action began almost casually. In the last hours of their march the Russians had wheeled right and crossed the river four miles downstream at Spasskoie; thus they were able to turn and face the French as they descended the road from Borowsk. Soon after daylight Docturov heard from scouts that a French detachment had been seen at the northern end of the town. Two Russian regiments moved forward and duly encountered a small advance-party from Delzons' 13th Division. They threw it out without much difficulty; but the French had no intention of giving up their positions of vantage and clung to the buildings by the bridge while waiting for the rest of the division to arrive and support them. It was essential for Docturov to finish his preliminary skirmishing before the main body of the French reached the river; for once the bridge was down and the Russians commanded the crossing, it would be hard indeed for Napoleon's troops to dislodge them. Provided that the bridge were broken, Maloyaroslavets offered the Russians a far more defensible position than the line of low hills they had had at Borodino. But, anxious though the Russians were to destroy the crossing over the Lutza, there seemed no way of shifting this determined handful of men; and the rest of Eugène's Corps, 20,000 men in all, were hastening to relieve them.

It was General Wilson who first spotted the reinforcements coming down the hill beyond the river, 'a dense body flocking forward as if quite at ease and unconscious of any serious opposition,' he wrote later. A round of grapeshot brought them to a halt, and two further rounds scattered them to seek shelter behind the buff of the ravine. The Russians took heart; at least they had gained a respite; perhaps they, too, might be strengthened before the 'dense body' took shape again. Docturov and Ermolov had both sent orderlies to Kutuzov urging him to hasten to Maloyaroslavets with the full force of his army. But an hour later there was still no sign of support and no one had prised the French from the bridgehead. By this time Eugène himself had arrived and ordered his guns to cover the bridge. More and more columns were filing down the road from Borowsk and it was beginning to look as if the Russians would soon lose their hold on the town.

With the heavy cannonade supporting him, Delzons sent his division down to relieve the two battalions which had held out for so long across the bridge. The Russians fell back, up through the town and over the crest of the hill to a plateau on the southern approaches, where Docturov had established his headquarters. The meadowland on the fringe of the town and beyond was marshy and at this time of the year it was only possible to move along certain well-defined causeways (as the German Fourth Army was to find when it came this way in another October 119 years later.) So long as Docturov held the southern causeway, Delzons' division could make no more progress than the Russians had done at the northern extremities of the town. The pattern of the battle was now alarmingly clear. For when the Russians had reached the comparative safety of their lines, Docturov summoned up regiments which had so far not been engaged, re-formed his assault troops and sent them to push their way back relentlessly into the town, past the church and the market-place and the dismal wooden houses once again. Delzons himself was killed, collapsing in the arms of his brother, who was himself shot a moment later. The fighting was ruthless and bloody, the French (says Wilson), 'infuriated by despair, the Russians by "the Moscow cry of vengeance!"'

Yet, despite the Russian counter-attack, the French still held fast to the bridgehead and Eugène sent General Broussier with the 14th Division to support their hard-pressed comrades of the 13th. Again the advantage swung away from the Russians and they retreated up the hill; there the battle stood suspended, as if each side sensed that it would never break out of the two points that constrained it. With the town in flames and terrified civilians fleeing amid the counter-charges, it was as grim a spectacle as the ramparts of Smolensk or the redoubts of Borodino. By ten o'clock Wilson calculated that Docturov's corps had already suffered 5,000 casualties, nearly one man in every three: there was as yet no sign of Kutuzov, seven hours of daylight still remained, and it was assumed that other corps in the Grand Army would be hastening to Maloyaroslavets. The prospect for the Russians was as chilling and as cheerless as the day.

Fortunately for Docturov and his men, General Raevski had started for Maloyaroslavets as soon as the first reports of battle reached him. He had not even delayed to gather all the units of his corps together and he reached the southern approaches to the town in the late morning with one full division and the main body of another. No time was lost. 'The Corps will penetrate into and carry the town by storm,' he announced on arrival. Once more the smoke-filled shell of a town fell into Russian hands; and once more the French repelled each thrust towards the bridgehead.

Across the river, too, there were fresh troops waiting to be thrown into the confused battle. Davout's corps stood ready in reserve and gave Eugène's men artillery support. But, as yet, Eugène felt no need of Davout's infantry. He was, of course, Viceroy of Italy and this time he turned to his last division, the 15th, which was recruited from the Veneto, the Romagna and the Dalmatian seaboard and led by an Italian, General Pino. To their commander's mortification, these troops had joined the Fourth Corps one day too late for the battle of Borodino; and he was eager for them to win honour. With Eugène's 'Italian Royal Guard' beside them, Pino's division forced its way over charred and broken bodies and into the square, where the buildings were burning like matchwood. By the late afternoon the Italians had cleared all the town of Russians. It was an achievement which won praise even from its adversaries: 'The Italian Army displayed qualities which entitled it evermore to take rank amongst the bravest troops of Europe,' wrote General Wilson in his account of the campaign. The wreck of Maloyaroslavets itself remained in Eugène's hands, but even these dauntless men could not expel the Russians from their position on the plateau. Yet the struggle for the town was over; as the light began to fade, the Russians wearily

The Burning of Moscow

'Russians Teaching Boney to Dance,' a contemporary English cartoon

counter-attacked, but they could gain no footing in the blazing streets.

Napoleon himself had witnessed the final phases of the battle from a vantage-point half a mile above the left bank of the river. The bitter conflict took him by surprise. He had spent the previous night at Borowsk, fifteen miles to the north, and the Saturday started for him with routine business, dictating to his secretaries. At six o'clock he had even found time to write a succinct, and not entirely accurate, review of recent events for Marie-Louise: 'My army is on the march. I have blown up the Kremlin and left Moscow. It did not suit my plans to make my winter quarters there. My health is good, the weather is fine, my affairs are going well.' He seemed as imperturbable as ever; and he did not bother to set out along the Kaluga road until ten o'clock. But the unexpected news that Eugène's Corps had met resistance ruffled his complacency. He could hear the sound of the cannonades as he rode southwards; and it made him uneasy. 'Is it then a battle?' he asked Davout with amazement. Together they hurried forward down the good, new road. And by one o'clock they stood watching, as the Italians began to drive Raevski and Docturov back through the town. The answer to his question seemed clear enough; now he wondered only how large was the Russian force.

Three hours later, Napoleon and his staff saw a movement far away downstream to their left; and through his glass he stared uncertainly at the dark mass of Kutuzov's army as it advanced slowly down the road from Spasskoie. It was the first time he had seen the enemy in full force since Borodino; but he had no desire now for a general action. Already it was late on a winter's afternoon and his men were weary. Moreover, he was still without Ney's corps and several other divisions were lagging behind on their way from Borowsk. That evening the Emperor retired to Ghorodnia, five miles back to the north, and set up headquarters in a log cabin, a weaver's hut beside the Kaluga road. Meanwhile, the two armies maintained a steady cannonade against each other's positions until nine at night and stray shells were lobbed spasmodically until midnight. General Wilson was an eye-witness of the whole scene from the Russian lines: 'After sunset the spectacle had been indescribably magnificent and interesting. The crackling flames – the dark shadows of the combatants flitting amongst them – the hissing ring of the grape as it flew from the licornes [mortars] – the rattling of the musketry – the ignited shells traversing and crossing in the atmosphere – the wild shouts of the combatants, and all the accompaniments of the sanguinary struggle formed an ensemble seldom witnessed.' And feeding the 'magnificent and interesting spectacle' were the bodies of twelve thousand men and the homes of three thousand families. It had been a savage and bitter engagement – and, as yet, it seemed curiously inconclusive.

Kutuzov had reacted slowly to Docturov's messengers and to the noise of the cannon, which was carried to his headquarters as clearly as to Napoleon. It was not until his midday meal that he clambered awkwardly into a drosky and gave the order to set out for the Kaluga road. He did not hurry, for so long as Docturov's corps could bar Napoleon's way, he was content. At heart, he had no desire for another great battle, a historic name to set beside Poltava and Eylau and Borodino itself. The sight of his own army filled him with misgiving. He dared not risk the infantry reinforcements in any decisive clash with the Grand Army, for these troops had been hastily levied and lacked the well-drilled steadiness of the old regiments. Docturov and Raevski, did, indeed, still retain under their command many hardened veterans steeled by a single-minded detestation of the invader, but even in these divisions there was a fair sprinkling of militiamen – Wilson had seen them bearing their pikes into action that very morning – and there were other corps so full of novices that no one could tell how they would fare in action. Yet if his infantry were far from perfect, Kutuzov could at least take comfort from the numbers and the skill of his cavalry and from the mobility of those irregular horsemen whom privately he mistrusted, but whom the French, with awe and apprehension, collectively termed 'Cossacks'. In Kutuzov's eyes a pitched battle would invite heavy casualties, while its issue would, at best, be uncertain; but to prod and nag the flank of the Grand Army by cavalry skirmishes, and to force it back down the devasted route through Smolensk, was to leave it at the mercy of Nature and its own imperfections. Such a strategy might not free Europe from the domination of France – he was less sure than his Tsar that this was a desirable object – but it would clear Russia's Empire of the invader and permit Tsardom to resume its historic mission as the champion of Orthodoxy against the Turk. For the man who had scaled the walls of Izmael was too old, and too Russian, ever to become a good European.

It is, of course, unlikely Kutuzov thought so far ahead, as he drowsed that day down the road through Spasskoie, although he argued in these terms with Wilson early next morning. For the moment, he was certain only that Napoleon must be prevented from penetrating any farther towards Kaluga and the granaries of the south. That night at eleven o'clock he summoned his staff and all the generals in the field to his bivouac and informed them that 'he had made up his mind to resist the advance of Napoleon . . . by a general action.' For three hours the Russian commanders prepared hastily for battle on Sunday. Then, at two in the morning, they were called once more to his tent. 'I have received information which has induced me to relinquish the intention of defending the ground in front of Maloyaroslavets,' he blandly announced. The army was to retire across the causeway towards Kaluga.

It was a bitter blow for the Russian officers, although from a man of Kutuzov's complexity, hardly a surprising one. His staff were irritably helpless and Bennigsen and Wilson openly critical. It made no difference. Kutuzov knew all the arguments well enough; he hardly needed Wilson to remind him that while the Russian defensive line was sound, a hurried retreat in the early hours might court disaster. And, shrewd assessor as he was of the ways of princes, he can have had little doubt how his 'inertia' would be interpreted in Petersburg. But he had made up his mind to retreat; and, whatever his generals may have felt, his own nerves were under admirable control.

'We will hold to the last, and at least save honour out of the wreck; but we are lost,' General Uvarov remarked to Wilson, as they left the incorrigible old warrior that Sunday morning. It was a creditable sentiment, even if a shade despondent for an audacious cavalry commander. Yet, on that day at least, it was not to be put to the test. As a pale sun broke fitfully through the smoke and mist, all was quiet around the ruin of Maloyaroslavets. Miloradovich and the rearguard remained in front of the town, as they had done outside Moscow after that other grim conference at Fili six weeks before. Two miles to the south-west the Russian army waited apprehensively, and in vain, for Napoleon to make the next move along the route to Kaluga. Only Kutuzov seemed serenely confident.

Seven miles away, at Ghorodnia, Napoleon, too, had spent a restless night. At eleven, Marshal Bessières returned from a close inspection of the Russian position beside the causeway. 'It is unassailable,' he told the Emperor bluntly. 'Three hundred grenadiers placed there would be sufficient to keep a whole army in check.' It was not the assessment for which Napoleon had hoped, but he knew that Bessières, who had fought across Italy and Spain, had a veteran's eye for the lie of the land. In such matters there could be no questioning his judgment. Yet it was hard to feel that Eugène's divisions had struggled fruitlessly in the burning streets. As a feat of arms, the capture of Maloyaroslavets ranked in the bulletins as a victory; need it be a wasted one?

The Emperor sent for Berthier; but the Chief of Staff could offer little comfort. He summoned Duroc and Caulaincourt; and the Grand Marshal of the Palace and the Grand Master of the Horse tendered advice to their sovereign in the weaver's cottage. 'I beat the Russians every time and never reach an end,' Napoleon complained, as he paced impatiently to and fro across the tiny room. For a quarter of an hour, as Caulaincourt waited, there was silence; only the steady tread of the Emperor backwards and forwards, a not unimpressive gesture in the salon of a palace, but ridiculously out of scale in a log cabin. Then, suddenly snatching up his hat, he announced that he would inspect the Russian positions for himself. It was still dark and Bessières and Berthier joined with Caulaincourt in convincing him that this would be a pointless expedition. Once more he resumed the restless prowling – a caged tiger, or a frustrated domestic cat?

Half an hour later nothing could hold him back. With Berthier and Caulaincourt at his side and General Mouton and General Rapp ahead, he rode off towards the Lutza. Although there were pale streaks in the eastern sky, they could see no more than twenty-five yards ahead in the half-light and, as the Emperor departed so impulsively, only a dozen mounted guards were ready to escort him. Less than a mile from Ghorodnia, his aides saw horsemen approaching; 'They were bunched closely together, we took them for French cavalry,' said Rapp afterwards. And then, as they closed in, shouting wildly, it was seen that their uniforms were half-oriental in cut. 'Halt, Sire! The Cossacks!' someone shouted. And the Emperor, Caulaincourt and Berthier waited with drawn swords in hand, as the Duty Guard rushed to arms.

It was more than fifteen years since Napoleon had been in such danger of death or capture. Fortunately, the enemy squadron – regular Tartar Uhlans, not Cossacks – had no idea that so rich a prize was theirs for the taking; they had been content to raid the baggage waggons and 'vehicles of luxury' with which, says Ségur, 'the road was covered,' and they had also captured some guns. The Guard descended on them with frantic zeal, so much so that one over-eager grenadier ran his sabre through Berthier's orderly officer, Captain Lecouteulx (who, surprisingly, survived.) It was a fierce action: 'We found ourselves directly in front of this host of savages, who drew back howling like wolves,' writes Bourgogne, who had been on guard all that night. The guns and the baggage were recovered and the Emperor rescued, unharmed. It had been a near thing. Bourgogne claims to have heard Napoleon joking with Murat over the narrowness of his escape; but that evening the Emperor had Yvan, the chief of his medical service, prepare for him a phial of poison (which was still in his possession in the dark days of 1814). He had no wish to be taken alive by the Cossacks.

All that Sunday the Emperor rode among the ruins of Maloyaro-slavets, inspecting the defences stormed on the previous day and crossing to the causeway where the embers still glowed in the abandoned camp-fires. Apart from Cossack outriders, who even raided his supply columns near Borowsk, there was no activity. It was clear that, as after Borodino, the enemy had packed up hurriedly and departed. On that occasion he had followed them into Moscow;

should he now advance to Kaluga? He could see that Kutuzov had evacuated a strong position; Bessières had certainly not exaggerated its effectiveness in his report. If the Russian commander was so reluctant to accept battle, why not force him into action? But was this possible? Could the old fox be made to fight against his inclination? Moreover, in less than a week it would be November; dare Napoleon risk pursuing a will-o'-the-wisp across all this open country at such a time of year? It was a difficult decision and when he arrived back at Ghorodnia at five in the afternoon he was so unsure of himself that he summoned a council of war.

Eugène, Berthier, Davout and Bessières all came that evening to the weaver's hut; and it seems as if others too participated, almost certainly Mouton, possibly Murat (under a cloud since the Winkovo skirmish) and probably Caulaincourt (to whom, perhaps, without realizing it, the Emperor was turning more and more as he saw how little he himself understood the Russian mind). Already the Emperor had made it clear that he was seeking winter quarters. Only two days previously he had signed the 26th Bulletin, which was now on its way to Paris, informing Europe that since Moscow was 'an unhealthy and impure cesspool,' the Grand Army was marching to new positions along the Dvina. Now the maps were spread out over the crude table. Without looking up, Napoleon posed the decisive question: should they march to Smolensk and Vitebsk by way of Kaluga, giving battle to Kutuzov if he barred the way, or should they retreat through Borowsk and Mozhaisk? He asked for their frank opinions.

Almost to a man, the marshals favoured retreat. Ségur, who was not present, paints a dramatic scene in which Murat, breathing fire and thunder, clashed once more with the icily calm Davout, while the Emperor interposed testily, 'We have done too much for glory, it is time to abandon thought of everything, apart from saving the army.' Probably Ségur invented the conversation, but he certainly caught Napoleon's mood. There were to be none of the histrionics of the conference at Vitebsk. Quietly the marshals gave cogent reasons for a withdrawal: the cavalry was tired; many of the guns and their teams were still at Borowsk, unable to keep up with the main body of the army; Mortier and the rearguard from Moscow were already falling back on Mozhaisk; and the days were getting darker and wetter and colder. Davout wanted the army to take an even shorter route to Smolensk, striking out north-westwards from Maloyaroslavets to Medyn and Viasma. It would have passed at first through country which had not been devastated – and it was, in fact, the line along which Kutuzov marched in due course – but no one else favoured sending so many carriages and guns and waggons across country in which there were no good roads and of which no one on the staff had knowledge. There seemed no alternative in their eyes to the route through Mozhaisk.

Still Napoleon hesitated. Perhaps he saw that such a movement would indeed mark a retreat; as the men retired over the field of Borodino and past the milestones of the advance, they would lose heart. He had wished to avoid an obvious withdrawal when he left the Kremlin; but now it was being forced upon him. Perhaps, too, he saw that he was actually declining battle, even as Kutuzov had done. It was a decision alien to his character. But by Monday morning he had made up his mind: he could delay no longer; the Grand Army would retire on Borowsk and fall back along the road by which it had advanced. At eleven that morning he turned his back on Kutuzov and by dusk he was in Borowsk once more.

The French claimed Maloyaroslavets as a victory, and technically no doubt they were correct. But it remained a name of ill omen for them. A few years later, when he came to write his account of the expedition, Ségur had little doubt of its significance. 'Can you ever forget, comrades,' he asked, in a fine rhetorical flourish, 'this fatal field which put a halt to the conquest of the world, where twenty victories were thrown to the wind, and where our great empire began to crumble to the ground?'

The Russians, too, gave their verdict. When the little town was rebuilt, a small plaque commemorated October 24, 1812. Like Kutuzov, it did not waste words: 'End of offensive, beginning of rout and ruin of the enemy.' Was it there still when the Hitlerite tide ebbed from Maloyaroslavets in 1942? There is at times a terrifying symmetry in History.

12

The Winter Trail

The Grand Army moved with ominous slowness from Maloyaroslavets back to Mozhaisk. Less than fifty miles separated the two
towns, and yet it took more than fifty hours to cover the distance.
It was not that the roads were bad in themselves; they were simply
incapable of carrying such a volume of traffic after the autumn rain.
The marching columns spilled from the paved surface into muddy
ditches and the heavy meadowland. Broken caissons blocked the
route and narrow bridges rocked perilously under lumbering
waggons as Davout's rearguard herded the stragglers along, away
from the Cossack raiders. Wherever the army passed it left a trail of
wrecked vehicles and abandoned equipment.

When Napoleon's men had set out from Moscow on October 19
they were heavily encumbered with booty. Waggons filled with
rum and brandy, tea and coffee and sugar accompanied each regiment. Almost every officer had at least one cart on which he had
loaded provisions for the winter and valuable trophies – gold and
silver ornaments, beautifully bound books, cloaks and furs, holy
relics. Castellane even made room for an iron bedstead. Colonel
Lejeune, an aide-de-camp of Berthier, had filched little and was, as
he says, 'one of the officers most interested in travelling without
impedimenta'; and yet he found that he needed six vehicles and no
fewer than twenty-five horses to convey his possessions westwards.
Lejeune, as a staff-officer of some standing, was fortunate in his
transport arrangements, but others had to be content with primitive
carts. Grossly overloaded, they began to sink into the first soft soil
and many were soon abandoned. The road from Borowsk to

Mozhaisk and beyond was littered with discarded treasure, ikons, candlesticks, books. Somewhere near Gzatsk on October 30 a column of grenadiers came across a collection of French classics bound in red morocco and gold which they picked up, browsed through and rejected; there was no space to spare for Voltaire and Rousseau in the knapsacks of the Grand Army.

The men in the ranks were already carrying an almost unbearable weight of trophies. One of them, the irrepressible Sergeant Bourgogne, has left an inventory. As well as his uniform, he had in his knapsack: several pounds of sugar; half a bottle of liqueur; a woman's Chinese silk dress; a woman's riding cloak; several gold and silver ornaments; some lockets; two silver-mounted pictures; a Russian prince's spittoon; and a piece of the cross of Ivan the Great. To lighten his load, he had felt justified in throwing away a pair of white parade trousers. His uniform appears, at the time, to have been mildly eccentric, for he was wearing a yellow waistcoat of padded silk and a cape lined with ermine. Beneath the cape hung a large pouch, into which he had crammed several more trophies, including 'a crucifix in gold and silver and a little Chinese porcelain vase.' Somewhere on his person were stowed a powder-flask, firearms, and a cartridge case; but, to his annoyance, he had been unable to find room for a specially tailored greatcoat and an ink-stand removed from Rostopchin's Moscow residence in the erroneous belief that it was silver. Fortunately, he was able to wrap up these possessions (and others unspecified) into a parcel which he entrusted to one of the grenadiers, who in due course restored them to him when the Guard had reached the comparative safety of Prussia. The Sergeant's company had filled a cart with provisions, and a looted silver punch-bowl, and left it in the charge of the sutler. She managed somehow to struggle with it to Mozhaisk, but a few days later it was lost in a snowstorm. There is no reason for supposing that other sergeants fared less well than Bourgogne, although as a member of the Old Guard he would have had better opportunities for good pickings than someone in a Westphalian or Portuguese or Italian regiment. But few can have reached their homes with so many trophies intact, for, while the contents of the knapsack suffered, he still had most of the other booty when he came to write his memoirs a quarter of a century later. It was indeed a bizarre procession that wound its way slowly westward across the boundless plain.

The rigours of the retreat had begun to take a toll of all this surplus baggage long before Mozhaisk was reached. The weather remained surprisingly good by day; there were even interludes of pale sunshine and at the end of the month Caulaincourt heard the Emperor drawing one last parallel to the climate of Fontainebleau, although this time with perhaps less conviction. But it was the long and endless nights that men and animals found intolerable, with the first frost clawing mercilessly into weary limbs clustered around the fires of a bivouac. Sometimes there were shouts of 'Cossacks!' as overstrained eyes sensed movement in a roadside copse, and the men were, indeed, terrified of these phantom horsemen (especially after the story of the Emperor's narrow escape passed through the ranks); but by now the men had come to know that their real enemy was 'General Winter', with whom they were engaged each hour of darkness even though he had as yet held back from them the torment of snow. It was, they felt, as they shivered in summer uniforms, an uneven and unfair contest.

Ségur writes of the army marching back from Maloyaroslavets 'with downcast eyes, as if ashamed and humbled,' while Napoleon 'morose and silent' rode in its midst. The Emperor was, however, still in good spirits at Borowsk on October 26; he wrote two letters to Marie-Louise, letting her know of Eugène's 'very fine scrap' and suggesting that she travel to Poland once he had set up his winter quarters. But, after leaving Borowsk, the Emperor sank into the deepest gloom. For six days he does not appear to have written to the Empress, the longest interlude since leaving her at Dresden in May. As he watched the slow passage of his troops, he seemed almost to become a fugitive within his own army. His magnetism lost its appeal; he was for the moment a petty tyrant and no longer a great commander. Near Vereya, south of Mozhaisk, he saw a fine château standing undamaged by the war. 'Since these barbarians like to burn their towns, we must help them,' he said bitterly; and two squadrons were despatched on his personal orders to set it ablaze.

Meanwhile the administrative incompetence of junior officers went unchecked and, apparently, unobserved.

It was while Napoleon was in this mood of nervous anger that a prisoner of unusual importance was brought to him. He had for many years regarded General Wintzingerode as a sworn personal enemy, one of the 'banished scoundrels' of Germans whom the Tsar had taken into his service and rewarded by his confidence. Now Napoleon heard that Wintzingerode had been captured. A lieutenant in the Young Guard attached to Mortier's Moscow garrison had discovered Wintzingerode, with a civilian cloak over his Russian uniform, seeking to induce the members of a French picket to desert, assuring them that they would be able to pass the rest of the war happily at peace in a country which was always generous in offering asylum to foreigners. Napoleon was furious and ordered Wintzingerode and his aide, a young officer named Narishkin, to be sent to him as he waited for a convoy of artillery to go by along the road north of Vereya.

Napoleon accused Wintzingerode of serving the Russians, even though born in a country which was now a French dependency (Würtemberg). In his eyes, he said, Wintzingerode was therefore one of his own subjects; he would be tried by court-martial for espionage and shot as a traitor. When Wintzingerode tried to justify himself, the Emperor lost his temper and all the guards heard him threatening the unfortunate prisoner. Caulaincourt writes that neither he nor Berthier had ever seen Napoleon so angry, and Ségur describes how, after Wintzingerode had retired with dignity and ahead of his escort, everyone was eager to reassure him and show sympathy. Murat and Berthier tried unsucessfully to calm Napoleon, who paced up and down with short, nervous steps, cataloguing grievances against Wintzingerode, some of which had originated more than three years before; fortunately, he does not appear to have known that it was Wintzingerode who had put an abrupt end to the Yakovlev mission.

By nightfall Napoleon had regained his self-control; the captive General should be sent as a prisoner-of-war to France, 'so as to prevent him from intriguing throughout Europe, with three or four other firebrands of his sort,' he explained with evident satisfaction. Yet in this Napoleon was to be disappointed. Wintzingerode and Narishkin did, indeed, set off for Smolensk and captivity; but three weeks later they were freed by Cossack raiders near Borisov. It was 1814 before they reached Paris – and then they came, not under escort, but as conquerors.

Napoleon did not stop at Mozhaisk. He preferred to press on along the road up which he had advanced seven weeks previously. By now, he had been joined by Mortier and the rump of the Moscow garrison, but the addition of several thousand men and horses to the long column hardly made the administrative task any easier. For the army was passing through a region where foraging was acutely difficult. To find fodder for the horses it was necessary to penetrate more than three miles on either side of the road and this carried the riders into land where the Cossacks and partisans were masters. Rather than risk capture and a cruel death, they preferred to feed the animals on stubble around the site of old bivouacs; but these meagre gleanings were not enough to sustain the horses for fourteen hours or more of travel each day, and the animal mortality rate was high. But with food painfully short, the men could at least find horse-flesh to ease their own hunger.

The Emperor was well aware of the plight of the soldiery. He relied on reaching the chain of depots from Smolensk westwards before the coming of the snow. He was, however, alarmed by the inability of Davout's rearguard to keep close up and considerably disturbed by reports of a Russian force under Miloradovich to his south-west. Fearing that he might be cut off from Smolensk, Napoleon was determined to push rapidly forward, even though it meant that the long column of his army stretched over sixty miles of road. At the same time, he ordered all the wounded from the Moscow garrison, Maloyaroslavets and the hospitals along the route to be sent ahead. Anything was preferable to leaving them at the mercy of the Cossacks or Russian irregulars, for fearful tales of atrocities had already reached headquarters. But the waggons and carriages which the Emperor provided were unsuitable for conveying sick men across such a bleak desert; short of food, short of medicine, short of dressings and exposed to bitter weather in overcrowded vehicles, their sufferings were horrible. How many died in these improvised ambulances can only be conjectured.

The morale of the Grand Army was crumbling rapidly; and

Napoleon at heart knew it. He spent Wednesday night (October 28) in a ruined mansion at Uspenskoie, four miles west of Mozhaisk. At two on the Thursday morning he sent for Caulaincourt and for three and a half hours they anatomized the campaign; it was as if the Emperor wished to reassure himself by disputing with the man who had intoned a respectful Jeremiad from the expedition's earliest days. Napoleon admitted that the soldiers were living on 'grilled horseflesh and a little thin soup,' but asserted that they would soon be replenished from the depots along the road to Vilna. The Russians, he maintained, were certainly in no state to give battle: 'it froze as hard for them as for us.' He spoke convincingly on the general prosperity of France, on how he would make good his losses by the spring and on the advantages of establishing a strong defensive line around Vitebsk. Yet, even amid his difficulties, Napoleon could not bring himself to abandon the illusion that an honourable settlement, guaranteeing French hegemony in Poland, was his for the asking. Did not Caulaincourt think, he asked, that a fresh approach to the Tsar might bring peace, once the purely Russian provinces were evacuated? 'No more than at Moscow,' came the frank reply. 'The news of our retreat will have made everyone exultant.'

Napoleon was, however, prepared to make one significant change of plan. Three days earlier from Borowsk he had written to the Empress indicating that he still intended to winter in Poland; now, after sixty hours of retreat, he had decided to return to Paris as soon as the army was well-established in a defensive position. He would once more become an Emperor, 'keeping a firm hand on Europe,' rather than a commander in the field. Napoleon had thus made up his mind, even before it snowed and with no crisis in his capital, that he would leave the army as soon as he could and set out for the Tuileries. And Caulaincourt, who was certainly no sycophant, told the Emperor that his proposed departure for France 'was the one thing which a faithful servant could advise'.

It would, nonetheless, be many more days before the Grand Army found refuge behind a defensive line. Meanwhile, the Emperor must stay with his troops. At dawn that Thursday – he can have slept little – Napoleon was on his way westwards once more, up to the heights where Ney and the Third Corps had spent a hideous night. For they had bivouacked above the ruined village of

Borodino. (Seven weeks ago an Order of the Day had promised 'abundance, good winter quarters and a speedy return to the homeland.') Heavy rain had uncovered bodies hastily buried in shallow graves soon after the battle; and now the twisted and broken remains of thirty thousand men littered 'the field of bloodshot fame,' carrion for beasts and birds. This time the Emperor rode on without a halt.

That night he reached Gzatsk. A consignment of Burgundy, originally despatched on the assumption that the Emperor was still in Moscow, awaited him in the town. No waggons could be spared to carry it back with the headquarter's staff. Napoleon ordered it to be shared by all who had reached the town; their spirits needed to be fortified that cold and sombre day.

Meanwhile, the Russians were beginning very slowly to appreciate that a disaster had swept down on their enemy. Five days earlier – it was the Saturday on which the main armies had been in action at Maloyaroslavets – a succession of explosions echoed round the hills outside Moscow. At dawn a small Cossack patrol, led by a young second lieutenant named Yazykov, crept cautiously towards the Dorogomilov Gate. It was deserted. The streets were silent. There was no movement in the Kremlin; it was damaged, but not seriously, for the French demolition squads had been mercifully inefficient. Only in the Foundling Hospital, where General Tutolmin still cared for his orphans, was there any sign of organized life. The last French garrison had gone. Hurriedly Yazykov set out for the headquarters of Docturov, who spread the news rapidly among the other army commanders. It reached Kutuzov when he was some miles south of Maloyaroslavets, still guarding the road to Kaluga. At first the old man refused to believe that the French had really pulled out of Moscow. Reclining on a camp bed in full uniform, complete with decorations, he made Docturov's orderly go slowly through every detail. Then he gave a deep sigh, sniffed, and turning to the ikon on the wall fervently thanked his Creator for answering his prayers. (Far away to the east in the town of Vladimir, Rostopchin too heard the news – and sent a police spy to see if it was safe for him to return to the burnt-out shell which, with impercipient possessiveness, he still dared to call 'my city'.)

Kutuzov reacted tardily to the French withdrawal from Maloyaroslavets, as if he distrusted all such tales of retreat, until convinced of the great news from Moscow. In falling back towards Kaluga he had lost touch with the Grand Army and he spent a couple of days vainly seeking Napoleon's rearguard along the road through Medyn (which, it will be remembered, Davout had urged the Emperor to follow). But soon scouts from the Cossack patrols let him know that the French were falling back towards the 'Big One', the main Smolensk road. And immediately, at Medyn, he settled the general pattern of pursuit.

His plan was simple and realistic. Apart from Cossacks and irregular bands, he had under his direct command rather more than 80,000 men. Although his infantry lacked experience, his cavalry was strong and, provided it could avoid the devasted strip along the Smolensk road, there was no reason why it should not find adequate hay and oats for the horses. Accordingly, he placed most reliance on lightly-armed and fast-moving horsemen. Miloradovich, with the Second and Fourth Corps, was to strike out to the north-west towards Gzatsk, while Kutuzov himself would move due west through Dubrovno or Viasma with the main body of his army. Ozhorovski, with a force of light cavalry, was to come round in an arc from the south-east on Elnya and seek to cut Napoleon's communications near Smolensk. Ataman Platov, as Hetman of the Cossacks, would harry Davout and the French rearguard from the east, while continuing to send raiding parties along the whole flank of the main column. Kutuzov still had no intention of fighting a pitched battle. The master-plan from Petersburg envisaged a grand enveloping movement. Kutuzov's task was to drive Napoleon back in a parallel pursuit, while Wittgenstein came down from Polotsk in the north and Chichagov (who had taken over the Third Army from Tormassov) was to advance from the south. If all went well, Napoleon and the Grand Army should be crushed before the end of the year on an anvil that stretched from the Dnieper to the Berezina.

The Russians were in full pursuit by October 30, when Napoleon was preparing to set out from Gzatsk. Miloradovich was already little more than ten miles to the south, but his horses had outpaced the infantry, who would take some three days to close up. Kutuzov was between seventy and eighty miles away, while Platov was in action from time to time against Davout, whose First Corps lay well to the rear of the main French column. It was, nevertheless, clear that Kutuzov had left it too late to seize Viasma ahead of Napoleon. But with the Grand Army dissipating its strength in a long, thin line, there was always the possibility that Davout, at least, might be cut off and eliminated. More and more, Kutuzov found himself depending on the Cossacks; and also, to his annoyance, on bands of partisans.

Like most Russian officers, Kutuzov respected the fighting qualities and horsemanship of the Cossacks, originally bearded freebooters from the lower Don, but supplemented by Tartars from the Crimea and wild Kalmuks and Bashkirs. Neither he, nor any other regular army commander, could ever understand their oriental code of behaviour or the reverential resignation with which they accepted every whim of their Hetman, Platov. If the French infantry kept its ranks there was little enough that the Cossacks could achieve. But against demoralized troops in open country and bad weather they made merciless harriers. To Kutuzov the Cossacks were colonial troops (as, in later years, the Spahis were to the French and the Gurkhas to the British) and, although there were many at his headquarters who deplored their savagery, he personally never doubted their value nor minimized the fear which they inspired in their adversaries.

He was less sure of the partisans. In his eyes they were a new-fangled creation, a translation into Russian of the Spanish guerrillas, the thrill of whose legendary exploits had sped swiftly across Europe. The partisan bands varied considerably in character and composition. The most successful of them were led by regular army officers, Colonel Davidov, Colonel Kudashev, Captain Seslavin and Captain Figner. It was Davidov who had organized the first partisan unit after witnessing the awful slaughter on his family's estate at Borodino; and he had made many successful raids on Napoleon's communications while the Emperor was at Moscow. But although he issued a call to the villagers to rise up and destroy the infidel invader, each of his actions was concluded satisfactorily because the peasants, when hard-pressed, could appeal for help from his permanent detachment of forty regular hussars and eighty Cossacks. Similarly, although it was Seslavin who had sent Kutuzov the news that Napoleon was advancing on Maloyaroslavets, the discovery had been made, not by any group of partisan villagers, but by a patrol of Cossack horsemen seconded to him from Platov's Corps. The genuine partisans, peasants in revolt, seemed to Kutuzov – and even more to his master in Petersburg – hardly distinguishable from brigands. The Russian land-owning class, of whom Kutuzov was a typical representative (except that he had some common sense), had never forgotten the revolt of the serfs under Pugachev in the 1770s, which had needed the intervention of Suvorov himself to restore order. The partisan movement seemed a likely nursery for other Pugachevs. There was, for example, Chetvertakov, a private in the dragoons who escaped from his escort after capture by the French and roused hundreds of peasants in a series of bitter raids. A few years before, he had been flogged as a trouble-maker; now the officer class feared that his barbarous methods would challenge all authority and not merely the tyranny of a foreign conqueror. To sup with the devil in this guise Kutuzov was determined to use a spoon of monumental length.

All these considerations prevented Kutuzov from actively encouraging the partisans during the retreat. He was gratified by reports that they were terrifying casual foragers and, with the regular Cossack regiments, spreading havoc among isolated detachments; but at no point did he include them in his general strategy. They remained an essentially spontaneous expression of Russian xenophobia; as such, they constituted a menace to the Grand Army up to the very edge of the Polish lands; but they were none the less an embarrassment and at times a liability to the Russian High Command. Even in this cruel and callous war, the delight of such men as Figner and Chetvertakov in bestiality shocked the sensibilities of hardened veterans and provoked counter-atrocities. It was as well for the invader to understand that the Russian people would never resign themselves to accept destruction and devastation; but it was essential for him to learn also that the Russian soldiery were not merely parade-ground automata. Sooner or later the prowess of Russian arms must be vindicated on the field of battle – but, perhaps, thought Kutuzov with his chilling realism, later rather than sooner.

By October 31 Kutuzov had reached Spas-Demensk, eighty miles from Medin. At Spas he issued a stirring proclamation informing the Russian army that the 'sacrilegious Enemy' was in headlong flight:

He is burning his waggons, abandoning his baggage and the treasures his impious hands have snatched from the very altars of the Lord. Desertion and famine spread confusion around him. The murmurs of his soldiers rise behind him like the mutter of threatening waves.

For the moment Kutuzov was well pleased. The news that reached him from his corps commanders was good and he had shaken off some of his more envious critics; for both Barclay and Bennigsen had been sent on sick-leave to Kaluga on the river Oka, a stream whose waters are rarely credited with therapeutic properties. Private enemies, of course, still remained at headquarters; Ermolov and Docturov had grievances, and there was always General Wilson, pen poised for another philippic to Petersburg. Moreover, even such loyal servants as Konovnitsin and Toll were at times exasperated by their commander's apparent imperturbability; and angry letters, hot with the valour of a palace far from battle, continued to pour in from the Tsar. But Kutuzov was unmoved by remonstrance or imprecation. Half asleep in a drosky, His Serene Highness was content to jog steadily westward, towards Wittgenstein and Chichagov and the long grey ribbon of the Berezina.

On that same Saturday as Kutuzov arrived in Spas, Napoleon entered Viasma, seventy miles to the north. It was four in the afternoon when he reached the town, taking the small garrison protecting the depots completely by surprise. The Emperor had travelled so fast that his personal guard was still some seventeen hours behind him; and that night Hessian sentries found themselves unexpectedly posted in his antechamber. He remained in Viasma for a couple of days.

The weather was fine, although there were ominous patches of thin ice floating down the river and the fields were coated with a thick frost. The town had been damaged by fire at the end of August, but enough buildings survived to provide shelter for the head-quarters' staff, while Murat's cavalry and the mounted artillery bivouacked in woods along the road. For once, food and forage were available for the men and their horses. It was a welcome respite. Napoleon even found time to deal with the trivia of Empire; and Maret, as foreign minister, was duly instructed to inform the French High Commissioner in Westphalia that the Emperor considered it ridiculous to transform the principal Protestant place of worship in the town of Cassel into a Catholic church.

There were, however, more pressing problems. 'Reports went in to him without ceasing. At midnight he was still quite active. . . I saw him up again at half-past three,' writes Captain Roeder, who commanded the Hessian Guard that night. Crisis threatened at two points on the map: in the east, Davout had been so hampered by stragglers and the weariness of his own troops that it would take the First Corps five days to close up if the Emperor maintained his speed along the Dvina. For there Wittgenstein's First Army Corps, reinforced by Steingell's 10,000 men, had tried to trap Gouvion Saint-Cyr and, although the Frenchman had inflicted heavy losses and even repulsed the initial Russian attacks, he had been forced to abandon Polotsk for fear of encirclement and withdraw towards Kamen. Moreover, Saint-Cyr himself, whom Napoleon regarded as one of his ablest subordinates, was seriously wounded and had handed over command to General Merle, a painstaking officer with an almost disconcertingly fine record of retirement in good order. These were serious blows to Napoleon, for Polotsk was only seventy miles from Vitebsk and in the very area in which he had intended to seek winter quarters. Merle's troops – Swiss, Croats, Bavarians – had fought valiantly, but they seemed a thin line to be holding such a vital region. Marshal Victor, with the Second and Ninth Corps, had hurried north from Smolensk to support Merle, but Wittgenstein's threat posed awkward questions for Napoleon: should he remain in Viasma long enough for Davout to close up, or should he hasten on to Smolensk and Vitebsk? Without waiting for Eugène or Poniatowski (let alone Davout) and ordering

Ney to remain in the Viasma area, Napoleon pressed forward with Murat, the Guard, and the tattered remnant of Junot's Westphalians.

As Napoleon left Viasma, Davout's rearguard was pulling out of Gzatsk, still more than forty miles away. He had already had one sharp engagement with Platov's Cossacks near the abbey of Kolotskoye and the horsemen still continued to plague him like a cloud of mosquitoes. But a greater danger was looming up; Miloradovich – 'the Russian Murat,' as Ségur called him – was within striking distance. West of Gzatsk lay the village of Tsarevo-Zaimishche, where Barclay had thought of making a stand in August. Now Miloradovich planned to cut off Davout's retreat in a narrow defile there. Had he done so, the First Corps could have been overwhelmed with ease, but the Russian infantry arrived too late. For the moment Davout was safe; but as he passed that night across a long earthen causeway, desperately seeking to extricate carriages from a marsh at the side of the road, the glow of enemy camp-fires lit his path and Russian cannon lobbed roundshot into the confused mass slipping on the frosted slopes. There had been 28,000 men in the five divisions of the First Corps when Davout set out from Moscow: now, a fortnight later, he was approaching Viasma with only 15,000. Already, for the rearguard, the withdrawal to winter quarters had become a cruel retreat. And still it had not snowed.

At eight o'clock on Tuesday morning, November 3, Miloradovich launched a fierce attack on the left flank of the French column, three miles east of Viasma. The point at which the Russian gunners struck was highly vulnerable; for their shot fell among the unfortunate horde of civilians who had fled from Moscow for fear of what would happen to them as 'collaborationists' once Russian authority was re-established in the city. Already in a desperate plight from want of food and clothing, the pathetic refugees were being hustled along behind Eugène's corps, but in front of Davout's, with Poniatowski's Poles urging them forward. As soon as the Russian cannonade began, they scattered in panic and Miloradovich was able to send his cavalry sweeping down on the road so as to cut off the whole of Davout's rearguard and some of the Poles. Nor was this all. When Platov heard the crunch of the guns, he too sent his horsemen forward so as to attack the First Corps from the east. With Russian hussars ahead of him and Cossacks behind, it seemed as if Davout was trapped.

Eugène and Poniatowski ordered their troops to turn and clear the road of the Russian cavalry. There was a sharp clash, the Russians wavered, and then as a Polish column made for the guns on their flank, they reared their horses back, and fled up the hill to the left; and the road was once more open for Davout. Perhaps, had Kutuzov sent another cavalry division to aid Miloradovich, as Wilson urged him to do, battle would have been renewed later in the day. The French certainly feared that a general action might develop, and Ney hastened back from the south-west of the town so as to cover the three French corps. But, although the Russians continued all day to harass the long column, they were never again to mount a determined attack on its flank.

As dusk fell, with heavy snowclouds looming up from the east and the frightened refugees seeking shelter in the town, Davout's corps at last approached Viasma. It had been a long and terrible march; the countryside was bare and even on the roads his men had been forced to struggle through the frozen ruts left by units which had passed that way on earlier days. They were near exhaustion, and yet that very morning they had fought with spirit. Suddenly there was an alarm in their rear, as someone sighted a force of Russian infantry: was this Kutuzov with the main body of the army? A crackle of musketry rang out and there was some desultory firing from a light battery. It was enough: without warning, the frayed nerves of the French cracked; and in utter confusion Davout's troops ran for the bridges and the illusion of safety afforded by Ney's covering force. Never before had any division in Bonaparte's armies broken in panic. But the Russian commander – a hot-tempered young general named Paskievich who much later was to win spine-chilling renown among the Poles and Magyars – found Ney firmly in position and halted his men among Miloradovich's advance-guard, for there was no sign of Kutuzov.

That night the guns boomed across the town and once more flames swept down its streets. Several times the weary French stood to arms, but the Russians had no intention of seeking another engagement. At last an ally was coming to them swiftly from the east. For, by the small hours of the morning, snow was falling over the ruin of Viasma, covering the four thousand corpses from the previous day's action, lying in the ruts and potholes and weighing down the canvas of the bivouacs. The cruellest enemy of all had begun to envelop the Grand Army.

Napoleon learned of the action outside Viasma while he was at a manor-house in the village of Jaskowo, forty-five miles to the west. His staff were alarmed by the news of disorder in the First Corps: 'From this incident must be dated our disorganization and misfortune,' Caulaincourt stated categorically when he came to write his memoirs a dozen years later. But at the time Napoleon himself does not appear to have understood its significance. He was angry with Davout, blaming him for having exposed the column to a flank attack by his slow withdrawal; and he ordered Ney and the Third Corps to take over the duties of rearguard. At the same time, he sent detailed directives to the corps commanders ordering them to march as he had done in Egypt fourteen years before: baggage-train in the centre; a half-battalion at the head, a half-battalion in the rear; and a strong escort in file on either flank. The various corps were to keep close up, with the guns and their crews massed between each of the moving squares. 'Treat this rabble of Cossacks as we treated the Arabs,' wrote Berthier bluntly to Ney. And yet, even as he put his signature to the letter, outside his window the snow fell remorselessly: for how long, under such conditions, would it be possible to keep the army in a rigid formation? It is curious that no clear code of instruction had been issued earlier in the retreat, at Borowsk, perhaps, or at Gzatsk.

From the reports he received of the fighting around Viasma, the Emperor concluded that Kutuzov and the main Russian army must be pressing hard on Ney's heels. He was therefore tempted to halt at Jaskowo, await the arrival of Davout, Eugène, Poniatowski and Ney, turn on Kutuzov and, taking him by surprise, steal victory from the week of discontent. He even dictated to Berthier an order of the day in preparation for such a battle. For a whole day he dallied at Jaskowo, but when he saw the state of the various corps, he decided that a general action might court disaster, and the long cavalcade resumed its march westward to Dorogobuzh. But the delay at Jaskowo had at least given the slower corps a chance to close up, and with Ney exhorting the rearguard, some sort of order was restored.

The weather remained for some days treacherous and unpredictable. At night it snowed, in the morning there was a damp fog, and by noon a fitful sun shone down on the monotonous landscape, so that it seemed as if a thaw were setting in and going became heavy for the guns and the waggons. But once darkness fell again, the temperature dropped and a frost returned. All who could clustered miserably round camp-fires, but too often the sick and wounded were unable to fight their way into the warmth and by dawn many had died. A pile of frozen corpses lay strewn around each bivouac as the columns moved relentlessly on with the coming of a new day. It was a grim progress.

On November 6 the Emperor reached the banks of the upper Dnieper at Mikhailewska; and that Friday the couriers brought startling messages from Paris. A fortnight previously, on the evening of October 22, General Malet, who had served under the Consulate with distinction until he suffered a mental breakdown, had escaped from a private asylum near Paris, published a forged decree of the Senate announcing the Emperor's death, shot and wounded the commandant of the Paris garrison and had both the Minister of Police and the Prefect of Police placed under arrest. All that night there was pandemonium in the capital; even the Minister of War (General Clarke) hurriedly swore an oath of loyalty to Napoleon's infant son, the King of Rome. But by ten o'clock the following morning General Laborde had marched troops into the centre of the city, released the police officials and seized Malet. As Napoleon saw speedily enough, this was the most inept coup d'état that had ever ruffled the not untroubled stream of Parisian politics. Malet was acting on his own; he had none of the elaborate apparatus of planning which was to help (or hinder) the plotters against Hitler towards the close of that other Russian campaign in July, 1944. Yet it was, nonetheless, an ominous event. For ten hours Paris had accepted, with little question, a pronouncement that Napoleon had perished; and immediately the elaborate machinery of the Imperial State ceased to function. Nothing else was capable of awakening the Emperor to the peril of his own isolation; for the efficacy of personal rule depends with shattering simplicity on the safety of the person. In the midst of a snowstorm in the depths of Russia it was disconcerting to learn how the capital reacted to a rumour of one's death. More than ever, Napoleon was determined to carry out the plan he had confided to Caulaincourt in the small hours of the morning at Uspenskoie: the army would go into quarters around Vitebsk and he would speed back across the continent to Paris.

At Mikhailewska he was barely forty miles from Smolensk. There the army would find food and shelter, and as he looked at the map that Friday evening he had every hope of reaching the city by Sunday afternoon. But the snow became worse with every hour that passed. There was no sun by day now – only a slippery surface to the road and deep drifts through all the fields. Horses fell to the ground and were too weary to rise again. 'The snow came down in enormous flakes. We lost sight not only of the sky, but of the men in front of us,' writes Sergeant Bourgogne. Nearly everyone was on foot, officers leading their mounts by the bridle, step by step. Even the Emperor at times abandoned his carriage and, wrapped up in a long Polish greatcoat, plodded forward through the snow, supported by Berthier or Caulaincourt or one of his aides. By two o'clock on Sunday afternoon the blizzard was so intense that Napoleon gave up the attempt to reach Smolensk and took refuge for some eighteen hours in a post-house several miles to the west of the city.

But by the Monday morning (November 9) it was at least possible to move forward along the road, although painfully slowly. Then, as the day advanced, the clammy fog turned into a light mist, and, at last, the sun broke through. Suddenly about noon it shone on the gaunt towers and long ramparts of Smolensk. A thrill of relief passed down the ranks – as it had done once before when a Russian city had come into view, picked out by the midday sun. Smolensk in retreat had none of the glamour of Moscow; but despite the desolation, it was a refuge. There were rations to be distributed and enough roofs to house the sick and wounded. And there was no sign of the enemy.

It was not until the following day that Napoleon learned that the Russian First Army Corps had captured Vitebsk.

13

Krasnoe and the Berezina

The news from Vitebsk was disturbing. It was barely eighty miles from Smolensk and, back in August, Napoleon had covered the distance between the two towns in three days' riding. Already Wittgenstein's advance troops were creeping dangerously close. With Chichagov coming up from the south-west, Miloradovich to the east and Kutuzov lumbering ponderously along somewhere to the south, there was a strong possibility that the Grand Army (or what was left of it) would be trapped in the very region which the Emperor had intended to retain as his base of operations in 1813.

If the news was alarming, it was also totally unexpected. Napoleon had been acutely conscious of the potential menace afforded by Wittgenstein's First Army for some two months. But he considered that he had taken adequate counter-measures: Marshal Victor, with the Ninth Corps, formed a central reserve in the triangle Vitebsk-Orsha-Smolensk; he was to defend the main supply line to Moscow from partisan raiders; and he was to move, if necessary, to the support of Saint-Cyr and Oudinot, who were watching Wittgenstein in the north, or Dombrowski, who was guarding Minsk in the south. Even when Napoleon heard in Viazma of the loss of Polotsk, he still believed that Vitebsk could be held, and indeed that Polotsk itself would soon be recovered. All dispositions were taken on the assumption that contact could be maintained between Smolensk and Vilna along the most direct route, through Vitebsk. Victor duly left Smolensk with 21,000 men for the Dvina; General Baraguay d'Hilliers, whose division consisted of fresh troops newly arrived from France, was ordered back from an exposed position at Elnay so as to strengthen the reserves at Smolensk; and Eugène's Fourth Corps was sent out across country from Dorogobuzh to assist Victor in front of Vitebsk. Each of these units swiftly ran into trouble, if not disaster.

Marshal Victor, Duke of Belluno, was a singularly unfortunate commander. Robbed through Joseph Bonaparte's excessive caution of a triumph over Wellesley on the parched slopes of Talavera in 1809, he had been caught up for another three years in the interminable Andalusian fandango, only to be summoned eastwards to Warsaw just as the Spanish campaign was reaching a climax. Once in Poland, he was assigned, rather belatedly, the Ninth Corps which was one-third German and one-third Polish, with a leavening of Dutch, and for good measure, some refractory French conscripts newly released from prison-camps. Understandably, Victor had no great confidence in his men; he had always believed in strict discipline and sound training and this composite force looked distinctly unpromising on parade. Moreover, Victor himself, though a first-class tactician and as careless of his own safety in combat as any other marshal, was always hesitant on independent missions. Like everyone else, he was uncertain of Napoleon's intentions and at the time he left Smolensk, he had no idea that the Grand Army was in a state of exhaustion. But he understood well enough the Russian plan. From his own scouts he had heard that Wittgenstein's line of advance seemed to be directed due south, down the Ulla river towards Chichagov's army which, Victor believed, was in some places little more than eighty miles away. Accordingly, Victor placed the Ninth Corps between Wittgenstein and Chichagov, around the town of Tchasniki, where they joined 14,000 men of the Second Corps, under Oudinot. Strategically, Victor had taken the right decision, for Wittgenstein was indeed eager to make contact with Chichagov and was fulfilling the directive sent to him from St Petersburg. But these dispositions sealed the fate of Vitebsk. Tchasniki lay sixty miles to the south-west and Victor could give no assistance to the isolated garrison. On November 7 Vitebsk was captured by a comparatively small force detached from Wittgenstein's army. Sporadic skirmishes continued between Tchasniki and Sienno, but they reflected credit on neither of the opposing commanders. As snow enveloped the formless ridges which constitute the watershed between the rivers of the Baltic and the Black Sea, so Victor and Oudinot were gradually forced back and back towards the Berezina, losing guns, losing men taken prisoner, perhaps even losing heart.

Baraguay d'Hilliers, retiring from Elnya, fared even worse. Napoleon had counted on Baraguay's division to restore the shattered morale of his own men as they rested at Smolensk. But, on the same day as the fall of Vitebsk, one of Baraguay's brigades two thousand strong, blundered into an ambush set by Russian irregulars and was forced to surrender. The brigade was led by General Jean-Pierre Augereau, younger brother of one of the most publicized generals of the revolutionary armies. It was a humiliating incident felt keenly by all the French officers and an unexpected success to elate the Russians and vindicate the effectiveness of partisan bands. Other units also lost men and material and by the time Baraguay reached Smolensk his troops had been as heavily mauled as the divisions which had struggled down the frozen trail from Viasma. Augereau remained a Russian prisoner, but Baraguay, who had ignored elementary precautions against a surprise attack, was already in Smolensk when the Grand Army straggled in. He incurred the full weight of the Emperor's displeasure; sent back to France in disgrace, pending a court-martial, he died two months later before further action could be taken. Napoleon continued to insist that the destruction of this division and the loss of Augereau's brigade, with its stores and supplies, made the whole Smolensk position untenable; but it is hard to escape the feeling that both generals were to some extent made scapegoats for the series of misfortunes which had fallen on the Grand Army.

Eugène, too, seeking to reach Vitebsk from Dorogobuzh, suffered considerable losses from Cossack raiders. He set off down side-roads with Platov in full pursuit. By November 9 he had reached the frozen marshes of the river Vop. The Vop itself had a thin coating of ice, there were no bridges and nothing with which to construct one. His Italian Guard, veterans who had distinguished themselves at Maloyaroslavets, won fresh glory; they waded through the bitter water, cracking the ice with their chests as they struggled towards the farther bank. Their guns were soon bogged down and all the heavy waggons had to be abandoned, many of them fused with primitive (and damp) booby-traps. Grimly Eugène pressed on, with his pursuers defeated in equal part by the conditions and by the indomitable resolution of his Italian and Croatian troops. But, though he shook off Platov and halted a column of regular cavalry which had crossed the river by a bridge several miles upstream, Eugène realized that his corps was in no state to reach Vitebsk. After pushing on north-westwards for nearly fifty miles to the small town of Dukhovschina, he swung south again and brought his survivors down to Smolensk as darkness fell on November 13. At the first muster after Eugène's corps entered Russia in June it had comprised more than 45,000 men with 116 pieces of artillery; by the time it returned to Smolensk there were 7,000 men still bearing arms and only twenty guns.

Despite the gloomy reports which kept on reaching him, Napoleon spent much of his four days in Smolensk wrapt in impassive silence. There were, of course, occasional explosions of temper: Baraguay and Augereau served as convenient whipping-boys in moments of frustration; and a general who proposed lightening the burden on the horses of the Guard by blowing up some of the artillery, discovered to his discomfiture that beneath the Imperial greatcoat there still stirred the spirit of a gunner. Now and again he spoke optimistically of the immediate future; he was cheered by the notion that there was a force of Polish 'Cossacks' somewhere around Smolensk waiting to escort the veterans of Moscow into safe winter quarters; he commented favourably on the milder weather; he argued that the Russians must be in an even worse state or they would have made a determined effort to wipe out the Grand Army before it reached Smolensk. At heart, he continued to believe that Fortune would soon smile on him again; and each morning he rode confidently through the slippery streets, a Maître Pangloss on horseback. It was, complained Caulaincourt, almost as if he wished to preserve the city rather than evacuate it.

To the soldiery, Smolensk that November wore a mask of comfort, sometimes hideous and desperately thin. For the town was as much a ruin as Moscow. Snow made it hard to distinguish between the roads and the open spaces where there had been houses; and Bourgogne comments on the ease with which one could suddenly sink through the snow into empty cellars. He himself literally fell into a den of thieves and was lucky to escape with his life; others were less fortunate, some were killed outright, some were murdered, and some broke their legs and lingered on in cold and agony. It was a selfish community. Money, of course, could purchase luxuries. The Imperial wine-merchant had seen that Smolensk was well-stocked with brandy and there was a flourishing black-market. In the centre of the city the Old Guard set up a fair – comment enough on the demoralization which had spread to even the finest regiments. You could buy liquor or the complete works of Voltaire or women's shawls or coffee; and there was still a glut of church ornaments. Only the necessities of life were in short supply. General Charpentier, the Governor of the town, had heard of the approach of the army no more than five days before it arrived. He had gathered in as much food and fodder as possible and ordered any bakers he could find to set up improvised field-kitchens. But he had not realized that the troops were little better than a rabble and there was no proper system of distribution. As ever, the Imperial Guard fared well; yet for most of the men, and especially for those who were not French by origin, survival depended on quick wits and heavy blows.

Although it was possible to find shelter for most of the desperately sick, the majority of the regiments remained under canvas. Not all were even in the city: Davout's corps, for example, were on the road to Krasnoe and, by the evening of November 12, Ney and the rearguard had only reached the old battlefield of Valutino, where the ridge of hills offered some protection. Fortunately, although it was still bitterly cold, the weather remained dry. Within Smolensk itself, accommodation was poor and diversions few. 'We have a vile lodging,' wrote Castellane in his diary on November 13, 'One is condemned to be either frozen or smoked out, seated before this cursed stove.' But at least he had the company of Count Narbonne, who, in a long life, had assembled a salty collection of scandalous tales – and Narbonne, for his part, was still accompanied by the harp-plucking courtesan he had befriended in Moscow, Madame Grandier. But there were not many in Smolensk with such pleasant distractions.

Napoleon had not yet abandoned his plan for another campaign against Russia in the spring. Although he spoke once more to Caulaincourt of returning to Paris, he still hoped to find permanent quarters along the Russian borderland for his troops. Muster-rolls indicated that he retained under his command in Smolensk some 50,000 effective troops. (When he had been there in August, the muster had been more than three times as high.) It was no longer possible to hold Vitebsk and Smolensk, but he believed that with help coming from Poland and from his Austrian allies, he could even now establish a winter line along the rivers Dvina, Luchesa and Dnieper. If this could be done, there remained only seventy miles of retreat. Adequate supplies should be available from the stores collected in Minsk. After despatching urgent messages to Victor and to Maret in Vilna, on November 13, he sent Junot ahead with the Westphalians and Poles down the road to Krasnoe and Orsha. The following day he set out himself with the Guard, leaving Eugène to follow with his weary Italians on the 15th and Davout a day later, although Ney might delay even longer if he felt it advisable to blow up the walls of Smolensk before he departed.

In this region of Russia there are a number of low hills between the rivers. In good weather these gentle undulations gave the normal traveller no problems; they were a relief to the monotony of the landscape; but the first icy days of November made the winding road treacherous. Horses, inadequately shod, tumbled, slid and, unable to clamber up again, perished exhausted in the snow. Famished men died at their sides. 'All along our way we were forced to step over the dead and dying,' wrote Bourgogne of that first day's march after leaving Smolensk. And yet, despite all the horrors, the Emperor and the Guard somehow covered sixteen miles before the light failed, Napoleon setting up headquarters in a ruined hut in the village of Korytnia, while the Guard bivouacked in nearby woodland.

Between Korytnia and Krasnoe, however, the Emperor was to meet a new and unexpected threat to the Army's existence. At Smolensk he maintained that the Russians were giving up the pursuit; now he was to learn otherwise. For Miloradovich had in fact by-passed Smolensk and made a direct thrust for the Krasnoe

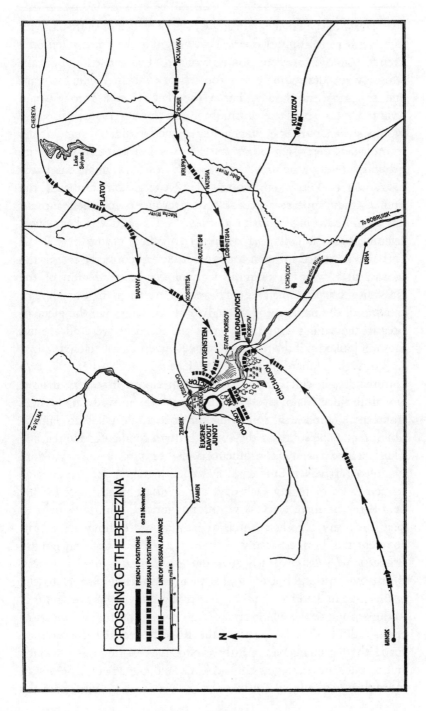

CROSSING OF THE BEREZINA

FRENCH POSITIONS ▮▮▮▮ on 28 November
RUSSIAN POSITIONS ▮▮▮▮
⟶ LINE OF RUSSIAN ADVANCE

miles
0   3   6

N

MINSK

To BOBRUISK

USHA

Berezina River

UCHOLODY

CHICHAGOV

OUDINOT

ÉUGENE
DAVOUT
JUNOT

KAMEN

ZEMBIK

To VILNA

VICTOR
VESELOVO

WITTGENSTEIN

STARY-BORISOV
MILORADOVICH
BORISOV

LOSHNITSHA

RADUTSHI

KOSTRITSA

BARANY

PLATOV

Lake
Selyan

CHEREYA

NATSHA

KRUPKI

Bobr River

Nacha River

BOBR

MOLIAVKA

KUTUZOV

223

road ahead of the French. Already Cossacks were close at hand, with light artillery to support them. That very day they descended on a French convoy, capturing some of the trophies carried away from Moscow and destroying a waggon which contained valuable maps and topographical studies. For a moment it seemed to Captain Lyautey, whose battery was caught in the ambush, as if the Russians would sweep over the French like a sudden tidal wave. Horses stumbled against each other and he was himself thrown to the ground, although the snow was so soft that he was unhurt and able to remount. Yet, even though the Russians outnumbered the French, they appeared incapable of pressing home their success. Twice more during the grim journey the Cossacks attacked: once, Lyautey even thought that he heard an officer crying out 'Paris! Paris!' as he urged his men forward. If he had correctly caught the words, they were an ominous sign of the determination of the Russians now that their enemy seemed to be in flight. Though weakened, the battery got through; but after nightfall the glow of fires in the winter sky showed that the Russians were all around them. It looked as if the road to Krasnoe was effectively closed.

Although neither Napoleon nor Kutuzov realized it, the two commanders-in-chief spent that night in closer proximity than at any time since Maloyaroslavets. Kutuzov had moved slowly west from the Viasma area, following the road to Mogilev for ninety miles, far to the south of the route through Smolensk. He reached Elnya, where he rested for some forty-eight hours, on the day before Napoleon arrived at Smolensk. So far he had continued to average sixteen miles marching each day, despite the blizzards, but for the next week he made very slow progress indeed, with long halts to keep his army together. Some of his staff were indignant at this apparent tardiness, especially Wilson. But Löwenstern, an émigré Prussian well-disposed towards the commander-in-chief writes, 'Kutuzov kept stubbornly to his plan, advancing parallel to the enemy. He refused to take risks, preferring rather to expose himself to the censure of the whole army.' And even Wilson, the severest of critics, admits that by the time the Russians reached the Krasnoe road, 'the regiments were nearly as effective as when they set out'; and he calculates that they still had some 80,000 men in the field with more than 600 cannon. Kutuzov had as yet saved his men from the

Tsar Alexander I

A scene from the retreat

worst privations; they approached Krasnoe in far better shape than their adversaries and by dusk on Sunday, November 15, they were within two miles of Napoleon's headquarters. To many Russian officers it seemed as if the moment had come to fall on the demoralized invaders and destroy them, but both Kutuzov and Miloradovich remained in awe of Napoleon's reputation. They saw the events of the next three or four days through a cloud of irresolution and uncertainty; and chroniclers of the campaign have not spared their reputations. 'Krasnoe,' wrote the intrepid Davidov, scathingly, 'should, in all justice, be called a three-days' search for hungry and half-naked Frenchmen: insignificant detachments like mine could boast some trophies, but this was not the case with the main army.'

In a sense, Davidov was right. Krasnoe was not a battle, as Borodino or even Maloyaroslavets had been; it was the scene of a series of indecisive skirmishes fought out in mist or failing light through thawing snow. The action was begun by Miloradovich, who planned a similar trap to the one he had set beyond Viasma. Protected by a ravine, he lay in wait for the French columns west of Korytnia that Sunday afternoon. As Napoleon and the Guard passed through the village of Rianka, his cannon opened fire but he did not dare send his cavalry against the ranks of the Guard and Napoleon arrived unscathed at the town of Krasnoe, although the Russians ruthlessly disposed of several thousand stragglers they encountered along the road, and also seized a dozen abandoned guns.

Napoleon now realized that he was in grave danger, not so much from the immediate threat of a frontal assault – although he had discovered from prisoners that Kutuzov was at hand – but from the scattered formation of his own troops. Eugène, for example, could not reach Krasnoe until Monday evening (November 16) and there would still be the separate corps of Davout and Ney, not due until even later. Eugène received heavy treatment from the guns and cavalry of Miloradovich near the hamlet of Merlino. His corps escaped from the Russian trap only by turning Miloradovich's left flank under cover of darkness. The heavy casualties among Eugène's men presaged disaster for Davout and Ney, since it was likely that the Russians would bring up reinforcements to block the route to Krasnoe.

Eugène's arrival stirred Napoleon to action. For the first time since the retreat began, he determined to seize the initiative. Early on Tuesday morning he sent his cherished Old Guard back towards Smolensk to strike at Kutuzov while Davout and the First Corps were approaching Miloradovich's position. This French counter-attack surprised Miloradovich: he had intended to send out cavalry to cut the escape route westwards out of Krasnoe; now, hastily withdrawing his own headquarters, he countermanded his orders and there was a sharp clash on the outskirts of the town. But nothing could prevent Miloradovich from falling on the First Corps and it suffered heavy casualties. Davout himself lost maps and papers; as some of them related to central Asia and the invasion of India, their capture had little immediate relevance to the battle. But Davout was furious that the enemy should also have taken possession of his marshal's baton. It was despatched speedily to St Petersburg, a much admired trophy.

After conferring with Davout, Napoleon decided that afternoon to break off the action and press on swiftly towards Orsha, fearing that he might otherwise be encircled. It was a hard decision, for there was still no news of Ney and the rearguard. Davout, who had sent back scouts to warn Ney of the danger ahead, was to remain in Krasnoe as long as possible in the hope that Ney might break through Miloradovich's position.

Orsha is forty miles from Krasnoe and the roads remained almost impassable. Napoleon reached Lyadi that night, a small town technically beyond the boundary of Russia proper and in Lithuania. The last mile into Lyadi lay along a sunken road down a steep hill, and it was so icy that the Guard was treated to the inelegant spectacle of the Emperor and his staff leaving Russia on their backsides, like schoolboys on a slide. 'The many arms offered to the Emperor,' writes Caulaincourt, with a blush of apology, 'provided no adequate support.' Fortunately, says Lyautey, there were still many people living in the town, most of them Jewish, and they had food and clothing to sell. From now on the Grand Army hoped that it would be in less hostile country.

Napoleon reached Orsha shortly after midday on the Thursday, November 19. Davout had been forced to evacuate Krasnoe on the previous morning, still without making any contact with Ney.

Napoleon feared disaster. 'His heart was full at Ney's misfortune and of despair at abandoning him,' writes Ségur. 'I would give the three hundred millions I have in gold in the vaults of the Tuileries to save him,' declared the Emperor somewhat boastfully. Some well-shod horses might have been of more practical value.

Ney's withdrawal from Smolensk remains an epic. He was always at his best in command of a comparatively small unit of hard-pressed troops. A furious fighter, as intrepid as Murat, with the same will to seek glory, but less natural showmanship, he was quick to size up a situation and to exploit any hesitation in his adversary with ruthless energy. Unfortunately, in Smolensk, Ney had quarrelled bitterly with Davout over accusations of looting made against his troops, and he was now on as bad terms with Davout as Murat had been earlier in the campaign. Inevitably, this rift prevented close co-operation between the First and the Third Corps, and Davout was blamed among his fellow-commanders for not giving Ney and the Third Corps more determined support. The fault was not, however, entirely Davout's. Ney, in a temper, was perversely obdurate; he scorned the warnings sent back to him from Davout and resented his advice to hasten the retreat.

It was not until the morning of November 17 that Ney left Smolensk, having exploded mines under the ramparts before his departure. He had 6,000 combatant troops with him and several thousand desperate camp-followers. The following afternoon his leading division, advancing through a heavy mist, came under fire from the batteries Miloradovich had placed along the Krasnoe road. The French troops – men of Ricard's 18th Division, detached from the First Corps – fell back on the main body of the Third Corps, although their resistance was so determined that Miloradovich did not realize that he had engaged only the vanguard of Ney's force. Hence by the time Ney himself reached the Russian position, Miloradovich had considerably strengthened it, giving Paskievich the command of a battery of two dozen cannon which were placed facing down the road while other guns remained on escarpments to each side. Miloradovich sent a messenger to ask for Ney's sword: 'A Marshal of France does not surrender,' Ney replied haughtily and ordered his men forward.

For five hours the French tried to force their way through to Krasnoe. With fog muffling the sound of cannon, orange flames showed waiting lines of Russian horsemen silhouetted against the rocks of the ravine. The French successfully dislodged the Russians from two positions, but Paskievich's guns remained unassailable. The mist lifted, the Russian lancers counter-attacked, and Ney was forced to summon his men back; they had suffered grievously. Once more a Russian major under a white flag sought his surrender, informing him that the French had already left Krasnoe and that both the First Corps and the Imperial Guard had been destroyed in the fighting of the previous three days. Ney was unimpressed, although he insisted on detaining the officer as shots were exchanged during the parley.

If Krasnoe was abandoned, there seemed to Ney no point in making another assault on the Russian lines. Leaving his camp-fires burning and his heavier guns spiked, he struck out northwards beside a small frozen stream known as the Lossmina. That night the clouds came down and a sudden snowstorm set in, covering the tracks of his men as they stumbled forwards. Momentarily he was lost, but he ordered the ice of the stream to be broken so as to discover the direction in which it was flowing and then followed it, confident that sooner or later he would reach the Dnieper. As he neared the river, the weather cleared and with one of those unpredictable changes of temperature which always caused havoc, a slight thaw set in once more. The Dnieper remained frozen, but the ice was thin and treacherous. Some men were drowned as the ice cracked under them. The sick and wounded, most of the non-combatants and all the surviving guns and waggons were abandoned. Only a few horses were able to reach the other bank. And even when Ney and his men were across the river, they were still far from safe. For Platov and his Cossacks continued to raid them by night and day for the rest of the march, bringing up light artillery on sledges to pour grapeshot into their thinning ranks. Twice the French were forced to make bayonet charges on the Cossack gun-positions. At last, a Polish officer, riding ahead of the corps, entered

Orsha on November 20 and Eugène sent out a strong detachment to disperse Platov's Cossacks and bring Ney and the survivors of the march into the town. Out of 6,000 men who had left Smolensk with the Marshal, there remained only 900 combatants under arms when they reached Orsha.

Nevertheless, despite all these losses, the Emperor was elated by the news that Ney had succeeded in rejoining the main body of the army. Borrowing a title first bestowed on General Lannes fifteen years previously – for by now even his phrases had lost their thrill of originality – Napoleon described Ney as 'the Bravest of the Brave.' Ney was, of course, gratified, but anger smouldered within him at what he regarded as neglect shown towards his corps by the other marshals. His own comment on the march at the time was brief, pungent, and, in its purest form, unprintable.

It is probable that Napoleon deliberately encouraged the rejoicing at Ney's survival in order to offset the effect of unpleasant information which reached him on November 20. Two days previously he had heard a rumour that the city of Minsk, where great supplies had been accumulated, had fallen to the 'Army of Moldavia', under Admiral Chichagov. Now the report was confirmed. This was an even harder blow for Napoleon than the loss of Vitebsk. The Russians were closing in the net around the Emperor; it began to look as if he had escaped encirclement at Krasnoe only to be caught farther to the west, along the line of the Berezina.

Napoleon had consistently underestimated the danger from Chichagov, feeling instinctively that Wittgenstein to the north was a more serious menace. Perhaps he was right; Chichagov's military record was hardly impressive. He was a favourite of the Tsar, who made him Minister of the Navy and in 1811, during the war with Turkey, he had been given extensive powers as 'Commander-in-Chief of Moldavia, Wallachia, and the Black Sea Fleet.' The Turkish campaign ended before his prowess could be tested as a soldier on land, but the Tsar had already marked him out for further advancement. At Vilna, before Napoleon crossed the Niemen, the Tsar actually proposed that Chichagov should be entrusted with the task of raising a revolt among the South Slav subjects of Napoleon's Austrian ally. It is probably as well that this scheme was abandoned for Chichagov, who had been educated in England (and was, in time, to become a naturalized Englishman), was contemptuous of everything Slavonic. Yet Chichagov – or his staff – showed considerable administrative skill. During September he brought 34,000 veterans of the Turkish War up from Moldavia to the town of Ostrog, some three hundred miles away. There they made contact with the Russian Third Army south of the Pripet Marshes. The Third Army, which was commanded by Tormassov until the end of September, had been for some weeks engaged, in a somewhat desultory fashion, with Schwarzenberg's Austrian Corps along the border of Galicia; but Austrian participation in the war, always suspect, had by now become virtually nominal and Chichagov found that he could move his troops in an arc west of the Pripet Marshes without encountering serious opposition, provided that no Russian force threatened Austrian territory. Chichagov was thus able to approach Brest-Litovsk with his skill as a tactical commander on land still untested.

It was while in camp to the east of Brest-Litovsk that Chichagov took a vital decision. He divided his army into two separate corps: General Sacken was to contain Schwarzenberg along the river Bug with some 27,000 men; Chichagov himself with the remainder of his force would wheel eastwards and seek to uncover the whole right wing of the Grand Army. On October 29 – the day on which Napoleon was re-crossing the field of Borodino – Chichagov and the Army of Moldavia struck out to the east, heading towards Slonim, a hundred miles away, and Minsk, ninety miles farther still.

Five days later Chichagov was in Slonim and his horses were ready to continue the journey to Minsk. It was a strange march. In some ways it was appropriate that an Admiral should be in command, for the corps moved forward like a squadron of cumbersome and top-heavy warships. Only rarely was Chichagov in contact with the enemy – or, indeed, with anyone else. An aide-de-camp got through to Wittgenstein, but both Kutuzov and the authorities in St Petersburg heard nothing but rumours of his movements, and Napoleon and Marshal Victor heard no more. Chichagov's field commanders railed against his imperious character and extravagant projects; he was breaking most of the rules of their trade and they were certain he was courting disaster. And yet in eighteen days he was able to lead an army of 30,000 men across two hundred miles of open country in virtual isolation and with the weather worsening the farther he advanced. Small wonder that the arrival of the Army of Moldavia in the province of Minsk caused consternation.

The city of Minsk itself had suffered little from the earlier fighting in the campaign. Enough food and supplies had been collected there in the previous ten weeks to sustain the Grand Army throughout the winter months. But little had been done to defend the town. Napoleon believed that it would be safeguarded against any threat from the Army of Moldavia by Schwarzenberg and the Austrians, but they were fully occupied with Sacken's troops. The garrison of the city consisted of a mere handful of Würtembergers and Poles, 4,000 men at the most. At first, the Governor of Minsk refused to believe stories that reached him of a large Russian Army advancing from the south-west, and when Chichagov's troops appeared, he barely had time to escape from the town. The garrison offered only token resistance, for their commander, Bronikowski, saw that he was heavily outnumbered and wanted to save his men and guns until they could receive reinforcements from Victor's corps in the north. On November 16 Chichagov entered Minsk, Bronikowski hastily withdrawing to guard the western bank of the Berezina at Borisov.

As soon as he heard that Minsk was once more in Russian hands, Napoleon knew he must hasten to the Berezina. 'For the first time, the Emperor struck me as uneasy about the future,' writes Caulaincourt. And well he might be; for at that moment, with three Russian armies converging on the river and his own troops little better than a fugitive horde, it seemed probable that his whole empire might tumble to pieces along the banks of the Berezina and he himself be brought captive to a triumphant Tsar in Smolensk. In Borisov there was a vital bridge across the river. At all costs he must get there before the Russians. With the river behind him and the bridge destroyed, he could still reach Vilna and safety.

Others too, were hurrying to Borisov. The first to get there, after Bronikowski, was a division of Poles commanded by Dombrowski and sent south by Oudinot. But Chichagov was not far behind. His advance-guard reached the river on November 21, taking the two Polish generals by surprise. Dombrowski counter-attacked and held the bridge for several hours, even though outnumbered by a force three times the size of his own. But, as night fell, he was forced to retire; and the bridge remained in Chichagov's hands. It was a further heavy blow to Napoleon. For mile upon mile of the central stretch of the Berezina there appeared no other way to cross; either the river cut a deep channel between high banks or it overflowed into swamp and marshland. 'This damned sailor brings me nothing but bad luck,' complained Napoleon when he heard the news; it was an understatement. Significantly, he ordered the destruction of surplus baggage and the burning of official documents and private papers.

So far all had gone well for 'this damned sailor'; but now he was to meet stiffer opposition. On November 22 Marshal Oudinot with 8,000 men of the second Corps, coming from the north, reached the village of Natsha, which was twenty miles east of Borisov, and it was there that he received news of Dombrowski's unsuccessful attempt to recover the bridge. These troops of Oudinot's corps were comparatively fresh and still well-disciplined. As yet they had encountered little bad weather. They included several battalions of Swiss, who had already distinguished themselves in action against Wittgenstein, and two divisions of Poles, many of whom knew the region well. Moreover, at Natsha, Oudinot was joined by General Corbineau's cavalry brigade which arrived after a remarkable cross-country journey of ninety miles from a position astride the Vitebsk-Vilna road. In the course of the march Corbineau had successfully crossed the Berezina at a ford shown to him by Polish peasants opposite to Studenka, seven miles north of Borisov. For the moment, Oudinot was too pre-occupied with the problem of the Borisov to appreciate the significance of the information Corbineau had brought to him; but a few days later it was to prove the salvation of the Emperor.

That Monday afternoon, November 23, one of Oudinot's cavalry detachments, the 4th Cuirassiers, caught sight of Russian horsemen as it approached the village of Loshnitsa, halfway between Natsha and Borisov. They were Chichagov's advance-guard, under Count Pahlen. The cuirassiers attacked immediately and, taking Pahlen's men by surprise, drove them back helter-skelter down the road to Borisov. In the confusion Pahlen, who had only taken command of the division on the previous day, was borne along unrecognized by his men and totally unable to halt them. Early in the evening the Russians dashed into Borisov shouting '*Frantsusyi*! *Frantsusyi*!' in panic. Chichagov, comfortably accommodated in the best house in the town, was about to dine with his officers, silver plate on the table. The meal remained untouched; within minutes, Chichagov had fled across the bridge on foot. For a moment it even looked as if Oudinot would capture the bridge intact, but one of the Russian commanders had the presence of mind to have it cut and fired as the French galloped in. Once on the right bank of the Berezina, the Russians felt secure; but they had lost a thousand men taken prisoner and more than three hundred waggons filled with supplies. Oudinot's troops found plenty to eat and drink that night.

As yet, Oudinot had won little distinction in the campaign; he was an infantryman, ill at ease in a war of movement. But now he acted with quick intelligence. He sent Corbineau, with infantry and bridge-building engineers, north to Studenka to discover if it were possible for an army of 60,000 men to ford the river there. At the same time he sent out reconnaissance parties to look for other crossing points upstream and downstream from Borisov. Chichagov's troops did little to hamper him.

While the 4th Cuirassiers were chasing Pahlen and Chichagov back across the river, Napoleon arrived at Bobr, little more than thirty miles away. He was cheered by the reports which reached him. He had confidence in Oudinot, and he believed that he had outpaced his pursuers. Kutuzov, Miloradovich and the main Russian Army were certainly lagging behind; they had been delayed by their attempt to cut off Ney, and were still more than forty miles east of Bobr. Even Platov and the Cossacks were giving little trouble; occasionally they raided Davout and the rearguard, but they were some fifteen miles from Napoleon's own position. The nearest Russian force of any danger was Wittgenstein's Corps, at Chereya, twenty miles to the north; but Victor and the Ninth Corps were firmly astride the road from Chereya to Bobr and Wittgenstein seemed disinclined to attack; he was, in fact, remarkably ill-informed of what was happening. Napoleon still had hopes that Schwarzenberg would threaten Minsk and cut off Chichagov; and he had, indeed, already thrashed Sacken on the borders of the Pripet Marshes. A few nights previously Napoleon's staff were mournfully regretting that there was no balloon available for the Emperor to escape the Russian net; now he was prepared to laugh at their fears and to talk privately to Caulaincourt of his projected return to Paris.

The rank and file of the army remained, of course, in a sorry plight. At Orsha there had been more food than in Smolensk and a rather better system of distribution, although it had broken down in a general anarchy of drunken pillaging. Many veterans were plodding westwards only half-conscious of what was going on; they had hallucinations, sometimes of food and drink, sometimes of their families, sometimes of smart parades in elegant cities. Hunger and fatigue taxed their minds like sun-stroke. Many were, at the same time, feverish from dysentery and in agony from frostbite. Captain Roeder of the Hessian Guard was one of these unfortunates: that Monday, on the way to Bobr, his horse was drowned as she slipped through the ice while seeking a drink of water; and Roeder completed the journey by walking for eight hours on swollen feet, sick, delirious, and racked by violent coughing. There was little order about the retreat, units had become inextricably confused. Some of the men – Sergeant Bourgogne among them – were lost, travelling aimlessly through the Russian waste, finding their way from heap upon heap of discarded kit, navigating themselves by a trail of crumpled corpses. Here and there, they were helped by friendly Polish peasants; always, even in this living nightmare, they feared the death that Cossack raiders would inflict on their broken bodies. Behind the rearguard, clinging pathetically to the slim protection of Davout's corps, came the great horde of stragglers, women and children among them, frightened and cold and hungry. Already there were stories of cannibalism. For five days the snow-clouds had held off, but on the night of November 23–24 the temperature dropped suddenly and a blizzard swept down on the Bobr road. With each mile that they trudged between the dark mass of forest, the cold grew more intense; fallen bodies were swiftly hidden by drifts of snow. At times the cruel grip of winter seemed almost merciful.

The return of the heavy frost, although fatal for so many wretched stragglers, was militarily an advantage for Napoleon. For when Corbineau had arrived back at Studenka he found that the warmer weather had made a remarkable difference to the ford which he had crossed only three days previously; the icy water was five feet deep and he could see flooded marshland extending for a mile and a half beyond the opposite bank. But the falling temperature and the heavy snow changed the situation once more. Both the Berezina and the marshes began to freeze over, although beneath the ice the river remained dangerously deep. Corbineau began as best he could to make preparations for constructing a bridge, but he had few tools and no iron and there was little that could be done. In personal interviews with the Emperor and with Oudinot he urged a rapid crossing of the river and a retreat to the Vitebsk–Vilna road along the route he had just taken. But Napoleon hesitated, maintaining later on that he had not been properly informed of Corbineau's knowledge of the area. In reality he was tempted once more by the thought of marching on Minsk, hoping that the Russians would not have destroyed all the supplies accumulated there and that he would make contact with Schwarzenberg. This, however, as he knew well enough, would have been a gamble; and he had already taken too many chances in the campaign. By the evening of November 24 he decided to make for Vilna. Work was to start immediately on constructing two bridges near Studenka, but it was essential to prevent the Russians from massing troops on the opposite bank. To deceive Chichagov, Oudinot was ordered to send patrols to make noisy demonstrations at every crossing point along the river. At Studenka the preparations were to go ahead with as much quiet and secrecy as possible.

Throughout the campaign Napoleon had retained as part of his headquarter's staff General Eblé's sappers, the engineers who had thrown the bridges across the Niemen in June. Eblé himself had, almost incredibly, preserved a couple of field forges and several waggons loaded with bridge-building equipment and coal. By the evening of November 25 Eblé and his pontoon-builders were at

Studenka, assisted by every able-bodied engineer still with the army and even by a detachment of seamen who had been seconded to the Grand Army before the passage of the Niemen and shared its fortunes ever since. They started work that night, hidden from the enemy on the opposite bank by the deep escarpments that overhang Studenka like a cliff. Iron supports were turned out from the forges and carpenters hammered away at trestles for the pontoons. Soon they ran out of wood. Infantrymen were made to tear down the houses of the village to supply their needs. It was not enough and other buildings were demolished in Veselovo, the next village upstream. Throughout the night there was ceaseless activity; it seems extraordinary that Chichagov's scouts were not alerted.

Napoleon spent that night at Stary-Borisov, some five or six miles away, on an estate belonging to Prince Radziwill. But Oudinot was at Studenka, anxiously watching in case the Russians moved troops north to the opposite bank. From the hillock above the village he could see the long bend of the Berezina and the marshland beyond. The night was clear, although a strong wind drove across the sky a few clouds tinged with the glow from Russian fires downstream. The moon picked out the tips of fir-trees with frozen sharpness and gave a spectral candescence to the ice-floes on the river. Apart from the muffled hammering of workmen down in the dip of the land, there was no sound. Facing Studenka was a solitary Russian outpost and watchers on the French side thought they could count no more than four guards manning it. All remained still as the grey dawn broke, and the Emperor and Berthier came to share Oudinot's watch beside the river.

By eight o'clock it was light enough for the sappers to begin placing the first trestles in the icy water. The task was a difficult one, for the depth of water was uncertain and variable. Suddenly men would sink up to their shoulders and some were washed away in the current; once they lost their foothold there was little chance of saving them from drowning. The pontoons had to stretch for a hundred yards across the stream and work continued on both bridges simultaneously. To prevent the Russians taking counter-action Napoleon had ordered Oudinot's artillery to be massed on the escarpments above Studenka. And, as the first engineers waded into the river, Polish lancers succeeded in fording the stream so as to clear the opposite bank. Later in the morning three hundred infantrymen from Oudinot's corps were ferried across the Berezina on hurriedly constructed rafts. But throughout the morning the Russians took no action.

The first bridge was completed by one o'clock in the afternoon and Oudinot led the remainder of the Second Corps across, accompanied by Dombrowski's division. It took another three hours to finish the second bridge, but by four o'clock it was possible to start moving across all the guns of the Second Corps and any other artillery that could be found. During the afternoon Oudinot had been in contact with Russian patrols and he was anxious to secure the bridgehead against a possible Russian counter-attack.

All had gone remarkably smoothly for the French that day (November 26). Napoleon had given orders that stragglers and non-combatants should be halted at the approaches to Studenka, so that the fighting men might cross the river first, with as many horses, limbers and guns as possible. The various regiments therefore moved over the pontoons in good order that Thursday. But in the evening the sheer weight of the artillery made some of the trestles in the second bridge collapse. Eblé roused half his weary men once more and personally led them into the water, where for three hours they struggled to repair the bridge, working by the light of the moon and in a temperature which, on land, had fallen far below freezing-point. The guns began to go across again before midnight, but at two in the morning the bridge broke for the second time, and Eblé had to waken the rest of his men and spend four more hours toiling among the wreckage.

Victor arrived in Studenka with two divisions of the Ninth Corps on Friday morning, November 27, having left another division under General Partouneaux to act as rearguard in Borisov. There was, as yet, no sign of Wittgenstein – nor, indeed, of any Russian troops on the eastern bank of the river – and Napoleon decided that as soon as he made contact with Victor, he would move the rest of the survivors of the retreat across the Berezina. The Guard was to cross first, followed by the corps of Junot, of Eugène, and of Davout (Ney and the remnants of the Third Corps had gone over the bridge with Oudinot on the Thursday afternoon). So long as the bridges were kept clear for the movements of the organized units, Napoleon gave permission for isolated groups of stragglers and camp-followers to make the journey. He personally crossed with the Guard in the late morning and sought to check each formation that came off the bridge, so as to gain some idea of the condition of his army. Victor and Eblé remained in Studenka trying to keep order among the thousands jostling to get on the bridge, but, once the Emperor and the Guard had gone, discipline rapidly gave way to chaos and when darkness fell there were screams of panic from the horde, and men and women were crushed to death in aimless rushes for the bridgehead. And that night, the temperature dropped even lower.

Few survivors of the Berezina seemed to have retained clear impressions of the actual crossing of the river. Bourgogne, who had found his way back to the regiment only two days before, was weak and dazed; he believed that he crossed the bridge alone and on foot in the middle of the night, meeting no one but the pontooneers who were keeping it in repair. The Hessian Captain Roeder, too, was wretchedly ill; but he remembered mounting a pony with no bridle and a broken stirrup, and clinging to its neck as his sergeant-major led the creature by the mane through a mass of men and horses. 'I do not know which way we came,' he scrawled that night in his diary, 'I could not notice it.' Baron Fain, a dozen years later, maintained that as Napoleon himself went across, with Murat by his side, a ray of sunshine broke through the snow-filled sky to light the Emperor's path, but it seems to have gone unperceived by less romantic chroniclers; Castellane, who was with Napoleon's suite, merely records that when he reached the far bank he had an awful meal and found it excellent.

Yet there were some who remembered the Berezina in its full glory and horror. Captain Lyautey, who was still in remarkably good health, led his battery across towards noon on Friday in a long column which had to make frequent halts; once he found himself next to a young Russian officer who had been captured in the recent cavalry skirmishing, and was able to give the Russian a little food from his small stock of provisions. And Captain Dumonceau, of the French lancers, who did not cross until later that afternoon, re-membered having to use the flat blade of his sword to clear a path and having to dismount and lead his horse so as to avoid shaking the bridge; there was no guardrail and the pontoon sagged alarmingly, almost to water level; a broken cart and dead horses had to be thrown into the river before the lancers could reach the right bank of the stream.

Napoleon had hoped that the crossing would be completed by Friday night. Had this been possible, several thousand lives would have been saved, but Victor was still without Partouneaux's division, which had been left to hold Borisov, and he continued to hold Studenka to await his coming. By now, however, the Russians were approaching. Wittgenstein had cut across country to approach Studenka down frozen trails from the north-east and had made an arrangement with Chichagov by which they would launch a concerted attack on the French bridges on the Saturday morning, November 28. Ermolov had reached Chichagov's headquarters with a cavalry detachment from Kutuzov; Platov was already at the approaches to Borisov with his Cossacks; and Miloradovich was not far behind. The Russians were thus able to concentrate more than 60,000 men against 8,000 French around Studenka and possibly 20,000 combatants on the western bank of the river.

Partouneaux had set out from Borisov at five o'clock on Friday afternoon. In the darkness, his troops took the wrong road and blundered into Wittgenstein's advance-guard. The Russians had seen the French column riding confidently forward and had remained hidden in the forest so as to surround them. Although Partouneaux's men held out for several hours, they never had a chance of breaking through, and more than 4,000 of them, with their commander, were forced to surrender.

Victor, of course, knew nothing of this. The rear column of the Partouneaux division did, however, follow the correct route to Studenka, and Victor assumed that disaster had overtaken the rest of the force. But he was unable to get the men across the river before the Russians opened their attack at dawn on Saturday.

There was hard fighting throughout the day on both banks of the river. Napoleon watched Chichagov mount a clumsy attack on Oudinot's troops. The Russians were repulsed easily enough, although Oudinot himself was wounded once more and had to hand over command of his corps to Ney, who by the end of the day had sent Chichagov reeling towards the Minsk road. Around Studenka the result was at times in doubt because Wittgenstein had considerable artillery power. At one point Napoleon even sent a division of the Guard back across the Berezina to support Victor, but Wittgenstein failed in each of his attempts to capture the bridges. Victor was hampered by the crowd of stragglers and refugees who had jammed the approaches to the bridges as soon as the first shots were fired that morning. Somehow Eblé succeeded in clearing the bridges soon after darkness fell and Victor managed to evacuate his troops overnight.

Napoleon had ordered Eblé to destroy the bridges at seven o'clock on Sunday morning but, as there was no sign of activity in the Russian camp, Eblé delayed taking action for as long as he could. Desperately the remaining stragglers and camp-followers tried to fight their way on to the bridges and some succeeded, but many were crushed to death or fell from the bridge into the ice or collapsed with exhaustion. At half-past eight Eblé finally set fire to the two bridges. Half an hour later the Cossacks descended on the poor wretches who had been unable to escape. In due course the Russians counted beside the river corpses of more than 13,000 members of the Grand Army or French followers and the remains of twice as many horses.

Despite the fearful loss of life, the Russians were denied a decisive military victory, just as Napoleon had been at Borodino. Chichagov was inexperienced and over-confident, Wittgenstein ignorant of what was going on and too awed by the legend of Napoleon to risk an assault on his army, the size and strength of which he grossly overestimated. Kutuzov, too, came in for much criticism. He only arrived on the Berezina two days after the bridges had gone up in smoke – and even then he reached the river some twenty miles south of the point where Napoleon crossed it. Kutuzov, however, believed that his duty was to free Russia from the invader. He was never prepared to fight a European war. After Orsha, Napoleon was technically beyond the borders of Russia proper. Kutuzov's only fear was that he might swing south and seek, as Charles XII had done, to wait in the Ukraine until he could resume his offensive in the spring. If Napoleon had turned towards Kiev, he would have been entering the province about which Kutuzov cared most, the region where he and men like him had fought out Russia's eternal war against the Turk. Constantly Kutuzov had warned Chichagov of the danger of Napoleon marching on Bobruisk. He believed that Wittgenstein could protect the Baltic provinces; let a German defend the German lands, Russia's destiny lay to the south.

It was a point of view which few could understand; it infuriated Tsar Alexander and puzzled Napoleon. For the moment, however, reflections on grand strategy could wait. The war was still going on. Vilna was one hundred and forty miles away. There were no formations of regular troops in the area, and, almost incredibly, the Russians had done nothing to destroy the three long bridges over which his men must march; but each day the frost grew more and more severe and blizzards clawed mercilessly at their famished bodies. It was a long way to Paris.

14

'His Majesty's Health Has
Never Been Better'

In London on November 27, the day Napoleon crossed the Berezina,
a leading article in *The Times* declared:

> The French army has abandoned any idea of establishing itself for
> the winter, in any part of Russia; and is in full retreat out of the
> lands of that empire. We are ready to believe that whatever can
> be done by military science in conducting the retreat, has been
> effected by the united efforts of the French Generals, who alto-
> gether constitute a greater body of talent and experience than
> any other army of the world can boast; but we look, in this
> instance beyond the skill of the General – we look to the physical
> powers of the soldier – we picture to ourselves a Provencal, a
> Tuscan or a Neapolitan struggling from day to day with the snow
> and the frost, toiling through the marshes, and fording the half-
> frozen torrents which, as he advances, swell gradually into
> impassable rivers; we see his hopes failing, his strength exhausted,
> his constitution broken.

The most recent news from Russia was nearly a month old when this
passage was written and it is therefore a remarkably accurate and
sympathetic piece of imaginative prose. It was, in fact, only during
the previous weekend that people in Britain heard for the first time
of the battle of Maloyaroslavets and began to realize that, despite the
fall of Moscow, the whole Russian adventure was becoming a

catastrophe for the French. The impact of this news was startling; it seemed to cheer a bleak winter with the prospect of an early peace. There was an immediate outburst of admiration for 'our Russian ally,' voiced at the lowest level by popular songs or crude captions to simple cartoons. But there was, too, a genuine sympathy for the Russian people and a consciousness that they were suffering cruelly from the war. Within a few weeks, two public subscriptions for relief work in Russia had been announced in the press: the Prince Regent gave £2,000; Liverpool, the Prime Minister, and Castlereagh, the Foreign Secretary, gave a hundred guineas each; and so, too, did the proprietor of *The Times*. Ordinary Londoners could bring their contributions to two taverns in the city; lists of donations in contemporary newspapers include £8.13.6 from workers in a Limehouse factory and an anonymous shilling 'for a Poor Man of Kutuzov's Army.' The Russian Ambassador, Count Vorontsov, was moved by the generosity and respect shown towards his compatriots. Even before the end of November he wrote, in a letter to his son (who was at Kutuzov's headquarters), 'You cannot imagine the enthusiasm there is here for the Russians.'

By Christmas the adulation had become almost hysterical. Every day brought encouraging news. 'The Tyrant is in Flight,' declared *The Times* with rare brevity on November 29, and a week later it was rejoicing because the French were known to have evacuated Smolensk. Inevitably, rumour and conjecture led to wild stories. But *The Times* remained cautious. An article on December 9 was judiciously guarded:

> Davout is said to be dead of his wounds: so, it is added, is St-Cyr. Rumour, indeed, has not spared Buonaparte. He is dead, or taken, just as it suits the fancy of the narrator; but at all events, his misfortunes are dwelt upon with pleasure, and his downfall is anticipated with delight, in every part of the Continent except that degraded and demoralized country which seems fitted only for slavery.

And eight days later, with news of the fighting around Krasnoe and of the arrival of Davout's captured baton in St Petersburg, *The Times* was still offering portentous advice:

In speaking of the successes of the Russians, we are obliged to abate the excess of our joy, not from doubt of their magnitude or reality, for upon these our countrymen may rely; but from mere apprehension lest the vicissitude of human affairs, which does not usually suffer mankind to exult beyond measure upon any occasion whatever, should, by we know not what unexpected reverse, abate somewhat of the transcendent felicity which is promised the world by the overthrow and disgrace of its most detested and detestable tyrant. We shall only say, therefore, in so many words, that Buonaparte is wholly defeated in Russia: he is conquered, and a fugitive.

The City of London and the ancient universities were, however, far less circumspect. On December 11 a story ran through the City that Napoleon had died three weeks previously and that a peace emissary had recently landed at Dover: Consolidated Funds promptly rose 1 per cent on the strength of the report. At Oxford a don laid a heavy wager in bottles of port that the Emperor was either dead or a Russian prisoner; and the Fellows of Trinity College, Cambridge, were so elated at the apparent fall of Napoleon that they climbed on to the High Table in a raucous display of bibulous patriotism.

It was, of course, natural that the British, who had been at war for so long, should magnify the discomfiture of Napoleon. More ominous was the reaction on the Continent. For sensational tales were circulating in the greater cities of France and of the German and Austrian lands, tempting reluctant allies to strike unheroic attitudes as they sought to sift fact from fabrication. The official press in Paris offered reassurance where it could: troops and supplies were reported to be moving steadily through Poland; and there were desperate hints that a bulletin containing good news was on its way westwards. But the credence already given in October to Malet's announcement of the Emperor's death emphasized the fear and uncertainty in the capital. Rumours multiplied: in November, for example, it was being said that Napoleon had suffered a mental collapse and had been placed under restraint by his marshals; and in the following month two men who claimed to be fugitive officers from the Grand Army were seized by the police for asserting that he had been shot by Berthier. So long as few letters or despatches came through from the army, it was hard to counter these stories, however improbable they might seem to be. And, of course, side by side with these rumours travelled a growing anxiety for husbands or sons or lovers in the ranks of the Grand Army; the suspension of casualty lists was a very negative comfort.

There was, too, another danger in the Emperor's long absence. For a month after leaving Smolensk, Napoleon and many of his advisers and senior officials were little more than lost phantoms in the snow, isolated from every department of state. Under these conditions the elaborate machinery of administration which Napoleon had constructed could not work efficiently and the diplomatic representatives of France could not conduct their business with any authority. Perhaps it was inevitable that shadows of treachery should begin to fall over the Empire. In Berlin, voices of critical discontent, muted so long as Napoleon's mastery remained unchallenged, were no longer silent; and in Vienna Metternich was already seeking to reserve a seat for the Emperor Francis beside the angels of retribution. Even in France no one could be certain of the Prince of Benevento (who had once been Citizen Talleyrand) or the Duke of Otranto (who was always Joseph Fouché). It was high time that the Emperor returned to the Tuileries.

Napoleon had sensed as much long before the Malet conspiracy alerted his companions. But he refused to consider handing over his powers to another commander so long as the army was east of the Berezina. Once across the river, the military danger eased. With the Russians suffering as much as the French and their allies from want of food, fuel and clothing, there was little risk of pursuit by Chichagov or Wittgenstein, let alone Kutuzov. The problem now was to reach a route along which there would be posting stations with horses groomed and ready for the journey. Slowly the army veered north-westwards and began to move on Vilna, where Maret, the foreign minister, had maintained a capital in miniature for the past three months.

It was to Maret that Napoleon, on November 29, despatched a

courier from Zembik with a desperate note to make Vilna ready for his weary troops: 'The army is large but broken up in a terrifying manner. It needs fifteen days to reform under its flags. . . Food, food, food – without it there are no horrors that this undisciplined mass will not commit in Vilna. Perhaps this army will not rally before the Niemen. As things are, it is possible that my presence in Paris is essential for France, for the Empire, even for the army. Give me your opinion. . . There must be no foreign representatives in Vilna; the army is today not a fine sight.' It was a message of grim honesty.

These snow-filled days of early December stood out vividly in the memories of all who participated in the retreat, although few found it possible to render in words an account of all that they had seen. There had, of course, been periods of intense cold both before and after Smolensk, but there were also many days on which the temperature crept above freezing point and a thaw set in. (It is significant that the Berezina never froze over completely until after the army had left its bank.) Meteorological records show that over the whole of November the average temperature was only a few degrees below normal in the Russian lands (22.7° Fahrenheit in St Petersburg and 28.4° Fahrenheit in Riga); but with the coming of December the frost became unusually severe and remained so for the rest of the winter. The men of both armies sensed it at the time. Officers on Napoleon's staff, for example, noticed that Murat's face bore a scar; it was the relic of the Egyptian campaign, a sabre-wound normally not visible but now standing out as a livid line across his frozen cheeks. And in the Russian camp Wilson wrote, 'The cold was intense – the thermometer twenty-seven and thirty degrees below freezing point, with sky generally clear, and a subtle, keen, razor-cutting, creeping wind that penetrated skin, muscle and bone to the very marrow, rendering the surface as white and the whole limb affected as fragile as alabaster.'

In such a climate only the Cossack horsemen were hardy enough to offer fight, and even they had lost much of their spirit. They would fall like a pack of wolves upon a straggler, rob him, strip him virtually naked and leave him to perish in the bitter cold. Any small and determined platoon with bayonets at the ready was enough to deter the Cossacks at that stage of the retreat; for they had no need to skirmish with armed detachments, there were always men falling back along the route. Some, of course, had lucky escapes: Captain Roeder, for example, was spared because the Cossacks mistook a ribbon of the Hessian Order of Merit on his chest for the Russian Order of Vladimir, a decoration bestowed by the Tsar in person; and some – very few – were captured by generous Russian officers who did what little they could to ease their suffering; but for most it was a cruel death. The overall impression of the survivors was one of indescribable horror; almost certainly the traditional image of groups of forlorn men – dirty, unkempt and weary – struggling through the virgin snow is too kind to the eyes.

On Wednesday, December 2, while churches throughout the Empire dutifully offered *Te Deums* for the eighth anniversary of his coronation, Napoleon watched the remnant of the Grand Army file by for the last time. It was not a parade; there were no trumpets or drums; no elegant uniforms; no smart dipping of eagles borne proudly at the head of regiments. A line of bearded men, some muffled in furs and cloaks and some in tatters, plodded past the Emperor and his bodyguard as they stood on a slope above the river Vilia. That night Captain Castellane jotted down in his diary an unofficial muster-roll. The Old Guard, which had numbered 10,000 men on leaving Moscow, was now reduced to 2,000. The Young Guard, 8,000 infantry and horsemen six weeks previously, had 300 men under arms that day. Only Oudinot's and Victor's troops retained any smartness. Colonel de Fezensac led the 4th Regiment of the Line, 3,000 strong, into Moscow; that Wednesday, Castellane saw Fezensac's regiment represented by four men bearing its eagle; 200 others were still stumbling forward through the frozen wilderness, but the Emperor spared himself the sight of the stragglers.

Next day Napoleon reached Molodechnok. There he found dispatches awaiting him from Paris and reports from Warsaw and Vilna. The news they contained was bad: it had proved impossible to raise a regiment of Polish Cossacks; and there was no immediate prospect of support from Schwarzenberg and the Austrians. The

Emperor finally took his decision. That night he told Caulaincourt he intended to set out for Paris within the next forty-eight hours.

To retain his personal prestige Napoleon needed to select carefully both the moment at which he would leave the Grand Army and the timing of his return to Paris. Once before he had been accused of deserting his troops – and, significantly, the Egyptian Campaign was as much in his thoughts during the retreat as Austerlitz had been on the way to Moscow. In 1799 he had turned the tables on his detractors by seizing supreme power in the state; now it might prove hard to retain it. Then he had arrived in Paris within eight days of the news that he had defeated the Turks at Aboukir; this time he would be preceded by tidings of disaster – unless, of course, the withdrawal across the Berezina could be shown as a triumph snatched from defeat. But Napoleon had already taken the first steps in stage-managing his own return to France. On the previous evening he dispatched Berthier's aide-de-camp, Colonel Anatole de Montesquiou, to France with instructions to reassure the Empress and to inform Paris 'of the victory of the Berezina, won by the Emperor against the combined armies of Admiral Chichagov and General Wittgenstein.' Montesquiou also conveyed with him eight captured Russian flags as trophies of success.

With Montesquiou on his way to France, Napoleon began to put the last touches to the document in which he intended to inform the world of all that had happened in the retreat from Smolensk, the Twenty-Ninth Bulletin. By an ironical coincidence it happened to be seven years to the day on which he had signed the flamboyant announcement of his victory at Austerlitz; but, for once, Napoleon seems to have had little difficulty in avoiding an evocation of past glories. 'I will tell all,' he declared to Caulaincourt. 'It is better that these details should be known from me than from private letters.'

The Twenty-Ninth Bulletin did not, of course, reveal the whole truth. It preserved the illusion of a great army falling back corps by corps and it made no mention of the fugitive horde trailing in its wake. Nevertheless, it admitted frankly that the survivors were exhausted and without the means of waging war. In less than two thousand words Napoleon described Ney's withdrawal across the Dnieper and the epic bridging of the Berezina. He told of the 30,000 horses which 'had perished within a few days'; of the

Cossacks 'making off, like Arabs in the desert, with all the waggons and carriages that strayed from the road'; of 'the cruel mischance' which had lost the Partouneaux division in the night near Borisov. But time and time again he emphasized one point – the severity of the weather and its effect on the troops:

> The frost, which had begun on November 7th, suddenly became more intense, and from November 14th to the 15th and the 16th, the temperature fell to 16°C. and 18°C. below freezing. . . This army, so splendid on the 6th was totally changed by the 14th, with almost no cavalry, no artillery, no transport. . . . Those men whom Nature had not hardened against all chances of fate and fortune seemed shaken; they lost their cheerfulness and good humour and saw ahead of them nothing but disaster and catastrophe. Those on whom she had bestowed superior powers kept up their spirits and normal disposition, seeing in the various ordeals a challenge to win new glory.

For an admission of failure there is no doubt that the Twenty-Ninth Bulletin was a remarkably stirring document. Yet the last sentence seems, at first glance, terrifyingly callous; for, after listing the sufferings of the men, the Bulletin concludes, 'His Majesty's health has never been better.' As a statement of fact, this was not far from the truth. At all events, the Emperor was certainly fitter than he had been in September. Care had been taken throughout the retreat to ensure his comfort. It was a question of honour for Duroc, his General Master of the Palace, Caulaincourt, his General Equerry, and, indeed, his personal servants. He continued to be served with his favourite Burgundy, Chambertin, and he was regularly supplied with white bread, rice and lentils, and beef or mutton. Moreover, although forced to travel on foot on dangerous stretches of road with a rough-hewn larch staff to hand, his carriages remained intact (even the one bearing his private commode). But the phrase was inserted in the Bulletin not to stress any distinction between commander-in-chief and ranker or Emperor and subject. It was intended to put an end to the rumours of his death, insanity or capture. Europe had to learn that although Fate may have struck hard blows at the army, she had decreed the Emperor's preservation; was he not, after all, the Man of Destiny?

Early on December 5 the Emperor reached the small town of Smorgonie. There he completed arrangements for his departure and for the future command of the Grand Army. His marshals accepted the need for him to return to Paris. Berthier was unhappy at not being allowed to accompany him, but Napoleon made it clear that he valued Berthier's staff work too highly to remove him from the army at this crisis in its fortunes. Selection of a commander-in-chief posed serious problems. Murat's relations with Davout were habitually strained and he had quarrelled with Eugène, but he was idolized by the troops and feared by the enemy. Ney had proved once more that he was a tenacious rearguard fighter, but he was angry with most of his fellow marshals, unable to speak to Davout except in choleric terms, and suspect as a commander of large units. There remained Berthier, who had been Napoleon's shadow for so long that it was hard to think of him as an independent commander, and Davout, whose appointment would have sent most of his fellow-marshals scurrying back across Europe in high dudgeon. Probably the wisest choice would have been Eugène, who had shown energy and resource throughout the retreat. He had, however, two disadvantages: his family relationship to the Emperor made men under-value his merits; and he was a comparatively junior field commander, never awarded a marshal's baton.

In the end, Napoleon sought the advice of Berthier (as so often). To Berthier it seemed that the natural leader was Murat, the only man apart from the Emperor himself to be a living legend. The other marshals did not share Berthier's confidence in Murat; they had no doubt of his courage in action, only of his common sense. Privately they made their views known to Napoleon, but he had made up his mind and was adamant – and in a hurry. Eugène even wrote a formal letter of protest to his step-father, receiving in reply a curt note of paternal rebuke. Murat was duly made commander-in-chief. It proved a disastrous appointment.

At ten o'clock that night, December 5, Napoleon left Smorgonie for Vilna and ultimately for Paris, eleven hundred miles away. There was no ceremonial; the departure was so sudden that poor General Mouton, who was to follow with Duroc and Fain in a second carriage, had no time to say farewell to his nephew. The Emperor travelled in one of his larger carriages with Caulaincourt as a companion and an escort of the Guard for the first stages of the journey. Beside him as an outrider was a courageous Polish noble-man, Count Dunin Wonsowicz, whom Napoleon had selected as an interpreter, for he spoke fluent German as well as his native language. The Emperor slept soundly as the cavalcade moved slowly through the snow-covered countryside.

The first halt was at Oszmiana, fifteen miles away, and they reached it at midnight. There Napoleon had a lucky escape. For at nightfall Seslavin's band of partisans had made a surprise raid on the town and the Russians were believed to be still in the vicinity, although by now some distance from the road. After a two-hour wait Napoleon set out again, this time accompanied by a hundred Polish lancers. But the horses kept slipping on the icy surface and, as they approached Vilna shortly before dawn, there were only fifteen men still with the carriage.

Napoleon was travelling incognito. He did not wish the people of Vilna to know that he had left the army and he refused to go into the town, contenting himself with a long interview with his foreign minister in one of the suburbs. At noon they were off once more, travelling all that Sunday through the region where young recruits had perished from hunger and cold and fatigue at night, even in June. Now, in the long hours of darkness, ice formed inside the Emperor's carriage and although he had fur boots, a heavy rug and woollen clothing, he was shivering desperately when they reached Kaunas at five on the following Monday morning. It had taken them seventeen hours to cover seventy miles. That same morning Napoleon took the road to Marienpol and re-crossed the Niemen, finally leaving the Russian Empire close to the spot where Eblé had built his pontoon bridges 166 days previously.

There are steep hills between Kaunas and Marienpol and with sheet-ice on the road it was hard going. At one point the Emperor and Caulaincourt had to get out of the carriage and help heave it up the slope. There seemed little prospect of getting through roads piled high in snow in so heavy a carriage. But at Gragow, a few miles beyond Marienpol, Caulaincourt was fortunate enough to discover a sledge. It was closed in but uncomfortable; it had, however, the great merit in the Emperor's eyes of running swiftly over the snow. Leaving a coachman to bring his carriage on to France later, Napoleon clambered into the cage-like box with Caulaincourt and Wonsowicz. No other members of the party which had left Smogornie could keep up with them. Travelling night and day, they began to make good progress across the Grand-Duchy of Warsaw. All the time, Napoleon talked incessantly – of the Continental System, of the wickedness of the English in forcing him to renew war after the Peace of Amiens, of a plan to convert the Senate into a House of Peers, of the restoration of Poland, of the absurd way the British were wasting men in the Iberian Peninsula, of the double-dealing of the Spanish rulers, and of Talleyrand's intrigues and cowardice. Occasionally his thoughts would wander back to the present campaign: 'It is the winter that has been our undoing. We are victims of the climate.' Carefully he was cultivating the legend implanted in the Twenty-Ninth Bulletin; pride in his own invincibility made him believe it.

On Thursday, December 10, Napoleon descended suddenly and unexpectedly on Warsaw, to rate his ambassador there, the Abbé Pradt, for having failed to induce the Poles to raise more troops – the phantom regiment of Polish Cossacks still obsessed him. But he stayed in Warsaw for only eight hours, setting out that night for Poznan and Silesia. With an ermine cap pulled down over his forehead and muffled in a cloak of green velvet, Napoleon sped over the Polish snows from relay-post to relay-post like one of his own couriers. Once, on the Friday, he thought of turning aside from the road and resting at the country house of Countess Walewska, who had borne him a son two years before – he was, in time, to become foreign minister under the Second Empire – but Caulaincourt had no taste for such distractions and they continued on their journey. (The Countess had, in fact, already gone to Paris with her child.)

With each mile that they travelled, the worm-eaten woodwork of the sledge box gaped wider and wider open, so that the icy wind swept in on them and they began to wonder if the whole vehicle would disintegrate before they reached the frontier. At Kutno it did, indeed, break and the Emperor turned his charm on two pretty Polish girls while a shaft was repaired. Dispatches and letters awaited them at Poznan and Napoleon relieved the tedium of the next stage by reading aloud to Caulaincourt the insipid banalities of Marie-Louise: 'Haven't I got an excellent wife?' he exclaimed proudly. There were some anxious moments as they crossed a strip of Prussia near Glogau, for Napoleon had little confidence in Prussian loyalty and Caulaincourt thought the men at the posting stations were unco-operative, but they arrived safely at the borders of Saxony (although once more the sledge shaft snapped). As darkness fell on December 13 they knew that they were approaching the Elbe and at midnight the ramshackle sledge lurched into the deserted streets of Dresden.

The Emperor was back in the city where he had held court to Europe seven months previously. Now no one met him. The weary travellers rode slowly through the town, hunting for the official residence of the French Minister. They could not find it, but at last Caulaincourt spotted one house with a light in an upper storey. Stiffly he clambered down and rang the bell. A window opened. 'The house of the French Minister?' he called up at a head in a nightcap. The window slammed down again; and it took them another hour to find their destination. But there was still no rest for one of the party. Wonsowicz was sent round to the King of Saxony's palace. Frederick-Augustus, always punctilious, hurried out of bed, called for a sedan chair from the public stand and was carried to the Emperor. It had been an exhausting night and Napoleon received his royal guest in bed. Outside in the antechamber dictated letters awaited signature: stern pleas to the rulers of Austria and Prussia, orders for Warsaw, and dispatches to be sent to Murat and Berthier – for somewhere, five hundred miles to the east, there remained the skeleton of an army.

Napoleon's departure had left most of the troops unmoved. To a few he had always seemed a talisman of success and they saw his absence as the final misfortune; but others were too occupied with their existence from hour to hour to be troubled by such affairs. With drifting snow piling up along the roads, questions of high policy appeared strangely irrelevant. The immediate task was to reach Vilna, somehow.

At various moments in the retreat, Napoleon had hoped to find a city in which his shattered army could rest and recuperate. Smolensk had proved to be a ruin and Vitebsk and Minsk had fallen into enemy hands before he could reach them. There remained, ultimately, only Vilna. Secure behind mediaeval walls and virtually undamaged in the summer campaign, Vilna seemed ideally suited for a convalescent fortress. With a massively defiant citadel, solid houses built of stone and not wood, ample supplies and a score of monastic buildings in which troops might be quartered, there appeared no reason why the city should not sustain a siege through the winter months until new armies, marching to its relief, began the campaign of 1813. Napoleon himself, knowing the condition of the troops, was in the later days far from optimistic; but, even so, he had told Berthier that he expected Murat to halt at Vilna for at least a week and probably for longer.

The administrative officials in Vilna had received more warning of the arrival of the army than the authorities in any of the other towns along the route; and they had systematically prepared to receive it. The city had enough meat and flour to feed the army for several months and considerable stores of clothing and equipment, including no less than 30,000 pairs of boots. The Governor of Vilna, the Dutch General, Dirk van Hogendorp, had requisitioned ruthlessly. All the monks were moved into one building and at the entrance to the town large posters informed the men of each army corps to which monastery they were to report. Had there remained any order or discipline in the army, it could have been re-organized before the Russians were able to offer any serious challenge.

The vanguard of Murat's army reached Vilna on December 8, the commander-in-chief travelling in a coach surrounded by the Guard, as the Emperor himself would have done. As they approached the town gates the crush produced chaos, with the fit caring only for themselves, as the stragglers had done on the banks of the Berezina.

Murat and Berthier were forced to go ahead on foot. There was no sign of order. Men sought shelter and food where they could. They seized brandy, and collapsed dead from the effect of the spirits on their weakened bodies. They warmed themselves in front of blazing fires, and frostbite turned to gangrene. Murat and Berthier found it impossible to check the chaos. By the time Davout arrived, he had to force his way in through a gap in the walls because the congestion in front of the gates and down the main streets was so bad. All orders were ignored and the system evolved by the Governor never had a chance to function. Berthier, normally so clear-headed and self-disciplined, was on the verge of a nervous collapse. Early next morning he wrote a dispatch for transmission to the Emperor: 'Sire, I must tell you the whole truth. The army is in a complete state of chaos. The soldiers cast aside their guns because they cannot hold them; officers and men think only of protecting themselves from the terrible cold.' The warning which Napoleon had sent to Maret on November 29 was fully justified: the army was certainly 'not a fine sight.'

Lyautey had been impressed when, at Oszmiana, his battery had been met by fresh troops sent out from the Vilna garrison to assist the army back into the town. 'We were surprised,' he wrote, 'at the quality of their bearing.' But two nights of bitter cold sapped their morale and they were soon absorbed in the general misery and chaos. Castellane was amazed at the contrasts within the city: at the Governor's palace he dined well, with good wine and cream in his coffee; out in the streets it seemed as if some hideous carnival were in progress.

All that day and the next the sound of gunfire could be heard above the din in the city. Cossack horsemen and partisan detachments were at the approaches, some with light cannon mounted on sledges. Seslavin's band even pushed within the city boundary on December 9, but there were too few of them to constitute a serious menace and they were thrown out again. Orderlies brought disturbing news from Ney's rearguard to the commander-in-chief, and Murat was at his wit's end. This was not the type of warfare to which he was accustomed. That evening there was a general alert and his nerve cracked. He dared not risk the Russians gaining control of the hills along the road to Kaunas. Giving orders for the city to be evacuated that night, he hurried to the gates and Berthier dispatched the indefatigable Eblé to blow up the stores of ammunition in the arsenal. Castellane noted in his diary, as if he could not believe it, the panic which had seized Murat and Berthier. By the next morning they were on their way to Kaunas. Thousands of sick men were left in Vilna to await the coming of the Russians; most of them perished.

The road to Kaunas had been hard going for Napoleon and Caulaincourt; it was to prove impassable for most of the guns and waggons still remaining with the army. Five miles out of Vilna there is a steep hill. Loose snow lay over a sheet of ice and the horses could get no footing. Cossack raiders were in the adjoining woods and Platov was skirmishing constantly with Ney and the rearguard. It was impossible to save the guns and only a few waggons could be dragged over the hill. Even the army pay-chests were abandoned. When Platov appeared, the French fled wildly towards Kaunas, only the attraction of loot saving them from the Cossack riders on their light ponies.

By the time Murat reached Kaunas, the Niemen was completely frozen over and the town seemed indefensible. As at Vilna, there was plenty of food and clothing and some artillery. Berthier gave orders for the men to be re-armed but, as the troops received their muskets, they threw them away again and went in search of food and spirits. Half-drunk and half-dazed the troops made for the bridge, few realizing that they could just as easily cross the river on the ice. Once more men were trampled under foot as the horde surged around the bridgehead. In despair, Murat wrote to the Emperor: 'Every human effort to check the disorder is hopeless: one can only resign oneself.' And placing a battery on the left bank of the river to cover Ney and the only troops who still showed any spirit, he crossed the Niemen on December 13 to set out out for Königsberg.

As on the Dnieper, so on the Niemen it was left to Marshal Ney to offer the last resistance. He reached Kaunas, with Platov and the Cossacks hard on his heels, just as Murat was crossing the river. He had several thousand men with him, but probably little more than 800 who were in any condition to fight. Throughout the day he held off his pursuers, even when they went over the Niemen and began to harass him from the western bank. Then after dark he crossed the river into Prussian territory, the last of the invaders to

Marshal Ney

Napoleon, by Meissonnier

leave the Tsar's Empire. It was December 14 – and from Dresden, as though from some other world, there were dispatches on the way for 'King Murat', commander-in-chief of an army that had ceased to exist.

Napoleon remained in the French Minister's home in Dresden for only five hours. With Wonsowicz and Caulaincourt he left it before dawn on December 14 – the same dawn in which Ney was seeking to rally the rearguard in Kaunas. The sledge was by now such a wreck that it was abandoned and they travelled in one of the King of Saxony's carriages, mounted on runners so as to glide easily over the snow. Once more Napoleon talked endlessly, a verbal autobiography to while away the hours and prevent his mind from pondering the imponderable. That evening they rested at Leipzig – it was a city he was to see again in ten months' time – and then drove on through the night into Thuringia, where the snow was less deep and the runners snapped off the carriage. At Erfurt they obtained a landau and travelled in comfort towards the French frontier. On December 16, just short of the Rhine, they met Montesquiou returning from Paris where, on the previous day, he had broken the news of the victory of the Berezina. Now he followed them back to the capital. Napoleon was well satisfied. The Twenty-Ninth Bulletin would be published the next day. The French people would look for details of his triumph and, before they had taken in the horrors of the retreat, he would descend unexpectedly upon them, reflected in glory.

At Mayence – Mainz – Napoleon was back on what he regarded as the soil of France, counting the hours that it would take them to reach the Tuileries. They supped at Verdun, where he gave an audience to old Kellermann, who had saved the Revolution at Valmy a generation ago, and on December 18 they began to follow the Marne through the steep wooded hills to Château-Thierry. But the pace was too fast for the landau. Barely fifty miles from Paris, the axle broke and at Meaux Napoleon was forced to transfer into an old posting-chaise, a cumbersome carriage swinging between two enormous wheels.

Now at last he was approaching Paris. Eagerly anticipating a rapturous welcome, he had changed into the green uniform of the Foot-Grenadiers, although he was still muffled in a heavy velvet cloak. Shortly before midnight the posting-chaise swung under the Arc du Carrousel at the gallop and through the main gateway into the Tuileries. No sentry halted them and they walked unchallenged down the colonnade to the Empress's apartments. Caulaincourt tapped on the glass door. A porter in a nightshirt emerged; he could not recognize the strangers in the dim candlelight and fetched his wife. Napoleon stepped forward and threw back his cloak. 'It is He Himself,' exclaimed the porter's wife, in consternation, 'it is the Emperor.' The cry was taken up around the palace. Someone hastened to awaken Marie-Louise; and Napoleon sent Caulaincourt off to get some rest. The great adventure, which had begun as a Carolingian epic, was to end like an Italian opera.

15

Laurels and Legends

The Russian campaign was over. Napoleon had lost nearly half a million men and over 150,000 horses. Probably as many as a thousand guns had been destroyed and countless waggons and supply depots had gone up in smoke. By the time the Emperor reached Paris, the survivors of the retreat, some 20,000 in all, were making their way back to Königsberg, Marienwerder and Thorn or across the Polish lands to the Vistula. There were still 40,000 men on the river Bug – mainly Schwarzenberg's Austrians who had fallen back to Bielystok from the Pripet Marshes – and another 25,000 under Marshal Macdonald in front of Riga. But, otherwise, all that remained of the Grand Army were captives. Yet, if the campaign had ended, the war had not. Within sixteen months the Russian Army was to advance from the Niemen to the Seine and Tsar Alexander was to become the first foreign conqueror to enter Paris since Henry v of England, four centuries before.

Throughout the weeks of Napoleon's retreat the Tsar had remained in the Winter Palace at St Petersburg and taken no part in military operations. Before Tarutino he had approved the general strategic plan drawn up by his advisers for cutting off the Grand Army as it passed through the district of the long rivers, west of Smolensk; but thereafter he was prepared to pray for victory and await an answer to his supplications. Sometimes he would send off an astringent dispatch to Kutuzov or busy himself with administrative details; but on most days he spent hours poring over the maps in his study, impatiently wondering why no news of Napoleon's capture had reached him. At last, on December 18, that same Friday on which the Emperor was completing his journey to Paris, Alexander set out for the headquarters of his army. Travelling by way of Polotsk, he arrived at Vilna on December 23, three days before his thirty-fifth birthday. There Kutuzov awaited him, having reached the town with the main body of his army on December 13.

The Tsar and his commander-in-chief had not met since the black days of August; and in Vilna they greeted each other with every outward display of courtesy and mutual admiration. They embraced; they wept tears of gratitude and relief. There were formal banquets, ceremonial investitures, elegant balls. And all the while the two men continued to distrust each other, knowing that they could never forget the tensions of the recent past, nor agree on conduct for the immediate future. The Russian people had needed a saviour and now that the French had withdrawn from the lands of the empire they believed that they had found one in Kutuzov. His policy – it could not in all honesty be called a strategy – had ended in the triumph of liberation; as he had foreseen amid the despair of Fili, the sponge had absorbed the torrent. But Alexander had wished for something more dramatic. He had dreamt of receiving Napoleon's sword in surrender; he had hoped to arrive at his frontier as the arbiter of Europe. Now, instead of celebrating a decisive victory, he was to end the year snowbound in the city where he had waited at midsummer, uncertain, as he had been then, of the effectiveness of his army in battle or of the wisdom of taking the initiative.

Real differences of policy separated the two men. Kutuzov was convinced that his task, and that of the men he commanded, was done. Russia had saved herself by her exertions; was it in her interest to save Europe by her example? To liberate the German lands would be to entangle Russia in problems for which she had no solution and from which only the other peoples of the continent could benefit; her true destiny lay in Asia. Alexander, and all who had been with him in St Petersburg, thought otherwise: he wished to end French hegemony for all time; to assert the might of the State Peter had created and Catherine had built up over the centuries; and to ensure that in the vacuum caused by the fall of Bonaparte, the head of the House of Romanov-Holstein should be accepted as the new Augustus. In time, Alexander's ambition was to prove of greater moment for Europe and for Russia than Napoleon's march to Moscow. The Romanov dynasty could never free itself again from the affairs of the West – nor, indeed, prevent its subjects from receiving and absorbing western ideas.

But it was by no means certain, in December 1812, that Russia was in a position to carry the war into Prussia and the Grand-Duchy of Warsaw. For the Russians, too, had suffered in the preceding months. General Wilson estimated at the time that Kutuzov's army had sustained 45,000 casualties since leaving Krasnoe, and the Soviet historian Predtechensky maintains that two-thirds of the Russian troops who marched from Tarutino to Vilna were lost, the majority of them sick in hospital and in no fit state to take part in any military enterprise for some months to come. There were some 35,000 men watching Macdonald's corps around Riga and Schwarzenberg's troops on the river Bug, but they were heavily outnumbered by the forces opposed to them. The combined Russian armies in the Vilna area totalled no more than 65,000 men that Christmas, of whom 27,500 were directly under Kutuzov and the rest fairly evenly divided between Chichagov and Wittgenstein. Ten thousand recruits were on their way from depots within Russia, but according to Wilson only 1,500 completed the journey and many of them were too ill for active service when they reached Vilna. It was hardly an impressive vanguard with which to undertake the liberation of Europe.

Yet on January 15, 1813, Alexander sent his troops across the Niemen in pursuit of the French and 'to liberate from oppression and misery even those nations who have taken up arms against Russia.' Tired, worn-out and fearful of what would happen that summer if Napoleon could take the field with a new army, Kutuzov followed in their wake, still nominally their commander but too ill to assert himself.

Alexander had counted on dissension among Napoleon's allies; and he was right. On the last day of 1812 General Yorck, who commanded the contingent of 18,000 Prussians in Macdonald's corps, reached an accommodation with the Russians by which his men would withdraw from the war, holding the area between Memel and Tilsit as neutral territory. His king, Frederick William III (the 'blockhead drill-sergeant' whom Napoleon had treated with such patronizing contempt at Dresden in May) hesitated to support Yorck; but, sensing the mood of his subjects, he fled from Berlin to join the Tsar at Kalisch in what had been Prussian Poland. On March 16 Prussia duly declared war on France. Slowly Europe was turning against Napoleon, now that the Russian disasters had destroyed the myth of his invincibility. Swedish troops at last crossed the Baltic and it was clear that the Austrians, although still nominally allied to Napoleon, would make little more contribution to his campaigns.

Napoleon, however, had over-awed all outward discontent at home. By the spring of 1813 he had raised another army to fight in Germany. It was a remarkable achievement of improvisation. Half-trained conscripts were thrown into new regiments, veterans were summoned back from retirement, men were drafted from the National Guard, from the gendarmerie and even from the navy. Some – although in Berthier's opinion not enough – were withdrawn from Spain. Napoleon buried himself in work as though the business of war would consume the shame of the winter's privations. By April 15, when he left Paris, he had completed arrangements for concentrating a quarter of a million men between the Elbe and the Main. They were short of cavalry, they were short of guns, and for the most part short of experience; but they still outnumbered the combined Russian and Prussian armies by two to one. A decisive victory in Thuringia or Saxony would enable the Emperor to impose peace on continental Europe. Perhaps even now he could do something for Poland; for as he journeyed that Spring down the familiar road towards Saxony – it was a month earlier than in 1812 – much of his old confidence returned and he seemed to look upon the new campaign as a resumption of the 'Second Polish War,' which had begun with such an eloquent proclamation in June and lost itself in the smoke of Smolensk in August.

Thuringia was a region over which armies had marched many times in the past. Napoleon himself knew it well: at Erfurt he had acted as host to the Tsar in 1808; and farther to the east were the wooded slopes around Jena and Auerstadt where the Prussians were routed in 1806. But this time, on May 2, the opposing armies met near Leipzig, at Lützen, where Gustavus Adolphus of Sweden had been killed in battle in the Thirty Years' War. Once more Ney and the Guard clashed with the Russian Grenadiers, while concentrated artillery fire was loosed on Blücher's Prussians. Once more Napoleon rode among his conscripts, willing them into battle. And once more the French were left in command of the field with the Prussians and Russians retiring chastened across the Elbe and towards Silesia. Yet it was a tactical success rather than a victory; for the horses and riders who should have turned Lützen into a second Jena had perished in the winter snows. Without cavalry to pursue the defeated enemy there could be no final triumph.

At Lützen many former antagonists had found themselves renewing old conflicts: Ney and Wintzingerode; Oudinot and Wittgenstein; Lauriston and Tormassov; while, behind the battle line, Eugène and Miloradovich waited in reserve. But on both sides names were missing: Eblé had died of exhaustion in East Prussia; Admiral Chichagov was back in the Admiralty building at St Petersburg; Davout was keeping order in northern Germany; and Murat, after handing over his command to Eugène early in January, had retired to his kingdom of Naples. By now Kutuzov, too, had passed into legend. Throughout the early months of the year the old man had followed his troops gloomily into the German lands – 'We can cross the Elbe all right, but before long we shall re-cross it with a bloody nose,' he had predicted in March – but it was a hard winter for a veteran of sixty-eight and, on April 28, he died at Bunzlau in Prussian Silesia. There was genuine grief among the Russian troops and a less sincere display of sentiment on the part of the Tsar. It was not easy to find an acceptable successor. Alexander himself wanted Wittgenstein to be given command of both the Russian and Prussian armies, a proposal which King Frederick William was prepared to accept. But Miloradovich and Tormassov, who were both senior to Wittgenstein, resented his elevation. After a month of compromise and experiment, Alexander summoned Barclay de Tolly from St Petersburg, although the Tsar himself reserved the right to take final decisions over tactics and general strategy.

When Barclay reached headquarters the campaign appeared to be going badly for the Russians. On May 23 Napoleon won another victory at Bautzen, thirty-five miles east of Dresden, and Barclay considered retreating into Poland; it was, after all, the direction in which he was accustomed to travel. But Napoleon was once again unable to exploit his success. Now he was not only short of cavalry but of ammunition as well, and supplies were no longer coming through regularly from Paris. His marshals were sick of war, and there was no enthusiasm for the campaign in metropolitan France. Hence on June 4 he concluded an armistice with the Russians and the Prussians, hoping that it might lead to a general peace. It was, as he later admitted, a political and military blunder.

The Allies assumed that if Napoleon wished for a truce, his position must be weaker than it appeared. They benefited more than the French from the ten-week respite from battle. For the Armistice ended with a decisive addition to the manpower of the allied forces. Late in June, while a twenty-five-mile no man's land kept the opposing armies apart, Napoleon received the Austrian Foreign Minister, Metternich, at the Marcolini Palace outside Dresden. It was a stormy interview. At one point Napoleon angrily hurled his hat across the room: 'A man such as I am cares little for the life of a million men,' he shouted at Metternich, in an almost hysterical gesture of defiance. But Metternich, coldly assessing every variation in temperament, was not impressed. He was convinced that Napoleon's system was about to collapse and when he returned to Vienna he urged the Emperor Francis to break with his son-in-law. On August 12 Austria formally declared war on France; and Schwarzenberg, now thrown into opposition to Napoleon, led an army of more than 200,000 men across the borders of Bohemia to march on Dresden. The Second Polish War remained a historical curiosity; the German States were fighting for their liberation; and the French for survival.

There followed another seven months of war. Napoleon conducted the campaign brilliantly. In the last week of August he saved Dresden in a striking victory against the Austrians, Russians and Prussians; and, as the allied sovereigns saw through their glasses the long dark line of the Old Guard sweeping down the hill to the bridge over the Elbe, their nerves were shaken and they thought ominously of Austerlitz and Friedland and Wagram. But, if the old master could still conjure up magic, the gift had deserted his subordinate commanders and they fared dismally. As more and more German satellites cautiously cast aside his authority, Napoleon fell back on Leipzig. There, for three days in the middle of October, the nations clashed in battle. It made little difference to the French that the Saxons belatedly changed their allegiance while the fighting was in progress. If the Almighty was on the side of the big battalions, then an allied victory was predestined, for they had reinforcements ready and the French had not. A terrified corporal blew up the one remaining bridge before the French rearguard had crossed to safety. Macdonald successfully swam the Elster; Poniatowski, awarded a marshal's baton only a few days previously and wounded three times in the battle, was drowned; and 15,000 Frenchmen were taken prisoner. The rest fled westwards in disorder to protect their frontiers from invasion. When Napoleon finally crossed the Rhine on November 2 he had only 70,000 men still under arms; and typhus was raging among his troops.

Tsar Alexander pressed for an immediate invasion of France, but the Austrian and Prussian generals showed more circumspection. There was a pause for fruitless negotiation. At the end of November Caulaincourt was made Foreign Minister and for four months he did what he could to save Napoleon's throne and the natural boundaries of France. But no diplomatic skill could shake the Tsar's determination to seek retribution for the fall of Moscow by accepting the surrender of Paris; and as 1814 broke on a war-weary Europe the fighting still went on.

There were moments of panic in February as Napoleon won victories at Montmirail and Montereau and the invaders fell back on Langres. Even after the Allies resumed their advance on March 1 he still had hopes of cutting their communications and throwing them back across the Rhine in confusion. Perhaps he might have done; but luck – or caution – had deserted him by now. On March 23 a hurried note to Marie-Louise informed her of his plans; but the message was captured by a Cossack patrol; and the Allies were left in no doubt of his intentions. But what should they do? Their headquarters were at Vitry, a hundred miles from Paris. Ought they to march on the capital, or engage Napoleon? Schwarzenberg and

Blücher hesitated, but not the Tsar. That day he had received a message from inside Paris: 'You are groping about like children. You ought to stride forward on stilts. You are in the position to achieve anything that you wish to achieve.' It was unsigned; but the handwriting appeared to be Talleyrand's. The Allies pressed on to Paris itself; and on March 31 the Tsar was received by Talleyrand in the centre of the city. The flames of Moscow had, indeed, been avenged.

On April 6 his marshals induced Napoleon to sign an act of abdication. For a fortnight he lingered on at Fontainebleau, with Caulaincourt once more his main companion and only loyal associate. One night he swallowed the phial of poison he had ordered to be prepared after his narrow escape from capture on the eve of Maloyaroslavets. It made him sick, but in eighteen months it had lost all its potency and he survived. At last, on April 20, he said farewell to the Old Guard in the courtyard of the palace and set out through the forest on the long journey to Fréjus and Elba. Across the Belgian frontier King Louis XVIII, gross, old and almost forgotten, awaited a summons to the throne he had claimed for nineteen years. 'There is only one step,' Napoleon had remarked to Caulaincourt on the sledge, 'from the sublime to the ridiculous.'

Paris that spring had a disconcerting air of sublimated festivity. Its streets were filled with strange uniforms and improbable guests had moved into unlikely residences. Thirty-five thousand men marched past the Tsar and the King of Prussia, while in the square where Louis XVI had been guillotined Russian church dignitaries offered a solemn thanksgiving to God for the downfall of tyranny. Wellington came up from Toulouse, where the British redcoats had ended the Peninsular War; his blue frock-coat appeared oddly restrained as he moved among the green and gold of the Russian staff officers or the pantaloons and Circassian cloaks of the Cossacks. Napoleonic veterans were there, too, accustoming themselves uncomfortably to a new allegiance. There were at times moments of embarrassment;

thus Major Castellane noted in his diary that when he saluted Louis XVIII with a dutiful *'Vive le Roi!'* his column responded with the habitual full-throated roar, *'Vive l'Empereur!'*; and not all such errors were accidental. Nobility of the old and new dispensations met at ceremonial receptions, but mutual hostility kept them apart. Men who had fought for the Emperor found it easier to fraternize with the Russians than share in the celebrations of the returned émigrés. For the Tsar, at any rate, made little secret of his contempt for King Louis and the whole Bourbon baggage-train.

Alexander had marched on Paris in a sense of righteous vengeance, sustaining his wrath by a frequent reading of the Ninetieth Psalm. But, with a characteristically swift change of role, he was soon claiming to be the city's guardian and protector. All his actions were agreeable to the people of Paris. He walked without escort through the streets. He was seen at one of the balls to be partnering the Princesse de la Moskowa (as Madame Ney had become on the Marshal's return from Russia). He spoke to Lafayette of the need to abolish serfdom and to Kosciuszko of the merits of a free Poland. He visited the Empress Marie-Louise at Rambouillet and the Empress Josephine at Malmaison, and he was soon on terms of personal friendship with Josephine's children, ex-Queen Hortense and ex-Viceroy Eugène. When Josephine died of pneumonia at the end of May, the Tsar was genuinely moved; he despatched Russian guardsmen to escort her coffin to its resting place at Rueil. He proclaimed himself the friend of the French nation; and the French nation, singularly friendless that summer, took him at his word and to its heart.

Nor was his personal triumph limited to France, for in those months of relief and celebration, liberals everywhere hailed the ruler of All the Russias as their new Messiah. Already across the Atlantic he had received the accolade of virtue from the Federalists of New England. At a banquet in the Exchange Coffee House at Boston he had been lauded by the Honourable Harrison Otis and prayed for by Dr Channing; and, to the irritation of President Madison, the victories of the Russian armies were ostentatiously celebrated in Georgetown, D.C. To some, especially in Baltimore, it seemed treasonable to praise the ally of George III when the United States was still at war with Britain; but there was always hope that this 'wise and glorious Friend' might mediate in the senseless conflict.

On June 6, 1814, the Tsar and the King of Prussia crossed the Channel to Dover. It was a gusty day and Alexander was unceremoniously seasick. But his subsequent reception by the people of London offered adequate compensation for the indignities of the voyage. For three weeks *The Times* chronicled his peregrination with unctuous awe: his visits to Westminster and Greenwich, to the British Museum and the Royal Exchange; his religious devotions at the Russian Chapel and at a Quaker meeting-house; the day at Ascot races and the day at Oxford University; every trivial detail was reverently noted with the care of a hagiographer. He stayed at the Pulteney Hotel in Piccadilly: 'On ascending the steps of his hotel,' the readers of *The Times* were informed, 'His Imperial Majesty turned round to the people and condescendingly took off his hat.' There were banquets and visits to the theatre. On June 11 the audience of the King's Theatre in Haymarket applauded at the sight of his robes of scarlet and gold. It was a strange transformation for the frightened fugitive from Kammionyi Island – and the Prince Regent raged in a fury of jealousy and frustration.

Alexander, more than any of the other foreign visitors, shone with the lustre of victory. But the British people were also generous to the Russian troops who had elevated the Tsar to his position of predominance. On June 20 representatives of all the allied armies paraded in Hyde Park, but the loudest cheers were reserved for the Russians and more especially for the Cossack horsemen; for, coloured with the mystery of Asia, the Cossacks had captured the imagination of the city. Their leader, Platov, was fêted as though he were a commander-in-chief. He was honoured with a special performance at the Theatre Royal, Covent Garden, on June 21 in which – it was an odd choice – Grimaldi appeared in *Mother Goose* and there was a topical curtain-raiser *Fontainebleau or Our Way in France*. For a brief moment that June the hopes of the British public for a lasting peace seemed to rest in the Tsar's sense of divine mission. It was a union of illusions and autocracy; and it was far too good to last.

The marriage, in fact, barely survived its London honeymoon. Even before Alexander left Dover on June 27, it was noticed that he was no longer receiving such uninhibited adulation from the crowd, and his public and private remarks had alienated both the Tory Government and their Whig opponents. It was difficult to deal with a prophet who knew that the Almighty was a Russian and who sensed that His Ways, though mysterious, invariably provided for the spread of Russia's boundaries in Europe. As the peace congress began to assemble in Vienna that autumn, the distrust felt for the Tsar by the British ministers began to harden. In September the Prime Minister, Lord Liverpool, even went so far as to damn Alexander as 'half an American'; and by the end of the year the British were so alarmed at the Tsar's machinations in central Europe that they were prepared to conclude a secret agreement with the Austrians and the French to prevent the attainment of his objectives in Poland. There was a brief relaxation of tension during the Hundred Days, when Napoleon's return from Elba bound the Allies together once more and Barclay held an army in reserve in Saxony. But after Waterloo, with Napoleon secure on St Helena and a Russian army of occupation again in Paris, the latent suspicion speedily asserted itself; and every move in Russian diplomacy for the following decade seemed to justify it.

Public opinion moved less speedily than the British Government, but in time it went much further in denunciation of 'the barbarians of the North.' For gradually the English press began to realize that a new power, with countless reserves of cannon-fodder, had swept across Europe and reached the Channel coast. It was a rude awakening but, as though embarrassed by its earlier facile infatuation, the liberal press began to blacken everything Russian and see Russian intrigues in the remotest corners of the globe. No less a person than General Wilson joined the panic-mongers when he became a Whig member of Parliament in 1818. Although he delighted in wearing the insignia of a Knight Grand Cross of the Order of St Anne of Russia and of the Military Order of St George of Russia (Third Class), Wilson had no hesitation in warning the public of Russia's pretensions. He published a book in which, from his personal knowledge, he predicted a descent on India, the seizure of Constantinople, and the dominance of central Europe as stages towards mastery of the world by the rulers in St Petersburg. It was, in fact, Wilson who first conjured up the Russian bogey. Probably his creation was hardly more real than the idealized picture of Alexander in 1814; but it was to haunt England for many generations, until people forgot how it had come into being. Thus, in a curious way, fear of the limitless power of Russia became the final legacy of the Moscow campaign to European diplomacy.

Napoleon died on his granite rock in the South Atlantic in 1821, maintaining that a century later, with Europe overrun by the Russians, the English people would declare, 'Napoleon was right.' Some of his main lieutenants had pre-deceased him: Ney and Murat were shot as rebels in 1815; and Berthier, too, had died that summer, falling from a window in Saxony as he watched Russian cavalry marching off to meet the threat of the Hundred Days. Each year seemed to claim a distinguished name: Davout died in 1823, Eugène in 1824, Caulaincourt in 1827, Lauriston (in a dancer's dressing-room at the Opera) in 1828. And Napoleon's enemies were dying, too: Barclay de Tolly in 1818; Schwarzenberg in 1820; Rostopchin and Bennigsen in 1826. Tsar Alexander, mysterious to the grave and beyond it, was said to have collapsed suddenly at Taganrog on December 1, 1825, but there were strange tales that he had become a hermit and lived on in the wastes of Siberia for another forty years – a story which continues to intrigue Russian historians even in the nineteen-sixties. General Miloradovich became the one victim of the Decembrist revolt which followed within a fortnight of the Tsar's reputed death; and Admiral Chichagov settled in England, gave up his Russian nationality and lived the life of a country gentleman until 1849.

Some names from the past continued to exercise authority long after Napoleon's death – Metternich, for example, remained in power until 1848 and did not die until 1859. And there were others, less eminent, survivors who were still to win distinction; Castellane, who served successive rulers of France in Spain and Algeria and organized the defences of both Paris and Lyons, was made a marshal on the very day the Second Empire was proclaimed, December 2, 1852. He lived for another ten years, dying on the fiftieth anniversary of that September night when he had sought refuge from the flames of Moscow. Captain Lyautey, too, fought in Spain and Algeria and was promoted to General by Napoleon III. Ségur, on the other hand, lived out his life in the afterglow of the Russian campaign. He wrote his account of the expedition as early as 1825, was challenged to a duel by General Gourgaud for slighting the memory of the Emperor, was wounded, and survived until 1873, dying, aged ninety-two, a month later than Napoleon III.

It is, of course, difficult to trace what happened to the men in the ranks. In many country towns they were honoured figures, for by the eighteen-thirties the march to Moscow and its aftermath had become a romantic epic, as legendary as the victories of the Sun King. It was commemorated by cheap colour prints, by the light verses of Béranger and the heavy odes of Hugo, and by the novels of Stendhal (himself a veteran) and of Balzac. It was Balzac who, in *Le Médecin de Campagne* (1832) created Grenadier Goguelat, who could hold the villagers of Dauphine spell-bound as he told them of the magic appeal of the Emperor:

> Then there comes this call from him for us to go off and conquer Moscow, after all the other capitals, because Moscow has allied itself to England. Kings flock in to lick his boots – it's hard to say who isn't there! He wants to raise the Poles from their depths and they are our brothers. But then the mysterious Man in Red, who has crossed his path more than once before, warns him that friends will betray him and men abandon him. Moscow: the fire; the terrible retreat. They say he wept each night for his poor family of soldiers.

It was a simple but effective tale and Balzac had, no doubt, met many Goguelats in the provinces of France. One of them at least was induced three years after Balzac's novel was published to write down his reminiscences; for Sergeant Bourgogne had returned safely to Condé, his home near Valenciennes. During the last months of the Empire Bourgogne was granted a commission, but in later years it was the memory of his rank in the Imperial Guard that he cherished. He lived on until 1867, dying near St Omer, where young Philippe Pétain was at school.

In Paris the men who had been on the great retreat could be seen for years around the Palais Royal, gaunt figures, sometimes limping and often with fingers missing. There they frequented the Bonapartist Café Lemblin, where a veteran from Provence maintained the comradeship of the Grand Army over wine-stained tables and draught-boards. Once at least the survivors of the Old Guard went on parade: for in 1840 the Emperor's body was brought back from St Helena to the Invalides, and the grenadiers stood in homage beside the massive tomb which had been presented by Alexander's brother, Tsar Nicholas I. Napoleon had wished his ashes to 'rest on the banks of the Seine'; he could hardly have foreseen that they would be enclosed within fifteen feet of porphyry, stone from the Russian Empire. It was, perhaps, the last irony of the campaign.

Notes on Sources

(For full details of the books and articles listed below, see the Bibliography)

CHAPTER ONE: DRESDEN

For references to Napoleon's movements I have used L. P. Garros, *Itinéraire de Napoléon,* throughout the narrative, as it corrects and amplifies many of the earlier accounts; the Dresden interlude is covered on pages 369-373. There is considerable memoir material on the Dresden Congress: Fain, *Manuscrit,* vol. 1, pp. 61-69; Metternich, vol. 1, pp. 151-153; Caulaincourt, pp. 108-109; and Castellane, pp. 92-96. See also the article by Baron de Casse, which is based on the memoirs of the Queen of Westphalia. Additional material on Maret is in Ernouf, pp. 379-380 and 384. For the impression made by the Congress on a young citizen of Dresden, see Kügelgen, pp. 110-114. The most detailed historical account of the Congress is in Vandal, pp. 402-425.

For Alexander at Vilna, see the biographies of the Tsar by Strakhorsky, pp. 118-119; Almedingen, p. 129; and Waliszewski, pp. 13-18. A more personal impression of Alexander at this time is given by Countess Choiseul-Gouffier, pp. 9-10 and 27-28.

Narbonne's visit to Vilna is fully covered in the memoirs of his son-in-law, Rambuteau, pp. 67-68. For his subsequent report to Napoleon, see Fain, *Manuscrit,* vol. 1, p. 77.

CHAPTER TWO: THE UNDECLARED WAR

The general background of Franco-Russian relations is ably summarized in J. M. Thompson, *Napoleon Bonaparte,* pp. 310-325, and in chapter 9 of Geoffrey Bruun. For the Russian side, see the earlier chapter of Lobanov-Rostovsky. The fullest analytical treatment for the years 1807 to 1812 is in the 1,500 pages of Vandal; there are shrewd judgments on this classical work in Pieter Geyl, pp. 193-194 and 217-219. For the attitude of British public opinion towards Alexander, see Anderson, *Britain's Discovery*, pp. 213-214.

Alexander's letters to his sister were published by Grand-Duke Nicholas Mikhailovitch; the letter of Christmas 1810 is printed on p. 47. For Napoleon's contempt for Alexander in June 1811, see Caulaincourt, p. 71, and Vandal, p. 185. For Napoleon's Indian ambitions, see Tarlé, pp. 40-41 (English version, pp. 54-55) and Wilson's *Narrative*, p. 275; the quotation on his earlier dreams of 'marching into Asia' is from Rémusat, vol. 1, p. 274.

For the Kurakin interview of August 15, 1811 and the Council of State of the following day, see Vandal, pp. 211-216, and Caulaincourt, pp. 86-87. There is a translation of Napoleon's request for books on Russia in Thompson, *Napoleon's Letters*, pp. 263-264. On his intensive activity in preparation for the invasion, see Vandal, pp. 229-235, and *Correspondance*, vol. 23, nos. 18140, 18170, 18281, 18300, 18333, 18337, 18355, 18356, 18386 and 18400.

Alexander's activities in 1812 are covered by Almedingen, pp. 125-126, and Vandal, pp. 235-239. On the influence of Stein and the German exiles, see the article by H. A. Schmitt. On details of the historical architecture of St Petersburg (and later of Moscow) I have used the volume in the *Pelican History of Art* by G. H. Hamilton; Dr Hamilton points out, for example, on p. 182 that it was only in the nineteenth century that the Winter Palace was re-painted so as to give it the famous rust-red frontage. On Colonel Pfuel, see the caustic remarks of Clausewitz, p. 5, and of Waliszewski, pp. 22-26 and Tarlé, pp. 51-52 (English version, pp. 32-33). Vandal deals with the Tchernishev affair, pp. 41-42, 127-134 and especially pp. 311-322; and of Ernouf, pp. 345-348. On Kurakin's last efforts for a settlement, see Vandal, pp. 396-400.

Napoleon's letter of May 30 to Marie-Louise is no. 24 of the *Lettres*, p. 28, and of June 1, no. 27, p. 31. Napoleon's peripatetic writing habits are discussed by Fain, *Memoirs*, pp. 273-274. Fain records his delight at the Polish spring in *Manuscrit*, vol. 1, p. 80. Castellane notes his abrupt departure from Dresden on p. 96 of his *Journal*, his dislike of the Polish lands on p. 97, and of Posen on p. 98.

For Napoleon at Posen, see Brandt, p. 230; and for the *Chant du Départ,* Brandt, p. 232. For the pride of the artillery major at Thorn, Vandal, p. 241. Details of the movements from Dresden to the Niemen are in Garros, pp. 373-377.

Caulaincourt discusses Napoleon's meeting with Murat on pp. 115-117. For Davout, see Ségur, vol. I, pp. 97-104. On Davout and Murat, see Macdonell, p. 247. For the racial composition of the Grand Army, see Esposito and Elting, p. 107, and Wilson, *Narrative,* p. 12. On the enthusiasm of the troops for Napoleon in June 1812, see Caulaincourt, p. 118, and Bourgoing, *Souvenirs,* p. 69. On the Emperor's way of greeting veterans, see Ségur, vol. I, pp. 105-106.

Bourgogne's succinct analysis of the French soldier's character is on p. 27 of his *Memoirs.* The letters of the fusilier who thought he was going to India are quoted in Vandal, p. 454.

There is an eye-witness account of Napoleon's activities at Wilkowiszki in the Butkevicius memoirs which form the basis of the article by Martel. The proclamation of June 24, 1812, has often been quoted: conveniently, it may be found in C. de Grunwald, p. 15, or Ségur, vol. I, p. 115.

On preparations for the crossing of the Niemen, see Napoleon's instructions in *Correspondance,* vol. 23, no. 18839. The incident with the Polish priest is in Castellane, p. 104. On the weather, see *Lettres à Marie-Louise,* no. 41, p. 44. For Napoleon's use of a Polish uniform, see Castellane, p. 104, and *Correspondance,* vol. 23, no. 18755. There is a military assessment of the problems involved in the crossing in Bonnal, pp. 68-69. For Napoleon's fall from his horse, see Caulaincourt, pp. 119-120 and Ségur, vol. I, p. 121. The most interesting accounts of the crossing of the Niemen are in Soltyk, pp. 8-10; Dupuy, p. 166; Montesquiou, pp. 206-207; Denniée, pp. 17-18; and the first of the Lyautey articles, p. 489. *Lettres à Marie-Louise,* no. 42, pp. 44-45, records the arrival in Kaunas and includes the passage with which this chapter ends. The report of a Russian in Kaunas is quoted by Tarlé pp. 41-42 (English version, p. 57).

CHAPTER THREE: VILNA AND DRISSA

The most entertaining picture of Vilna during the visit of the Tsar is in Choiseul-Gouffier, pp. 10-45 and 55-57; it may be supplemented by Almedingen, p. 129; Strakhovsky, p. 118; and Waliszewski, pp. 14-15 and 21-23. Madame Narichkine's young brother, Serge Rostopchin, gambled away most of his money at Vilna; see the adverse comments in Narichkine, p. 110.

For the plan to encourage revolt among the Southern Slavs, see Tarlé, p. 24 (English version, p. 30), citing a letter from the Tsar to Barclay. Russian war plans in general are analysed by Colonel W. G. F. Jackson in *Seven Roads to Moscow,* Chapter 10. The fullest account of the Zakret ball is in Choiseul-Gouffier, pp. 48-60 and 89-90. Other eye-witness accounts are cited in Waliszewski, p. 33.

Accounts of Balashov's interview with Napoleon are given by Ségur, vol. 1, pp. 150-151 and Caulaincourt, pp. 128-132; see, also, Vandal, pp. 495-498 and 515-528 (using Balashov's own record). Tarlé, pp. 44-45 (English version pp. 60-61) doubts the authenticity of Balashov's report of the conversations on June 30. He argues that Napoleon would never have asked such a 'silly question' as, 'What is the road to Moscow?' This does not seem to me to be a valid objection; Napoleon's conversation was peppered with semi-rhetorical questions of this type. General Jomini records that during conversation at Vilna, Napoleon asked some of his entourage the distance to Moscow, even though he was fully aware of the answer (cf. Brett-James, p. 47). Napoleon clearly intended to alarm Balashov (and hence ultimately the Tsar) by a threat to march on 'Holy Moscow.'

Napoleon's letter to the Empress of June 26 is printed in *Lettres,* no. 43, p. 45. On the high casualties of horses between the Niemen and Vilna, see Montesquiou, p. 208. On the early days of the campaign, see Labaume, pp. 2-49; Bourgogne, p. 16; Castellane, pp. 108-109; and the criticisms of General Bonnal, pp. 74-76. For Napoleon in Vilna see Soltyk, pp. 35-38, Choiseul-Gouffier, pp. 90-97; and Caulaincourt, pp. 125-135. His letter to Tsar Alexander from Vilna is printed in *Correspondance,* vol. 24, no. 18878. (There is an English translation in Thompson, *Napoleon's Letters,* pp. 268-270).

For Bagration's escape from Davout and Jérôme Bonaparte, see Wilson *Narrative,* pp. 37-43 and *Correspondance,* vol. 23, nos. 18875 and 18877, vol. 24, nos. 18879, 18880, 18907, 18908: cf. the account in Jackson, pp. 106-113 and 123-131. The stinging rebuke to Jérôme

Bonaparte is printed in Thompson, *Napoleon's Letters,* p. 271. The accusation that Jérôme had missed a good opportunity is in *Correspondance,* vol. 24, no. 18901. The order for Davout to take command of Jérôme's Army is in *Correspondance,* vol. 24, no. 18911. The review of the Guard on July 8 was noted by Castellane, p. 113.

There are accounts of Alexander's activities at Drissa and Polotsk in Almedingen, pp. 132-133; Narichkine, p. 124; Wilson, *Narrative,* pp. 44-48; and Waliszewski, p. 48. The letter from his sister is in the Mikhailovitch correspondence, p. 76. The quotations from the Tsar's advisers at Drissa and Polotsk are cited in Tarlé, pp. 56-58 (English version, pp. 79-82). Clausewitz (pp. 41-42) discusses the indefensibility of Drissa.

Barclay's nickname in Russian (see Tarlé, p. 60) was *Boltai da i tolko.* Literally this means 'Talk-and-nothing-more-to-it,' but I have translated this rather freely as 'Bark-and-No-Bite,' since such a rendering seems to me to keep both the suggestion of a pun and the spirit of the phrase. The Russian soldiers delighted in playing on names in this way; thus, significantly, Bagration was known as *Bog-Rati-On* ('He is God of the Army').

For Napoleon's movements towards Vitebsk, see Castellane, p. 115 and p. 119. Caulaincourt comments on the deserted villages on p. 139. The letter to Marie-Louise of July 24 forms *Lettres* no. 56, p. 53. For the skirmish at Ostrovno, see Ségur, vol. 1, pp. 173-175, and Caulaincourt p. 139; there is also a description in Lyautey (first article) pp. 490-491, which includes the expressed hope of a battle on the following day. Napoleon's own high expectations are shown in the letter to Maret, *Correspondance,* vol. 24, no. 19008.

CHAPTER FOUR: PHANTOM OF VICTORY

Tarlé discusses the Russian evasion of battle at Vitebsk, pp. 81-82 (English version, pp. 118-119); cf. the contemporary report of Wilson, *Narrative,* pp. 95-96. There is additional information on the Russian attitude in E. von Löwenstern, pp. 101-104. See, also, *Correspondance,* vol. 24, no. 19016. The bravery of the French Ninth Regiment is well-documented: Fain, *Manuscrit,* vol. 1, p. 283; Caulaincourt, p. 140; Labaume, p. 71. The skirmish is also mentioned by Ségur, vol. 1, p. 178. Ségur has the most detailed account of the scene before Vitebsk and although he must be treated with caution later in the campaign there seems no reason for doubting his accuracy at this stage; thus he records Napoleon's parting words to Murat (p. 182) and his disappointment at capturing only one sleeping Russian (p. 183). Ségur's account should be compared with Labaume, p. 77 and Caulaincourt, pp. 141-142. See, also, Montesquiou, p. 213.

Ségur, vol. 1, p. 191, records Napoleon's announcement that he would treat the campaign as part of a three-year war. For Napoleon's vacillations, see Bourgoing, *Souvenirs,* p. 98. On life in Vitebsk, see Castellane, pp. 124-131; Bourgogne, p. 19; Fain, *Manuscrit,* pp. 288-308 (the Emperor's restless pacing up and down is noted, p. 307); Fezensac, *Souvenirs militaires,* pp. 218-222; Dupuy, p. 171; Labaume, pp. 50-67; and Caulaincourt, pp. 150-152. The request for 'light books' is in *Correspondance,* vol. 24, no. 19052. The experiment with roasted rye is described by Ségur, p. 208.

Ségur also has the most vivid account of the exchanges between Napoleon and his staff-officers (pp. 199-206), including, on p. 200, the passage complaining that his generals have grown too rich. See, also Caulaincourt, pp. 157-159. For Napoleon's departure from Vitebsk, see *Correspondance,* vol. 24, no. 19095; Caulaincourt, p. 161; and Castellane, p. 131, noting weather conditions. Caulaincourt (p. 528) records Napoleon's subsequent regret that he had not stayed at Vitebsk.

Tarlé has a full account of the meeting of Barclay and Bagration on p. 95 (English version, p. 137). See, also, the eye-witness accounts printed in C. de Grunwald, pp. 78-79; and compare Waliszewski, pp. 87-88. There is a long extract from the letter sent by Barclay to Arakcheyev on August 10 in Tarlé, p. 95. On Krasnoe see *Correspondance,* vol. 24, no. 19097; Ségur, vol. 1, pp. 222-225; and Burton, pp. 82-87. The retreat to Smolensk is described from the Russian side in E. von Löwenstern, pp. 108-111.

Descriptions of the appearance of Smolensk in 1812 are in Wilson, *Narrative,* pp. 103-105; Ségur, vol. 1, pp. 229-230; Fain, *Manuscrit,* p. 361. The action is described in Tarlé, pp. 97-100 (English version, pp. 141-145) and Foord, pp. 129-143. For contemporary accounts of the battle of Smolensk, see the following sources: Castellane, pp. 133-136; Caulaincourt, pp. 164-166; Lyautey (first article)

p. 493, with an account of the fraternization incident; Bourgogne, pp. 19-20; Ségur, vol. I, pp. 230-239; Douglas (journal of Charles François), pp. 235-236. Stendhal's remarks are quoted by Chuquet, p. 55. For the Fire, see: Ségur, vol. I, p. 239; Caulaincourt, p. 166, and Bourgoing, *Souvenirs,* p. 102. The comments of the Italian officer on entering Smolensk are quoted in Tarlé, p. 101 (English version, p. 147). Other accounts of the entry are in Fain, *Manuscrit,* vol. I, p. 378 and Ségur, vol. I, p. 239. Barclay's retreat overnight is described by Wilson, *Narrative,* pp. 90-91. On Valutino, see Brandt, pp. 259-262 and Caulaincourt, p. 167. For the Junot incident, see Gourgaud, p. 172, and Caulaincourt, pp. 168-169. Napoleon's remarks to Sébastiani are quoted by Ségur, vol. I, p. 252.

CHAPTER FIVE: THE TWO CITIES

Reaction to the invasion of Russia in London is discussed by M. S. Anderson, in *Britain's Discovery,* pp. 216-217; Dr Anderson prints the quotation from the Vorontsov Papers. The most interesting editions of *The Times* are those dated July 25, 27, and 31, and August 23 and August 24, 1812. For British official policy towards Russia, see Webster, pp. 96-97.

There is a good picture of conditions in St Petersburg in Madame de Staël, pp. 277-282 and pp. 332-339. The most interesting biographical material on Rostopchin is to be found in the book by his daughter, Madame Natalie Narichkine: his visit to England is described on p. 18; his actions as Governor of Moscow before the invasion on pp. 126-127. The Tsar's reluctance to appoint him Governor is mentioned by Waliszewski, p. 62.

For Moscow in general in 1812, see the attractive chapter in Fusil, *Souvenirs,* pp. 223-228, and the accounts in Olivier, pp. 31-32 and Waliszewski, pp. 64-67. For the early history of ballet in Moscow, see Slonimsky, pp. 4-5, and Roslavleva, p. 29 and p. 33.

Alexander's visit to Moscow is described by Narichkine, pp. 131-137; see, also, Olivier, pp. 35-39, and Waliszewski, pp. 71-74. The reminiscences of Vera Bakounina (then aged sixteen) are also interesting: see Bakounina article, p. 401. Tarlé gives examples of Rostopchin's distrust of the merchants, p. 110 (English version,

p. 161). Glinka's account of the meeting at the Sloboda Palace is printed extensively in R. F. Christian, pp. 67-68 and 72. Dr Christian's work is primarily a critique of Tolstoy – in this instance of Chapter XXII of *War and Peace*. For the retailer who wrote '5,000 roubles' in error, see Waliszewski, p. 73.

For the Moscow militia, see Narichkine, pp. 142-143. On Leppich see: Waliszewski, pp. 68-70, containing extracts from Rostopchin's letters; Narichkine, p. 148; and Olivier, pp. 34-35. The quotation on the advantages of conversion to Catholicism is from Narichkine, p. 100. The sending into exile of foreign residents is the subject of an appendix in Olivier, pp. 247-248. Narichkine prints vivid accounts of Rostopchin's reactions to the fall of Smolensk (p. 139) and of the autumnal dust-storms in Moscow (p. 151). For the reaction of the St Petersburg audience to *Phèdre*, see the extract from Arndt printed in Brett-James, p. 70. On the character and earlier career of Kutuzov see: Wilson, *Narrative,* pp. 130-131; Tarlé, pp. 115-118 (English version, 168-172). See, also, the critical review of Soviet historians' assessments of Kutuzov by Leo Yaresh in C. E. Black, pp. 271-301; and the study of Tolstoy's treatment of Kutuzov by Sir Isaiah Berlin in *The Hedgehog and the Fox,* pp. 46-51.

For the circumstances of Kutuzov's appointment as commander-in-chief, see: Waliszewski, pp. 93-94; Tarlé, pp. 113-114 (English version, pp. 165-167), which includes Shuvalov's letter of August 12; Strakhovsky, p. 127; and Almedingen, pp. 135-136. Alexander's letter to his sister explaining the background to Kutuzov's appointment is printed in full in Olivier, pp. 249-256.

On the Abo Conferences, see Scott, pp. 20-21, Webster, p. 98 and Waliszewski, pp. 95-96. On Wilson's meeting with the Tsar, see Wilson, *Journal,* pp. 36-37, and Wilson, *Narrative,* pp. 114-120. The British Ambassador's optimistic purchase of a three-year lease is documented by Webster (p. 99).

CHAPTER SIX: THE HOMECOMING OF COLONEL
DAVIDOV

Napoleon's stay in Smolensk is described by Caulaincourt, pp. 167,

170 and 172; and by Castellane, p. 141. For the orders mentioned in the second paragraph of the chapter, see *Correspondance,* vol. 24, nos. 19124, 19127, 19129 and 19138. The letter of August 24 to Marie-Louise is in *Lettres,* no. 78, p. 64.

For Dorogobuzh see: Caulaincourt, p. 175; Fain, *Manuscrit,* vol. 1, p. 422, and *Correspondance,* vol. 24, no. 19149; and for Viasma, *Lettres,* no. 82, p. 66; Montesquiou, pp. 219-220; Castellane, pp. 142-143; Bourgogne, p. 21; Fain, *Manuscrit,* vol. 1, p. 430; and Lyautey (first article), p. 494. On the exhausting character of the march, see Brandt, pp. 268-269, and Castellane, p. 175 and pp. 180-181.

For contemporary references to the dispute between Davout and Murat, see Ségur, vol. 1, pp. 237-239, and Caulaincourt, p. 171; the incident is described by Macdonell, p. 248. On the adulation felt for Murat by the troops, see Castellane, p. 142, and Dupuy, pp. 175-176. For Napoleon's conversational asides, see Soltyk, pp. 189-190. His letters to Marie-Louise of September 2 are in *Lettres,* no. 85, p. 68. The most detailed study of Napoleon's health and quotations from the medical reports of Mestivier will be found in Kemble, pp. 188-193. The famous 'God of War' phrase from the Brumaire speech will be found in *Correspondance,* vol. 6, no. 4388, p. 4.

Tarlé describes the arrival of Kutuzov at headquarters, pp. 118-119 (English version, pp. 174-175). The quotation from Clausewitz is on p. 115 of his *Campaign.* On Toll, see the extracts printed by C. de Grunwald, pp. 123-124; see, also, Tarlé pp. 123-124 (English version, pp. 182-183). Kutuzov's letter to the Tsar 'twelve versts' (i.e. eight miles) from Mozhaisk is printed among the selection of contemporary documents published by the Russians to commemorate the 150th anniversary of the battle, Altshuller and Bogdanov, *Borodino,* p. 64. The same book also contains Davidov's description of his return to his childhood home, p. 347. There is a useful review article on Davidov as a partisan-poet in *Revue des Etudes Napoléoniennes* for January, 1914, p. 412.

For the march from Viasma to Borodino, see Fain, *Manuscrit,* vol. 1, p. 445. Castellane's comments on the weather and on travelling conditions on September 4 are in his *Journal,* p. 147. (He records the death of Méda on the same page.) I have used five contemporary sources for the action of Shevardino: Thirion de Metz, pp. 175-178;

Lejeune, vol. 2, p. 204; Fain, *Manuscrit,* vol. 2, pp. 13-15; Caulaincourt, pp. 191-192; and Wilson, *Narrative,* pp. 136-138. Napoleon's reactions are noted in Ségur, vol. 1, pp. 318-320. His battle-order for Borodino is in *Correspondance,* vol. 24, no. 19181.

Kutuzov's letter to his wife on the eve of the battle is printed in Altshuller and Bogdanov, p. 87. For the religious ceremony with the veneration of the Ikon, see Ségur, vol, 1. pp. 328-329, Douglas (Journal of Charles François) p. 237 and Lejeune, vol. 2, p. 247. On Fabvier, see Caulaincourt, p. 191; and for the portrait of the King of Rome, see Bausset, vol. 2, p. 103.

For the strengthening of the Russian defences overnight, see the extract from the memoirs of Lieutenant Bogdanov included in Altshuller and Bogdanov, pp. 337-338, and for 'the long line of cavalry,' see Rodojitsky in the same book, p. 384. For the unfinished game of chess, see the extract from Girod de l'Ain's memoirs printed in Brett-James, p. 123. The proclamation on the eve of Borodino is printed, from the *Moniteur,* in *Correspondance,* vol. 24, no. 19182. There were at least two other versions; see Fain, *Manuscrit,* vol. 2, p. 20 and Tarlé, p. 127 (English version, p. 185). Both Fain (vol. 2, p. 19) and Ségur (vol. 1, p. 334) mention 'the sun of Austerlitz' remark. The fullest account of Napoleon's behaviour on the night before the battle would appear to be in Rapp, pp. 200-202.

CHAPTER SEVEN:
'THE MOST TERRIBLE OF ALL MY BATTLES'

I have based my narrative of Borodino on the following eye-witness accounts from members of the Grand Army: Rapp, pp. 203-207; Dupuy, pp. 173-176; Labaume, pp. 138-179; Lejeune, vol. 2, pp. 208-219; Thirion de Metz, pp. 189-192; Montesquiou, pp. 221-222; Ségur, vol. 1, pp. 336-360; Caulaincourt, pp. 194-204; Castellane, pp. 148-151; Bourgogne, pp. 21-22; Fezensac, *Souvenirs militaires,* pp. 236-242; Fain, *Manuscrit,* vol. 2, pp. 22-43; and Douglas (Journal of Charles François), pp. 237-241. From the Russian side I have used two eye-witness accounts in Altshuller and Bogdanov: Raevski, pp. 380-384; and Rodojitsky, pp. 384-388 (including, on p. 386, the story of the major with the impediment in his speech). Wilson, *Narrative,* pp. 141-156, was, of course, also giving an account from the Russian side. On the disputed question of Russian casualty figures, see the article by Kats.

Secondary accounts of the battle will be found in Jackson, pp. 140-153 (with good sketch maps); Esposito and Elting, pp. 116-118 (excellent maps); Tarlé, pp. 130-139 (English version, 190-204); and Foord, pp. 197-219. The famous account in Tolstoy, *War and Peace,* Chapters 30 to 39, is critically examined by R. F. Christian (pp. 66-67) and by Sir Isaiah Berlin, pp. 29-31 and 42.

For individual national units at Borodino, see, for the Westphalians, Chuquet, pp. 71-75, and for the Poles, the article by M. Kukiel. Napoleon's description of the battle to Marie-Louise is in *Lettres,* no. 88, p. 70. Kutuzov's brief note to his wife is printed in Altshuller and Bogdanov, p. 121.

CHAPTER EIGHT: FILI

For St Petersburg that September, see Waliszewski, pp. 98 and 127-128. On Alexander personally, see Strakhovsky, p. 136. Cf. also, the extracts in C. de Grunwald, pp. 174-175. Kutuzov's report to Alexander on the battle is printed in Altshuller and Bogdanov, pp. 134-141.

Rostopchin's proclamation on the need for the people of Moscow to arm themselves is printed in Narichkine, p. 157; cf. Tarlé, pp. 154-155 (English version, pp. 224-225) and Olivier, pp. 41-42. For the exodus from Moscow, see Narichkine, pp. 158 and 165, and Garin, p. 26.

For the two versions of Rostopchin's meeting with Kutuzov at Fili, see the letter to his wife printed in Narichkine, p. 164, and the later account printed in the same book, pp. 161-163.

On the Council at Fili, see Tarlé p. 144 (English version, p. 211); this includes extracts from a summary of proceedings sent by Vorontsov to his father, the Ambassador to the Court of St James's. It is in this summary that the metaphor of the torrent and the sponge is used. There is an account in Narichkine, pp. 163-164 written by Rostopchin on information which appears to have reached him from the Tsar's uncle, the Duke of Oldenburg, or the Tsar's cousin, the

Prince of Würtemberg, both of whom rode into Moscow from Fili to see Rostopchin on the night after the conference. Narichkine also prints (p. 164) the letter in which Rostopchin fears he will 'die from sorrow.'

Napoleon's journey from Mozhaisk to the Poklonnaya Gora is described in Fain, *Manuscrit,* vol. 2, p. 45; Castellane, p. 153; and see also *Lettres,* no. 90, p. 72. For the scene on the Sparrow Hills, see Bourgoing, p. 111; Bourgogne, p. 27; Ségur, vol. 2, pp. 27-30; Lyautey (first article), p. 496; Brandt, pp. 285-286; and Dupuy, p. 181. On Murat and the Cossacks, see Caulaincourt, pp. 211-212; Fain, *Manuscrit,* vol. 2, p. 52; Ségur, vol. 2, pp. 31 and 34; Montesquiou, pp. 223-227; and the article by Marcel-Paon, p. 315. For the final evacuation of Moscow, see Garin, pp. 20-24, and Olivier, pp. 44-46.

There are accounts of Napoleon's activities at the Dorogomilov Gate in the following sources: Fain, *Manuscrit,* vol. 2, p. 54; Bausset, vol. 2, pp. 115-120; Gourgaud, p. 277; Caulaincourt, pp. 212 and 214; and Ségur, vol. 2, pp. 32-33 (including, on p. 32, the demand for the 'Boyars'). For the damp night before the entry into Moscow, see Lyautey (first article) p. 497. Bourgogne (p. 30) notes how the band played as the guard marched through deserted streets. Bausset mentions the fires on the first night in his memoirs, vol. 2, p. 121.

CHAPTER NINE: THE FLAMES OF MOSCOW

Bourgogne's vivid account of the start of the Fire is in his memoirs, pp. 30-36; see Caulaincourt pp. 216-217 for Napoleon's entry into the city, and cf. Gourgaud, p. 273. The details in Ségur, vol. 2, pp. 38-43 are confused and not always substantiated; but see Napoleon's itinerary in Garros, p. 392, and the note by Madelin to *Lettres,* no. 93, p. 78.

For the spread of the Fire to the Kremlin see: Caulaincourt, pp. 218-220; Ségur, vol. 2, p. 45; Montesquiou, pp. 234-235; Fain, *Manuscrit,* vol. 2, pp. 81-91; Gourgaud relates the incident in which Berthier induced Napoleon to leave the Kremlin (p. 278). See, also, Denniée, p. 95, and Boulart, pp. 260-261. For the plight of the refugees watching Moscow burn from the countryside, see Garin,

p. 31; and for an impression of the Fire from a distance, see Dumonceau, p. 154.

The fullest discussion of Rostopchin's responsibility for the Fire is
in the concluding chapter of Olivier, pp. 229-246; it may be compared with one of the earliest criticisms of Rostopchin, in Boutourlin,
vol. 1, p. 372. See, also, the comments of Rostopchin's daughter,
Madame Narichkine, on pp. 168-171 of her book. She also records
Rostopchin's remarks on leaving Moscow (p. 175); and for his later
views see the same book, p. 177. For Wolzogen and the fire-engines,
see Brett-James, p. 163.

On the Petrovsky Palace interlude, see: Labaume, pp. 228-229;
Castellane, pp. 155-156; Montesquiou, p. 236. Bourgogne (p. 44)
uses the phrase 'the Fair of Moscow' to describe the looting. For
Russian accounts, see Garin, pp. 52-66, and the article by Rambaud,
pp. 194-228. See Herzen for the adventures of his nurse (pp. 11-14).

For Napoleon's return to the Kremlin, see Caulaincourt, pp. 226-
227 and 229; Ségur, vol. 2, p. 54; *Correspondance*, vol. 24, no. 19209.
For estimates of the damage, see: Chuquet, pp. 82-83; Fain, *Manu-
scrit*, vol. 2, pp. 98-99; Brett-James, p. 146. Napoleon's account to
Marie-Louise is in *Lettres*, no. 95, pp. 79-80. On food supplies and
the views of Daru, see Caulaincourt, pp. 234-235, Bourgogne, p. 57,
Ségur, vol. 2, p. 87, and the comments of Olivier, pp. 108-109.
Napoleon's 'inventory' was included in his subsequent letter to the
Tsar, *Correspondance*, no. 19213. Napoleon's desire to find a re-
sponsible Russian official is recorded by Caulaincourt, pp. 227-228.
There is an eye-witness account of Rostopchin's behaviour at
Voronovo in Wilson, *Narrative*, pp. 178-180. See also Narichkine,
pp. 189-191, Caulaincourt, pp. 229-230, and Brandt, p. 300.

CHAPTER TEN: TWO CANDLES BY THE WINDOW

On the Tutolmin episode, see Caulaincourt, pp. 228-229; Fain,
Manuscrit, vol. 2, pp. 100-103; and Tarlé p. 196 (English version,
pp. 289-290). For events in St Petersburg, see Strakhovsky, pp.
137-138 and Olivier, pp. 130-132, pp. 172-173. For the Yakovlev
mission, see Caulaincourt, pp. 237-238, and Fain, *Manuscrit*, vol. 2,
pp. 104-106. Fain's account is corrected by Yakovlev's record,

edited in the article by Madame Stchoupak, pp. 45-48; see also Herzen, pp. 16-17. His pass is included in *Correspondance,* vol. 24, no. 19212 and the letter he carried to the Tsar forms no. 19213 (English translation in Thompson, *Napoleon's Letters* pp. 273-274).

Castellane records the device of the two candles on p. 161. For Kutuzov's movements and tactics, see the Tchitcherine article, pp. 17-18, and Waliszewski, p. 128. On Murat's confusion, and Napoleon's comments on his action, see Caulaincourt, pp. 238-245 and p. 256. Fain prints Berthier's letters to Sébastiani (*Manuscrit,* vol. 2, p. 177) and to Bessières (p. 185).

There are accounts of the events at Polotsk in Jackson, pp. 118-119, 122 and 134; and in Foord, pp. 177-182 and 299-305. For Napoleon and the Austrians, see Caulaincourt, pp. 257-258. Victor's appointment is in *Correspondance,* vol. 24, no. 19258. The 'Hessian Captain' is Roeder; see Helen Roeder, p. 144. The problems of administration and of the courier service are described by Caulaincourt, pp. 231 and 253, and by Fain, *Manuscrit,* vol. 2, pp. 130-131. For instances of Napoleon's broad interests while in Moscow, see the following documents in vol. 24 of *Correspondance*: on censorship, nos. 19268 and 19270; on Portugal, no. 19232; on Walcheren, no. 19279; on foreign affairs in general and problems forced on Maret, nos. 19230 and 19235. Maret's difficulties in trying to run the diplomatic service from Vilna are well illustrated in Ernouf, pp. 417-430.

The conference of October 3 is recorded, somewhat theatrically, by Ségur (vol. 2, pp 67-68) but may be compared with Caulaincourt's comments (p. 238). The October memorandum is in *Correspondance,* vol. 24, no. 19237.

For Caulaincourt's refusal to go to St Petersburg, see his memoirs, pp. 252-254, and Ségur, vol. 2, p. 70. On Lauriston's first mission, see the following sources: Fain, *Manuscrit,* vol. 2, pp. 106-108; Caulaincourt, pp. 254-255; Chuquet, p. 84; Ségur, vol. 2, pp. 70-72; Wilson, *Narrative,* pp. 184-190; Wilson, *Journal,* pp. 54-55. See also the account in Tarlé, p. 203 and pp. 206-207 (English version, p. 299 and pp. 307-308).

Napoleon's elation after Lauriston's return is noted in Caulaincourt, pp. 268-269, and in Ségur, vol. 2, p. 72. For remarks on the weather, the climate, and Fontainebleau, see Caulaincourt, pp. 249 and 271-272, and *Lettres,* no. 105, p. 86. Castellane comments on the fine autumn (p. 166). The request for 'good new books' is in *Correspondance*, vol. 24, no. 19236; and there are discussions of Napoleon's reading habits in general in Bausset, vol. 2, p. 188 and in Chuquet, pp. 96-97; Ségur's criticism is on p. 88, vol. 2.

For Marie-Rose Aubert, see Ysarn-Villefort, pp. 13-15; Montesquiou p. 230; and Olivier, pp. 98-100. For Tarquinio's entertainment of Napoleon, see Bausset, vol. 2, p. 130, and for other amusements devised for the Emperor, see Fusil, *Souvenirs*, pp. 256-257. On Napoleon's re-drafting of the statutes of the *Comédie Française*, see Ségur, vol. 2, p. 89. The French Theatre in Moscow is well documented: Bausset, vol. 2, pp. 127-130; Ségur, vol. 2, p. 67; Castellane, p. 167; and Montesquiou, p. 238. A programme is given in detail in Olivier, pp. 157-160. For the 'Dulcineas', see Bourgogne, pp. 56 and 62-64. Narbonne's courtesan is mentioned by Castellane, pp. 161 and 166. On the sorry state of Moscow, see Fezensac, *Souvenirs militaires*, pp. 244-246, and Vionnet de Maringoné, pp. 42-44.

Fain (*Manuscrit*, vol. 2, p. 152) reports Napoleon's acceptance of the need to find winter quarters. For Berthier's orders for the artillery and for moving the wounded, see Tarlé p. 209 (English version, p. 314). There is 'talk of India' in Bourgogne, p. 66. On trophies and the cross from Ivan Veliki, see the following sources: Caulaincourt, pp. 264-265; Fain, *Manuscrit*, vol. 2, p. 149; Castellane, pp. 170-171; Bourgogne, p. 59; Ségur, vol. 2, p. 78; and Vionnet de Maringoné, p. 57.

Caulaincourt (p. 261) deals with the timing of Napoleon's decision to leave Moscow. The Emperor's letter to Maret on his plans for retiring from Moscow is in *Correspondance*, vol. 24, no. 19275; his letter to the Minister of Police is in Tarlé, p. 210 (English version, p. 315). On Lauriston's second mission, see Caulaincourt, p. 277 and Castellane, pp. 170-171, supplemented by *Correspondance*, vol. 24, no. 19277. The skirmish at Winkovo is described by Tarlé, pp. 211-212 (English version, pp. 317-318), with contemporary references in Caulaincourt, pp. 279-282, and in Ségur, vol. 2, p. 92. For the Russian side, see the Tchitcherine article, p. 25.

Napoleon's instructions to Mortier are in *Correspondance*, vol. 24, no. 19286; his arrangements for departure are in no. 19284; and see also Castellane, p. 171. For the actual departure from Moscow, see the following sources: Castellane, p. 173; Caulaincourt, p. 290; Bourgogne, pp. 66-67; Fain, *Manuscrit,* vol. 2, p. 158; Montesquiou, pp. 243-244; Bausset, vol. 2, p. 140; and Ségur, vol. 2, pp. 94-95 (giving the substance of the conversation with Rapp).

CHAPTER ELEVEN: MALOYAROSLAVETS

On Alexander in St Petersburg, see Almedingen, p. 139, and Waliszewski, pp. 107-109; see also Mikhailovitch, pp. 76 and 83-88 for the correspondence between the Tsar and his sister. The interview between Alexander and Volkonsky and the subsequent letter to Kutuzov are summarized in Wilson, *Narrative,* pp. 203-205; cf. Tarlé, pp. 189 and 222 (English version, pp. 280-281 and 329) and Olivier, pp. 172-173. For Kutuzov's movements, see Waliszewski, p. 129, the Tchitcherine article, pp. 19-20, and Tarlé, pp. 213-214 (English version pp. 320-321). For the reply to the second Lauriston mission, see Fain, *Manuscrit,* vol. 2, p. 222 and Caulaincourt, pp. 277 and 292.

I have based the account of Docturov's expedition towards Fominskoie and subsequently to Maloyaroslavets on Wilson, *Narrative,* pp. 219-222. Wilson (pp. 222-228) also gives a vivid account of the battle of Maloyaroslavets. This may be supplemented by the following sources: Labaume, pp. 233-258; Lejeune, vol. 2, pp. 237-240; Soltyk, pp. 334-336; Ségur, vol. 2, pp. 100-106; Lyautey (second article) pp. 60-61; and Fain, *Manuscrit,* vol. 2, pp. 242-249. Carola Oman (pp. 342-343) includes extracts from Eugène's letters. Napoleon's letter to Marie-Louise on October 24 is in *Lettres,* no. 115, p. 93; his question to Davout is in Ségur, vol. 2, p. 99. Wilson's account of the night scene at Maloyaroslavets is in his *Narrative,* p. 229; he criticizes Kutuzov's hesitation and vacillation on pp. 230-234.

Napoleon's discussions with the marshals and generals at Ghorod-nia are described in Caulaincourt, pp. 297-298 and 303-304, and in Ségur, vol. 2, pp. 108 and 114-118. The incident in which Napoleon was nearly captured by Russian troops is well documented: Caulaincourt, pp. 299-300; Rapp, p. 226; Gourgaud, p. 330; Fain, *Manuscrit,* vol. 2, pp. 250-251; Bourgogne, p. 70; Ségur, vol. 2, pp.

110-111; and Vionnet de Maringoné, p. 60. For the rhetorical question about the 'fatal field,' see Ségur, vol. 2, p. 113. On the plaque at Maloyaroslavets, see Pares, p. 596.

CHAPTER TWELVE: THE WINTER TRAIL

For the impedimenta carried by the Grand Army at the start of the retreat, see Lejeune, vol. 2, pp. 234-235, Castellane, p. 178, and Bourgogne, p. 67. Bourgogne (p. 73) also noted the discarded French books near Gzatsk. The sufferings of the journey from Maloyaroslavets to Uspenskoie may be gathered from Caulaincourt, pp. 305 and 313-317; Castellane, p. 177; Rapp, p. 227; Ségur, vol. 2, pp. 135-137; and Lyautey (second article) p. 64. For the Wintzingerode incident, see the following: Caulaincourt, pp. 306-313; Denniée, pp. 115-116 and 120; Fain, *Manuscrit,* vol. 2, p. 157; Ségur, vol. 2, pp. 133-134. The correspondence with Marie-Louise on October 26 is in *Lettres,* nos. 116-117, pp. 94-95. Orders for the wounded are in *Correspondance,* vol. 24, no. 19308. Napoleon's conversation at Uspenskoie is related by Caulaincourt, pp. 317-320. The pitiable scene when the army re-crossed the field of Borodino is related in the following memoirs: Ségur, vol. 2, pp. 137-140; Bourgogne, p. 71; Fain, *Manuscrit,* vol. 2, p. 258; Lyautey (second article) p. 65; Montesquiou, p. 254; and Brandt, p. 306. Caulaincourt does not mention the re-crossing of the battlefield, which may suggest that the Emperor's entourage took the Old Road and so avoided the more harrowing scenes; on the other hand, it is possible that Caulaincourt was so affected by the sight of the ridge on which his brother had charged to his death that he chose to make no mention of it when he came to write his memoirs. But it is Caulaincourt (pp. 320-321) who records the distribution of wine and spirits in Gzatsk.

For Yazykov and the bringing of the news to Kutuzov that the French were in retreat, see Tarlé p. 219 (English version, p. 325), and Olivier, pp. 217-218. Madame Olivier also relates Rostopchin's caution over a return to Moscow (p. 223). On Kutuzov's plans at this time, see Wilson, *Narrative,* p. 234; Tarlé, pp. 221 and 241 (English version, pp. 328 and 356) and the extracts in C. de Grunwald, pp. 271-273. See also, Jackson, pp. 167-171 (with sketch-maps).

The fullest examination of the character of the partisan movement is in Tarlé, pp. 233-240 (English version, pp. 345-354); for contemporary material (mostly from Davidov), see Garin, pp. 88-94, and Altshuller and Bogdanov, pp. 347-348. Kutuzov's proclamation from Spas has been re-printed several times; conveniently it is in Caulaincourt, pp. 340-341. For differences at Kutuzov's headquarters, see Wilson, *Narrative*, p. 245 and Tarlé, p. 247 (English version, p. 365). There is additional material criticizing Kutuzov in Wilson, *Journal*, pp. 70 and 80.

For Napoleon's stay in Viazma, see Caulaincourt, p. 321, and Castellane, pp. 179-180; these should be supplemented by Roeder, pp. 163-164, (for the Hessian Guards) and *Correspondance*, vol. 24, no. 19311. On Saint-Cyr and Merlé, see Ségur, vol. 2, pp. 183-194, and Fain, *Manuscrit*, vol. 2, pp. 262-269; and for Victor, see *Correspondance*, vol. 24, no. 19312. The attack by Miloradovich on November 3 is narrated by Davout's chief-of-staff, Lejeune, in vol. 2, pp. 249-250. Cf. Ségur, vol. 2, pp. 148-155, and, from the Russian side, Boutourlin, pp. 184-194. Additional general information in the Tchitcherine article, p. 29, and in Fusil, *L'Incendie*, pp. 22-23; see also Carola Oman, p.345.

Caulaincourt describes the panic of the French on p. 324, adding the comment that this event marked the start of 'our disorganization and misfortune.' He prints Berthier's letter to Ney on the same page. For the collapse of discipline see, also, Denniée, p. 123. Napoleon's abortive plan for an attack at Jaskowo is discussed by Caulaincourt (p. 326). The most vivid accounts of the effect of the snow at this stage of the retreat are in Lejeune, vol. 2, p. 255, Bourgogne p. 77 and (with frozen tear-stains on every page) Ségur, vol. 2, pp. 155-159. For the Malet Conspiracy, see Caulaincourt, pp. 327-335, Ségur, vol. 2, p. 161, and Fain, *Manuscrit*, vol. 2, pp. 284-285. The approach to Smolensk is narrated in the following sources: Caulaincourt, pp. 335-337; Fain, *Manuscrit*, vol. 2, p. 288; Fezensac, *Journal*, pp. 79-80; Ségur, vol. 2, p. 175; and Bourgogne, pp.92-93.

CHAPTER THIRTEEN: KRASNOE AND THE BEREZINA

For the loss of Polotsk, see Foord, pp. 229-305, and for Victor's orders, *Correspondance,* vol. 24, no. 19326; see also Caulaincourt, pp. 339-340. For Victor's earlier career, see Macdonell, especially pp. 222-228. For the fall of Vitebsk, see Boisdeffre, pp. 220-225. On Baraguay, see Chuquet, pp. 133-139, Méneval, p. 71, and Caulaincourt, pp. 335 and 346. For Eugène, see Carola Oman, pp. 347-348, Caulaincourt, pp. 339-340; and Ségur, vol. 2, pp. 199 and 201.

There are several accounts of conditions in Smolensk: Pastoret, pp. 471-472; Vionnet de Maringoné, p. 65; Bourgogne, pp. 95-112; Castellane, p. 186; and the extract in Brett-James, p. 232. Napoleon's correspondence with Victor from Smolensk is in Fain, *Manuscrit,* vol. 2, pp. 341-343; and his letter to Maret is in *Correspondance,* vol. 24, no. 19336. For meteorological conditions between Smolensk and the Berezina, see the article by Angervo, based on official readings; cf. for Smolensk, Fain, *Manuscrit,* vol. 2, p. 299. On the departure from Smolensk, see the following: Bourgogne, p. 115; Roeder, p. 172; Fusil, *L'Incendie,* p. 26; Fain, *Manuscrit,* vol. 2, p. 289-290; Ségur, vol. 2, pp. 205-206; and Lyautey (second article) p. 68. For the grim conditions immediately after leaving Smolensk, see Bourgogne, p. 113. For Korytnia, see Montesquiou, p. 260, and Lyautey (second article) p. 72.

For Russian movements, see Tarlé, p. 246 (English version pp. 365-366), Wilson, *Narrative,* pp. 265-266, and the Tchitcherine article, pp. 28-30. On the battles of Krasnoe, see the following sources: Tarlé, p. 247 (English version, p. 367), quoting from Löwenstern and Davidov; Lejeune, vol. 2, pp. 262-263; Roeder, pp. 173-175; Bourgogne, pp. 123-128; Ségur, vol. 2, pp. 211-241; Castellane, p. 187; Vionnet de Maringoné, pp. 67-68; Caulaincourt, pp. 350-354; Gourgaud, p. 368; and the Tchitcherine article, pp. 30-33.

On Lyadi, see Caulaincourt, p. 359 (for the Emperor's undignified descent of the hill), Castellane, p. 189; and Lyautey (second article) p. 76. For the halt at Orsha, see Castellane, p. 190; Bourgoing, p. 152; Lejeune, vol. 2, p. 265; and Montesquiou, p. 265 (recording, among other points, that it was at Orsha that the portrait of the King of Rome was destroyed on the Emperor's orders).

For Ney's retreat and Napoleon's reaction to it, see the following sources: Ségur, vol. 2, pp. 255-269; Caulaincourt, pp. 361-371; Castellane, p. 189; Méneval, p. 77; Denniée, p. 146; Fezensac

Journal, p. 117; Fain, *Manuscrit*, vol. 2, pp. 324-325; and Wilson, *Narrative*, pp. 279-282.

For Chichagov's movements and his entry into Minsk, see his own memoirs, pp. 130-137; and compare the less glowing accounts in Langeron, pp. 1-4 and Rochechouart, pp. 145-146. Tarlé quotes Napoleon's remarks of irritation with Chichagov on p. 261 (English version, p. 385), and Caulaincourt records Napoleon's reactions to the fall of Minsk on pp. 347-348. For the burning of official French documents, see Méneval, p. 83. The best accounts of the re-taking of Borisov are in Langeron, pp. 47-55, Rochechouart, pp. 151-154, and Chuquet, pp. 179-183. For the suggestion that Napoleon might have escaped by balloon, see Caulaincourt, p. 374. On Corbineau's march, see Fain, *Manuscrit*, vol. 2, pp. 361-363 and Caulaincourt, pp. 381 and 383. On general conditions in the retreat at this time, see the following: Roeder, p. 182; Thirion de Metz, pp. 228-240; Douglas (François journal) pp. 257-258; Caulaincourt pp. 376-379; and Castellane, pp. 192-193. Bourgogne narrates his hair-raising adventures when he lost contact with the army in his memoirs, pp. 135-193.

For conditions before the crossing of the Berezina and the preparations for it, see the following sources: Ségur, vol. 2, pp. 286-296; Fain, *Manuscrit*, vol. 2, pp. 373-374; *Correspondance,* vol. 24, no. 19358; Castellane, pp. 194-195; Bourgogne, pp. 198-200; Montesquiou, p. 269; and, from the Russian side, the Tchitcherine article pp. 36-40.

I have based my section on the crossing of the Berezina on the following accounts by participants: Dumonceau, pp. 220-222; Thirion de Metz, pp. 247-254; Chuquet (for Roos), pp. 193-194; Douglas (for François), pp. 261-264; Bourgogne, p. 203; Lejeune, vol. 2, p. 276; Roeder, p. 184; Dupuy, pp. 203-204; Montesquiou, pp. 271-273; Bourgoing, pp. 155-156; Fain, *Manuscrit*, vol. 2, pp. 375-410; Lyautey (third article) p. 242; and the Turno article, pp. 114-115. See also the well-known accounts by Ségur, vol. 2, pp. 309 and 314-316, and Caulaincourt, pp. 385-388, and the brief reference by Castellane, p. 196. On the Partouneaux disaster, see Fain, *Manuscrit,* vol. 2, pp. 405-407, and Caulaincourt, pp. 388-392. For the tragic scenes beside the Berezina, see Rochechouart, pp. 159-160; Langeron pp. 71-72; Ségur, vol. 2, pp. 316-325; and the extracts in

Brett-James, pp. 261-262. For a defence of Kutuzov's hesitancy, see Tarlé, pp. 259 and 262 (English version, pp. 383 and 386).

CHAPTER FOURTEEN:
'HIS MAJESTY'S HEALTH HAS NEVER BEEN BETTER'

For the hysterical enthusiasm with which the British people greeted the news of Napoleon's retreat, see Thompson, *Napoleon Bonaparte,* p. 338 and Anderson, *Britain's Discovery,* pp. 220-221. I have used the files of *The Times* for the following days: November 27, 28 and 29, December 5, 9, 12, 17, 19 and 24. *The Times* printed reports which had reached it from Paris, as well as the views of the City of London and a splendid series of pontifical editorials.

Caulaincourt (pp. 393-395), gives the best narrative of the movement of the army from the Berezina towards Vilna. Napoleon's letter of November 29 to Maret is printed in *Correspondance,* vol. 24, no. 19362; for Maret's own difficulties in Vilna, see Ernouf, pp. 458 and 461-462; and compare the account of the Governor of Vilna, Van Hogendorp, p. 331-332. For Murat's scar, see Brett-James, p. 263 and for Wilson's description of the cold weather, his *Narrative,* pp. 342-343. On the confusion over the Hessian Order of Merit, see Roeder, p. 188.

Castellane describes the Grand Army filing past Napoleon on December 2 in his *Journal,* p. 199. For Napoleon at Molodechno, see Caulaincourt, p. 401. For the decision to send Montesquiou to Paris, see his memoirs, pp. 276-277 and *Correspondance,* vol. 24, no. 19364. Caulaincourt was in the closest touch with Napoleon during the period in which the Emperor was preparing the Twenty-Ninth Bulletin; see Caulaincourt's memoirs, pp. 399 and 402. The bulletin itself is printed in *Correspondance,* vol. 24, no. 19365. There are references to the high standard of comfort maintained for Napoleon in Vionnet de Maringoné, p. 64, and in several passages in Caulaincourt (see, especially, p. 414).

For the problems involved in selecting the new commander of the army, see Rapp, pp. 250-252, Ségur, vol. 2, pp. 328-330, and Caulaincourt, p. 409; for the orders, see *Correspondance,* vol. 24, nos. 19376 and 19377. Napoleon's letter of rebuke to Eugène is in the same volume, no. 19383. On events at Smorgonie, see also Denniée, pp. 166-167.

I have followed Caulaincourt's careful and detailed account of his journey with Napoleon to Warsaw, Dresden and Paris. It may be supplemented by Bourgoing's *Itinéraire,* which is based on the testimony of Wonsowicz. The Bourgoing book has additional information about the situation at Oszmiana, pp. 19-36, and the halt in Dresden, pp. 66-68. It is also a little fuller on the last stages of the journey (pp. 98-100). To these two accounts may be added the evidence of Castellane (p. 201) for the departure, Hogendorp for the halt in the suburbs of Vilna (p. 333), and Montesquiou (p. 292) for the crossing of the Rhine. There are several versions of the arrival in Paris, but I have followed the account of Caulaincourt as a principal participant; but compare the description in Carola Oman, p. 352.

For the march of the Grand Army from Smorgonie to Vilna, see Brandt, pp. 331-335, Lyautey (third article), p. 246, and Castellane, p. 202. The chaos in Vilna is well-documented: Hogendorp, pp. 334-338; Thirion de Metz, pp. 251-258; Fusil, *L'Incendie,* pp. 44-48; Choiseul-Gouffier, pp. 137-139; Lejeune, vol. 2, p. 212, Lyautey (third article), p. 249; Dupuy, pp. 205-206; and Castellane, pp. 203-206. For the virtual nervous collapse of Berthier, see Chuquet, pp. 259-260; see also Tarlé, pp. 264-265 (English version, pp. 389-391).

The attack by Cossacks on the army as it moved from Vilna to Kaunas is described in Thirion de Metz, pp. 259-263; Lyautey (third article), pp. 251-252; Vionnet de Maringoné, pp. 81-82; and Ségur, vol. 2, pp. 361-364. For events in Kaunas, see Thirion, pp. 264-267; Vionnet, pp. 83-84; and Ségur, vol. 2, pp. 366-372.

CHAPTER FIFTEEN: LAURELS AND LEGENDS

For estimates of the casualties in the Grand Army during the campaign, see Brett-James, pp. 264-265, Brunn, p. 189; and Tarlé, p. 269 (English version, p. 397). For Russian casualties, see Wilson, *Narrative,* p. 352, and the article by Predtchensky, p. 99.

For the Russians in Vilna, see the Tchitcherine article, pp. 47-53, and Rochechouart, p. 165. On the Tsar in Vilna, see the eye-witness accounts of Choiseul-Gouffier, pp. 149-153, Wilson, *Journal,* pp.

91-96 and Wilson, *Narrative,* pp. 351-358. For the proclamation when the Russian armies entered Germany, see Tarlé, p. 272 (English version, p. 401) and Wilson, *Narrative,* pp. 368-369. Wilson also prints correspondence about the Yorck incident (pp. 360-363).

I have followed standard accounts of the Leipzig campaign: Bruun, pp. 189-195; Markham, pp. 200-210; Thompson, *Napoleon Bonaparte,* pp. 347-354; and Esposito and Elting, pp. 127-144. Kutuzov's remark on crossing the Elbe is in Strakhovsky, p. 141. For the death of Kutuzov, see Tarlé, p. 273 (English version, p. 402). On the dispute over his successor see Wilson, *Journal,* p. 151.

Metternich's account of his interview with Napoleon at the Marcolini Palace, Dresden, is in his *Memoirs,,* vol. 1, pp. 185-192; compare the critical analysis in Nicolson, pp. 41-45.

For the invasion of France, see the following: Markham, pp. 210-216; Esposito and Elting, pp. 145-154, and Nicolson, pp. 73-83. Nicolson also prints, on p. 288, the secret message from Talleyrand to the Tsar; he cites the memoirs of the Comtesse de Boigne. For events at Fontainebleau, see Montesquiou, p. 335, Thompson, p. 360 and Nicolson, pp. 95-96.

On the Tsar in Paris and at Malmaison, see Castellane, pp. 254-255, Strakhovsky, pp. 149-154, and Stacton, pp. 87-90. For the American attitude to the Russian successes, see the Nagengast article, with events in Boston on pp. 304-305 and in Georgetown on pp. 307-308. On the Tsar's visit to England, see the rhapsodic pages of *The Times* for June 1814, the anonymous pamphlets listed below in the bibliography, and compare the accounts in Nicolson, pp. 111-116 and Anderson, pp. 222-223. For the attitude of the Foreign Secretary, see Webster, pp. 288-291. There is a handbill of the special performance for Platov preserved in the 'Nag's Head', James Street, Covent Garden.

On the growth of Russophobia after the Tsar's departure, see Gleason, pp. 50-56 and Anderson, pp. 222-223. For Napoleon's prophecies of Russian world-domination, see Herold, pp. 201-202. On the Tsar's mysterious death, see Nicolson, p. 279, the appendices to Strakhovsky, and *The Times* for November 15, 1965. There is some information on Chichagov's later years in England in his memoirs, p. 227. I have followed the device used by Geyl (p. 28) of condensing Goguelat's description of the Russian campaign in

Balzac's *Le Médecin de Campagne;* the original passage is in Chapter 3, pp. 130-133 of the edition I used. Prints of the veterans of the Old Guard at the Café Lemblin are preserved in the Musée Carnavalet in Paris.

Bibliography

1. COLLECTIONS OF OFFICIAL DOCUMENTS AND LETTERS

ALTSHULLER, R. E. and TARTAKOVSKY, V.: *Listovki Otechestvennoi Voini 1812 Goda* (Ak., USSR, Moscow, 1962).

ANON: *French Bulletins Relating to the War in Russia* (Sherwood, Neely, Jones, London, 1821).

MIKHAILOVITCH, GRAND-DUKE NICOLAS: *Correspondance de l'Empereur Alexandre I avec sa soeur.* (Papiers de l'Etat, St Petersburg, 1910).

NAPOLEON: *Correspondance de Napoléon I,* Volumes XXIII and XXIV (Plon et Dumaine, Paris, 1868).

NAPOLEON: *Lettres Inédites de Napoléon Ier à Marie Louise,* introduced by L. Madelin (Bibliothèque Nationale, Paris, 1935).

THOMPSON, J. M.: *Napoleon's Letters* (Dent, Everyman's Library, London, 1954).

2. MEMOIRS AND NARRATIVES OF PARTICIPANTS

BAUSSET, L. F. J., Baron de: *Mémoires anecdotiques,* vol. 2. (Baudouin, Paris, 1827).

BOISDEFFRE, MADAME DE: *Souvenirs de Guerre du Général Baron Pouget* (Plon, Paris, 1895).

BOULART, JEAN-FRANÇOIS: *Mémoires militaires du Général Baron Boulart* (Emile Colin, Paris, n.d.)

BOURGOGNE, A. J. B. F.: *Memoirs of Sergeant Bourgogne* (Cape, London, 1940).

BOURGOING, PAUL: *Itinéraire de Napoléon I de Smorgoni à Paris* (Dentu, Paris, 1862).

Souvenirs militaires du Baron de Bourgoing (Plon, Paris, 1897).

BOUTOURLIN, D. P.: *Histoire Militaire de la Campagne de Russie en* 1812 (Amelin et Pochard, Paris, 1824).

BRANDT, HEINRICH VON: *Souvenirs d'un Officier Polonais* (Charpentier, Paris, 1877).

CASTELLANE, BONIFACE DE: *Journal du Maréchal de Castellane,* vol. 1. (Plon, Paris, 1895).

CAULAINCOURT, ARMAND DE: *Memoirs of General de Caulaincourt, Duke of Vicenza,* vol. 1 (Cassell, London, 1935).

CHICHAGOV, P. V.: *Mémoires* (Franck'sche Verlags Buchhandlung, Leipzig, 1862).

CHOISEUL-GOUFFIER, COMTESSE DE: *Mémoires sur l'Empereur Alexandre I et sur l'Empereur Napoléon* (Dentu, Paris, 1862).

CLAUSEWITZ, KARL VON: *Campaign of 1812 in Russia* (John Murray, London, 1843).

DENNIÉE, P. P.: *Itinéraire de l'Empereur Napoléon* (Paulin, Paris, 1842).

DOUGLAS, R. B.: *From Valmy to Waterloo* (Journal of Charles François). (Everett, London, 1906).

DUMONCEAU, J. F.: *Mémoires,* vol. 2. (Au Coeur de l'Histoire, Brussels, 1958).

DUPUY, VICTOR: *Souvenirs militaires* (Calmann Lévy, Paris, 1892).

FABER DU FAURE, C. W. VON: *Campagne de Russie, 1812* (Flammarion, Paris, n.d.).

FAIN, P.: *Mémoires du Baron Fain* (Plon, Paris, 1908).
Manuscrit de Mil Huit Cent Douze (Delauney, Paris, 1827).

FEZENSAC, R. E. P. DE: *Journal* (Galliot, Paris, 1850).
Souvenirs militaires (Dumaine, Paris, 1863).

FUSIL, LOUISE: *L'Incendie de Moscou et la Retraite de Napoléon.* (Schulze and Dean, London, 1817).
Souvenirs d'une actrice (Société Belge de Librairie, Brussels, 1841).

GOURGAUD, GASPARD: *Napoléon et la Grande Armée en Russie* (Bossange, Paris, 1825).

HERZEN, ALEXANDER: *Erinnerungen* (Wiegandt und Gruben, Berlin, 1907).

HOGENDORP, D. C. A. VAN: *Mémoires du Général Dirk van Hogendorp* (Martinis Nijhoff, The Hague, 1887).

KÜGELGEN, WILHELM VON: *Jugenderinnerungen eines alten Mannes* (Herz, Berlin, 1870).

LABAUME, EUGENE: *Relation Complète de la Campagne de Russie en 1812*. (Rey et Gravier, Paris, 1816).

LANGERON, L. A. A.: *Mémoires* (Picard, Paris, 1902).

LEJEUNE, LOUIS-FRANÇOIS: *Mémoires du Général Lejeune*, vol. 2 (Firman-Didot, Paris, 1895).

LÖWENSTERN, E. VON: *Mit Graf Pahlens Reiterei Gegen Napoleon* (Mittler, Berlin, 1910).

MARBOT, ANTOINE-MARCELIN: *Mémoires* (Plon, Paris, 1895).

MENEVAL, C. F. DE: *History of Napoleon I* (Hutchinson, London, 1894).

METTERNICH, K. W. L., Prince von: *Memoirs*, vol. 1 (Bentley, London, 1880).

MONTESQUIOU, ANATOLE DE: *Souvenirs sur la Révolution, l'Empire, la Restauration et la Règne de Louis-Philippe* (Plon, Paris, 1961).

NOEL, J. N. A.: *Souvenirs militaires d'un Officier du Premier Empire* (Berger-Levrault, Paris, 1895).

RAMBUTEAU, P.: *Memoirs of the Count of Rambuteau* (Dent, London, 1908).

RAPP, JEAN: *Mémoires du Général Rapp* (Bossange, Paris, 1823).

REMUSAT, PAUL DE: *Mémoires de la Comtesse de Rémusat* (Calmann Lévy, Paris, 1893).

ROCHECHOUART, L. V. L.: *Memoirs of the Revolution, the Empire and the Restoration* (John Murray, London, 1920).

ROEDER, HELEN: *The Ordeal of Captain Roeder* (Methuen, London, 1960).

SEGUR, PHILIP DE: *History of the Expedition to Russia* (Treuttel and Wurtz, Treuttel, Jun. and Richter, London, 1825).

SOLTYK, ROMAN: *Napoléon en 1812* (Bertrand, Paris, 1836).

STAËL, GERMAINE NECKER DE: *Dix Années d'exil* (Plon, Paris, 1904).

THIRION DE METZ, A.: *Souvenirs militaires.* (Berger-Lavrault, Paris, 1892).

VIONNET DE MARINGONE, L-J.: *Campagnes de Russie et de Saxe* (Dubois, Paris, 1899).

WILSON, SIR ROBERT: *Narrative of Events during the Invasion of Russia* (John Murray, London, 1860).
General Wilson's Journal, 1812-1814 (edited by Antony Brett-James) (Kimber, London, 1964).

YSARN DE VILLEFORT, F. J.: *Relation du Séjour des Françaises à Moscou* (Olivier, Brussels, 1871).

3. GENERAL WORKS

ALMEDINGEN, E. M.: *Emperor Alexander I* (Bodley Head, London, 1964).

ALTSHULLER, R. E., BOGDANOV G. V., etc.: *Borodino* (Sovetskaya Rossiya, Moscow, 1962).

ANDERSON, M. S.: *Britain's Discovery of Russia, 1553-1815* (Macmillan, London, 1958).

BAINVILLE, JACQUES: *Napoleon* (Cape, London, 1932).

BERLIN, SIR ISAIAH: *The Hedgehog and the Fox* (Mentor Books, New York, 1957, originally published, 1953).

BLACK, C. E. (ED.): *Rewriting Russian History* (Atlantic Press, London, 1957).

BONNAL, H.: *La Manoeuvre de Vilna* (Chapelot, Paris, 1905).

BRETT-JAMES, ANTONY: 1812; *Eyewitness Accounts of Napoleon's Defeat in Russia* (Macmillan, London, 1966).

BRUUN, GEOFFREY: *Europe and the French Imperium* (Harper Torchbooks, New York, 1963, originally published 1938).

BURTON, R. G.: *Napoleon's Invasion of Russia* (Allen, London, 1914).

CHRISTIAN, R. F.: *Tolstoy's War and Peace* (Oxford University Press, 1962).

CHUQUET, A.: 1812; *La Guerre de Russie* (Fontemoing, Paris, 1912)

ERNOUF, BARON: *Maret, Duc de Bassano* (Perrin, Paris, 1884).

ESPOSITO, V. F. and ELTING, J. R.: *Military History and Atlas of the Napoleonic Wars* (Faber & Faber, London, 1964).

FABRY, L. G.: *Campagne de Russie (1812)* (Lucien Gougy, Paris, 1900).

FOORD, E.: *Napoleon's Russian Campaign of 1812* (Hutchinson, London, 1914).

GARIN, F. A.: *Izgnanye Napoleona iz Moskvy* (Rabochi, Moscow, 1938).

GARROS, L. P.: *Itinéraire de Napoléon Bonaparte* (Editions de l'Encyclopédie Française, Paris, 1947).

GEYL, P.: *Napoleon; For and Against* (Penguin Books, London, 1965).

GLEASON, JOHN H.: *The Genesis of Russophobia in Great Britain* (Harvard University Press, Cambridge, Mass., 1950).

GRUNWALD, CONSTANTIN DE: *La Campagne de Russie* (Julliard, Paris, 1963).

HAMILTON, G. H.: *The Art and Architecture of Russia* (Penguin Books, London, 1954).

HEROLD, J. CHRISTOPHER: *The Mind of Napoleon* (Columbia Paperback, New York, 1961, originally published, 1955).

JACKSON, W. G. F.: *Seven Roads to Moscow* (Eyre and Spottiswoode, London 1957).

JOMINI, HENRI DE: *Life of Napoleon* (Trubner, London, 1864).

KEMBLE, J.: *Napoleon Immortal* (John Murray, London, 1959).

LEFEBVRE, G.: *Napoléon* (Peuples et Civilisations, Paris, 1953).

LOBANOV-ROSTOVSKY, A. A.: *Russia and Europe, 1789-1825* (Duke University Press, NC, USA., 1947).

MACDONELL, A. G.: *Napoleon and his Marshals* (Macmillan, London, 1934).

MADELIN, L.: *Histoire du Consulat et de l'Empire, XII* (Hachette, Paris, 1949).

MARKHAM, FELIX: *Napoleon* (Mentor Books, New York, 1966, originally published 1963).

NARICHKINE, NATALIE: *1812; Le Comte Rostopchine et son Temps* (Golicke and Willborg, St Petersburg, 1912).

NICOLSON, HAROLD: *The Congress of Vienna* (Constable, London, 1946).

OLIVIER, DARIA: *L'Incendie de Moscou* (Laffont, Paris, 1964).

OMAN, CAROLA: *Napoleon's Viceroy, Eugène de Beauharnais* (Hodder & Stoughton, London, 1966).

PARES, SIR BERNARD: *A History of Russia* (Cape, London, 1947, originally published in 1925).

ROSLAVLEVA, NATALIA: *Era of the Russian Ballet, 1770-1965* (Gollancz, London, 1966).

SCOTT, FRANKLIN D.: *Bernadotte and the Fall of Napoleon* (Harvard University Press, Cambridge, Mass., 1935).

SLONIMSKY, YURY: *The Bolshoi Theatre Ballet* (Foreign Languages Publishing House, Moscow, 1956).

SOREL, A: *L'Europe et la Révolution Française, VII* (Plon-Nourrit, Paris, 1907).

STACTON, DAVID: *The Bonapartes* (Simon and Schuster, New York, 1966).

STRAKHOVSKY, L.: *Alexander I of Russia* (Williams and Norgate, London, 1949).

TARLE, E.: *Nashestvie Napoleona na Rossiyu – 1812 god.* (Sot.-Ekon., Moscow, 1938.)

(The English version – which does not include the source references – is entitled *Napoleon's Invasion of Russia*. It was published in the U.S.A. by the Oxford University Press, New York, in 1942.)

THIERS, A.: *History of the Consulate and the Empire*, XIV (Willis & Sotheran, London, 1857).

THOMPSON, J. M.: *Napoleon Bonaparte: His Rise and Fall* (Blackwell, Oxford, 1952.)

VANDAL, ALBERT: *Napoléon et Alexandre I* (Plon, Paris, 1897.)

WALISZEWSKI, K.: *La Russie il y a Cent Ans, Le Règne d'Alexandre*, vol. 2 (Plon, Paris, 1923.)

WEBSTER, C. K.: *The Foreign Policy of Castlereagh*, vol. 1 (Bell, London, 1931.)

4. ARTICLES IN PERIODICALS; i. MEMOIRS

BAKOUNINA, V.: Dvenadtsati God; *Russkaya Starina,* vol. XLVII (1885) pp. 391-410.

CASSE, BARON DE: La reine Catherine de Westphalie au Congrès du Dresde, *Revue Historique,* vol. XXXVI (1888) pp. 328-335.

LYAUTEY, HUBERT: Lettres d'un Lieutenant de la Grande Armée, three articles in the *Revue des Deux Mondes:* (i) December 12, 1962, pp. 485-500; (ii) January 1, 1963, pp. 58-78; (iii) January 15, 1963, pp. 240-254.

MARCEL-PAON, A.: 1812, Du Niemen au Niemen; *Revue des Etudes Napoléoniennes* for December 1933, pp. 305-320.

MARTEL, RENE: Napoléon en Lithuanie; *Revue de Paris,* no. 16, August 1932, pp. 897-912.

PASTORET, AMEDEE DE: De Witebsk à la Beresina; *Revue de Paris,* no. 7, April 1902, pp. 465-497.

TCHITCHERINE, A.: Tetrad; *Novy Mir,* 1962, no. 9, pp. 7-70. (This is a diary of the winter 1812-1813.)

TURNO, CHARLES: Souvenirs d'un Officier Polonais; *Revue des Etudes Napoléoniennes,* August 1931, pp. 99-116.

5. ARTICLES IN PERIODICALS; ii GENERAL

ANDERSON, M. S.: British Public Opinion and the Russian Campaign of 1812; *Slavonic and East European Review,* vol. 34 (1956), pp. 408-425.

ANGERVO, J. M.: How Cold was 1812; *The Times,* February 8, 1961.

GOLDER, F. A.: The Russian Offer of Mediation in the War of 1812; *Political Science Quarterly,* vol. 31 (1916) pp. 380-391.

KATS, B.: Podlinne Poteri Ruskoi Armii v Borodinskom Srazhenii; *Istorichevsky Zhurnal* (1941), nos. 7-8, pp. 122-126.

KUKIEL, M.: Les Polonaises à la Moskova; *Revue des Etudes Napoléoniennes,* January 1929, pp. 10-32.

NAGENGAST, W. E.: Moscow, the Stalingrad of 1812: American Reaction towards Napoleon's Retreat from Russia; *Russian Review,* vol. 8, no. 4 (1949), pp. 302-315.

PREDTECHENSKY, A.: Otechestvennaya Voinna 1812 Goda; *Istorichevsky Zhurnal* (1941), nos. 7-8, pp. 81-101.

RAMBAUD, A.: La Grande Armée à Moscou. Récits de témoins oculaires russes; *Revue des Deux Mondes,* vol. 160 (July 1873), pp. 194-228.

SCHMITT, H. A.: 1812: Stein, Alexander I and the Crusade against Napoleon; *Journal of Modern History,* vol. 31 (December 1959), pp. 325-338.

STCHOUPAK, N.: L'Entrevue de I. Iakovlev avec Napoléon; *Revue des Etudes Napoléoniennes,* July 1931, pp. 45-48.

6. FICTION CITED IN THE TEXT

BALZAC, H.: *Le Médecin de Campagne* (Cambridge University Press, edition, London, 1933, originally published 1832).

TOLSTOY, L.: *War and Peace* (Macmillan edition, London, 1954).

7. CONTEMPORARY PAMPHLETS IN THE BRITISH MUSEUM

The Christian Conqueror; or Moscow burnt and Paris saved. By a Country Gentleman of England (Longman, London, 1814).

The Christian Virtues of the Emperor of Russia and Others (Butterworth, Birmingham, 1814).

An Important and Authentic Life of Alexander, Emperor of Russia, from his Earliest Days to his Departure from England (Dean and Munday, London, 1814).

Index

Abo, meeting of the Tsar and Alexander at, 95–6

Adnet, M., French actor in Moscow, 91

Alexander I, Tsar of Russia, at Vilna in summer of 1812, 20–2, 42–6; attitude to France before 1812, 24–8; behaviour at Austerlitz, 29, 93; at Zakret, 44–5; in camp at Drissa, 56–58; leaves the Army, 58–9; general psychology of, 83–4; in Moscow, 84, 87–8; and Leppich, 89–90; in St Petersburg, 92, 96–7, 131, 133, 183–4, 259; and Kutuzov, 93–4, 131, 175–6, 184, 259–60, 263; and Bernadotte, 95–6; and Wilson, 96–7, 186; religious mysticism of, 183–4, 267; leaves St Pertesburg for Vilna, 260; and carrying the war into Europe, 260–1; and appointment of successor to Kutuzov, 263; and invasion of France, 265; in Paris (1814), 267; in Britain (1814), 268; rumours over death of, 270; mentioned, 37, 50, 51, 70, 105, 162–3, 164, 173

Alexander Nevsky, Russian national hero and saint, 93, 131, 173

Arakcheyev, Count A. A., Russian soldier and statesman, 29, 42, 57, 73, 75, 184

Armfeldt, General Gustav, Swedish soldier in Russian service, 42, 84

Aubert, Marie-Rose, meeting with Napoleon in Moscow, 177

Augereau, General Jean-Pierre, 219, 220

Austerlitz, battle of (1805), 24, 29, 46, 64, 70, 82, 93, 115, 129, 182, 248, 265

Austria, 18, 20, 31, 169, 230, 245, 247, 253, 259, 262, 265

Bagration, General Prince Peter, in early stages of campaign, 44, 53–5, 57, 59, 62–3; dispute with Barclay, 56–7, 72, 94; at Smolensk, 72, 75–76; serves under Kutuzov, 104, dispositions before Borodino, 110; mortally wounded at Borodino, 119–20; death of, 135; mentioned, 186

'Bagration Flèches', defensive works at Borodino, 110, 116

Balashov, General A. D., 42, 45, 46, 48, 49–51, 164

Ballet in Russia in 1812, 86, 161, 178

Balzac, Honoré de, 271

Baraguay d'Hilliers, General L., 217, 219, 220

Barclay de Tolly, General Mikhail, in early stages of campaign, 42, 43, 52, 55–6; friction with Bagration, 56–7, 71–3, 94; at Vitebsk, 61, 62, 65; at Smolensk, 71, 73, 75, 77; retires on the river Kolodnia, 78–9; hands command over to Kutuzov, 101; at Borodino, 124; at Fili, 137; on bad relations with Kutuzov, 186; sent on sick-leave to Kaluga, 210; appointed to succeed Kutuzov, 263; death of, 270; mentioned, 92, 104, 112

Barthemy, Colonel, negotiates with Russians outside Moscow, 180, 186

Bausset, Louis de, Prefect of the Palace, brings portrait of Napoleon's son to the Emperor, 114; arranges accommodation in the Kremlin, 143, 147; in charge of entertainments in Moscow, 178

Bavarians, 59

Bazhenov, V. I., Russian architect, 183

Beauharnais, see Eugène

Belliard, General, restrains Murat from assaulting Davout, 101

Bennigsen, General Count Levin, Hanoverian soldier serving in Russian army, early career, 29; adviser to